MW01614230

Words in Time

Words in Time

New Essays on Eliot's Four Quartets

Edited by
EDWARD LOBB

ANN ARBOR
THE UNIVERSITY OF MICHIGAN PRESS

Published in the United States of America by

The University of Michigan Press

1996 1995 1994 1993 4 3 2 1

Library of Congress Cataloging-in-Publication Data applied for

ISBN 0-472-10488-8

For Roosevelt O'Neal

1953–1991

Or puoi la quantitate
comprender dell'amor ch'a te mi scalda

Contents

Notes on Contributors

Jewel Spears Brooker is Professor of Literature at Eckerd College in St Petersburg, Florida. A former president of the T.S. Eliot Society, she is the author, with Joseph Bentley, of *Reading The Waste Land: Modernism and the Limits of Interpretation* (1990); she has also edited *The Placing of T.S. Eliot* (1991).

Donald J. Childs is Assistant Professor of English at the University of Ottawa. His articles on T.S. Eliot have appeared in many periodicals, including the *Journal of Modern Literature, ELH, Essays in Criticism, American Literature* and *Mosaic*.

Denis Donoghue holds the Henry James Chair of English and American Letters at New York University. His many books include *Ferocious Alphabets* and *Connoisseurs of Chaos*; his occasional essays on Irish, American and English literature have been collected in *We Irish* (1986), *Reading America* (1987) and *England, Their England* (1988). He has also written a memoir, *Warrenpoint* (1990).

Lyndall Gordon is a fellow of St Hilda's College, Oxford. She is the author of *Eliot's Early Years* (1977), *Eliot's New Life* (1988), *Shared Lives* (1992) and *Virginia Woolf: A Writer's Life*, winner of the James Tait Black prize for biography, 1984.

Cleo McNelly Kearns has a Ph.D. from Columbia University and is the author of *T.S. Eliot and Indic Traditions: A Study in Poetry and Belief* (1987). Her essays on modernism, literary theory and postmodern theology have appeared in many periodicals.

Michael Levenson is Professor of English at the University of Virginia. He is the author of *A Genealogy of Modernism: A Study of English Literary Doctrine, 1908–1922* (1984) and *Modernism and the Fate of Individuality* (1991).

A. Walton Litz is director of the Creative Writing Program at Princeton University and was Eastman Professor in Oxford

Introduction

The essays on *Four Quartets* gathered here are the work of critics and scholars from four countries – Canada, England, Ireland and the United States – and represent a variety of critical approaches. The first four essays are reconsiderations of individual quartets, while the remaining six deal with aspects of the whole sequence. All are published here for the first time, to celebrate the fiftieth anniversary of the *Quartets'* completion.

Criticism of *Four Quartets* has passed through three general phases. The first, extending from early reviews through to the late sixties, was largely one of explication and evaluation; it was during this period that many of the standard commentaries appeared and the *Quartets* were established as a benchmark of late modernism. The second phase included the reaction against Eliot's reputation and was marked by attempts to redefine the aesthetic of modernism in ways which would minimize Eliot's place, or, conversely, to expand the definition and recognize various 'modernisms'. The third phase, roughly coinciding with the recent ascendancy of critical theory, has involved renewed discussion of Eliot's early philosophical writings. Criticism of the *Quartets* in this period has emphasized the self-questioning nature of language and has tended, explicitly or implicitly, to blur or even obliterate the vexed distinction between modernism and postmodernism. It has also, in many cases, tended to ignore the status of poetry as poetry, and to treat all forms of literature as equivalent forms of statement.

These three phases are not wholly distinct, and perhaps represent states of mind as much as historical periods; but they do indicate some of the directions that critical discussion has taken, and some of the tensions involved in attempts to define Eliot's achievement and its relation to the age. What has been constant is the discussion itself: the importance of the *Quartets* has been acknowledged for fifty years, not least when they have been attacked. Like Pound's *Cantos*, in Basil Bunting's famous poem, they are the Alps – too big to ignore or dismiss.

The success of *Four Quartets* is still a matter of disagreement in part because, as Denis Donoghue points out in the first of the essays collected here, none of the critical procedures developed in the last fifty years has been responsive to the kind of poetry we find in the *Quartets* – or, at least, to one kind of poetry we find there. Eliot's boldest experiment in the *Quartets*, apart from the attempt to find analogies for what goes beyond language altogether, lies in what Donoghue calls 'the discrimination of concepts (not this precisely ... or even that)'. The passages in which these discriminations occur – the evocation of the still point in 'Burnt Norton' II, for example, or the passage beginning 'You say I am repeating' in 'East Coker' III – still strike many readers as woefully unpoetic, but the fault may be ours rather than Eliot's: as Donoghue notes, 'We have not yet devised a poetics of discourse in any way comparable to the several poetics of image, symbol, and structure.'

Whether such a poetics of discourse is possible remains an open question, but several of the essays in this volume explore Eliot's 'discrimination of concepts' in new ways. Cleo McNelly Kearns defines a complex logic of double negation in the *Quartets*, and traces its roots in both Eastern and Western apophatic traditions; her Derridean reading of *Four Quartets* (unlike earlier critics' deconstructive readings, which often seem imposed and artificial) reveals many of the links between deconstruction and a long tradition of scepticism about the theological dimensions of language – a scepticism which nevertheless accepts the challenge of speaking in significant, if difficult and paradoxical, ways. Donald Childs' essay outlines a different but related sort of mediation in the *Quartets*. Childs defines the poem's intellectual structure as one which both posits and criticizes accounts of experience which focus exclusively on the object or the subject. Eliot's double heritage of idealist and pragmatic thought, and his determination not to oversimplify, enable him to portray human being as necessarily suspended between impossible extremes – between a mysticism uncomplicated by epistemological problems and a reductive pragmatism which sees all belief as essentially a practical construction. Childs' reading of many passages in the *Quartets* gives us a new sense of the ways in which philosophical issues can inform figurative language. Using different sources and methods, Kearns and Childs work toward related conclusions about Eliot's 'discrimination of concepts'.

A common thread links three other essays in the collection,

each of which focuses on a different aspect of repetition in *Four Quartets*. Jewel Spears Brooker, building on her earlier work, analyses some of the ways in which Eliot moved beyond the aesthetic of *The Waste Land* to develop a structure in the *Quartets* based on repetition, relation and pattern; her analysis of some of the affinities between Eliot's work and that of Claude Lévi-Strauss is illuminating and suggestive. A. Walton Litz focuses on the implications of repeated form in the *Quartets* and in doing so extends our knowledge of Eliot's relation to Romantic doctrine, particularly in Coleridge and Stevens. Louis Martz, beginning with the repetition of the five-part structure of *The Waste Land* in the *Quartets*, traces the transformation of the prophetic voice in the earlier poem into the probing, meditative voice of the *Quartets*.

Another recurrent theme, not surprisingly, is that of time – not the philosophical time of the *Quartets*, but the more personal time of the poet's life and encounter with history. Michael Levenson details the movement, in Eliot's later poetry and criticism, from the spatialized eternal present of 'Tradition and the Individual Talent' to acknowledgment of the irrecoverable pastness of the past. The 'fault line' which he traces in Eliot's work is one which enables the poet to come to terms with the temporality of the self and 'thematize the necessity of change'. Lyndall Gordon's essay likewise shows us an Eliot reconciled to temporality, in this case the American past and the American writers whom he often appeared to have left behind. Her discussion of the theme of self-transformation in American literature, and of the American works which lie behind Eliot's European referents, provides a new perspective not only on 'The Dry Salvages' but on Eliot's entire *oeuvre*. Ronald Schuchard's detailed account of Eliot's relation to George Herbert shows another aspect of the poet's reconciliation with past masters: important changes in Eliot's aesthetic and spirituality grew out of his continual re-reading of Herbert and found expression in 'Little Gidding'. Finally, my own essay attempts to show the continuity between Eliot's early obsession with closed rooms and the theme of limitation in 'East Coker': here, too, the underlying theme is that of reconciliation in time.

I mention these threads of similarity in what is, after all, a collection of essays independently written by various hands, only to suggest that some of the main points in each essay are taken up, directly and indirectly, in many of the others; the critic's monologue is succeeded by dialogue with other critics and with the ideal reader to whom any such collection is addressed.

Edward Lobb
Kingston, Ontario

Acknowledgements

Quotations from unpublished manuscript material by T.S. Eliot in Professor Schuchard's essay are © Valerie Eliot, 1993, and are reprinted by permission of Mrs Eliot.

A Note on Abbreviations and References

The following abbreviations are used for parenthetical citation of Eliot's works in the text:

ASG   *After Strange Gods* (London, Faber, 1934)

CPP   *The Complete Poems and Plays* (London, Faber, 1969)

FLA   *For Lancelot Andrewes* (London, Faber, 1928)

ICS   *The Idea of a Christian Society* (London, Faber, 1939)

KE   *Knowledge and Experience in the Philosophy of F.H. Bradley* (London, Faber, 1964)

L1   *The Letters of T.S. Eliot*, vol 1 (1898–1922), ed. Valerie Eliot (London, Faber and Faber, 1988)

NDC   *Notes Towards the Definition of Culture* (London, Faber, 1948)

OPP   *On Poetry and Poets* (London, Faber, 1957)

SE   *Selected Essays*, 3rd edn (London, Faber, 1951)

SP   *Selected Prose of T.S. Eliot*, ed. Frank Kermode (London, Faber, 1975)

SW   *The Sacred Wood*, 2nd edn (London, Methuen, 1928)

TCC   *To Criticize the Critic* (London, Faber, 1965)

UPUC   *The Use of Poetry and the Use of Criticism*, 2nd edn (London, Faber, 1964)

WLF   *The Waste Land: A Facsimile and Transcript of the Original Drafts Including the Annotations of Ezra Pound*, ed. Valerie Eliot (London, Faber, 1971)

The following frequently cited works are also referred to by abbreviations:

CFQ   Helen Gardner, *The Composition of Four Quartets* (London, Faber, 1978)

EEY   Lyndall Gordon, *Eliot's Early Years* (London and New York, Oxford UP, 1977)

ENL   Lyndall Gordon, *Eliot's New Life* (London and New York, Oxford UP, 1988)

References to other works are generally incorporated in the text. The author's name and page or volume reference as necessary are given in round brackets: (Spender, 55) or (Grant, vol 2, 379), with full details in the bibliography at the end of the essay. If the author's name is mentioned before the passage cited, it is not repeated in the reference. If two works by the same author occur in the bibliography, the parenthetical reference includes the date of the work referred to, e.g. (Spender 1975, 45). Two or more works published in the same year are distinguished as 1970a, 1970b, etc.

Notes have been kept to a minimum, and are gathered at the end of each essay.

1

On 'Burnt Norton'
Denis Donoghue

For even when hours and days go by in silence and the phone
Never rings, and widely spaced drops of water
Fall from the eaves, nothing is any longer a secret
And one can live alone rejoicing in this:
That the years of war are far off in the past or the future,
That memory contains everything. And you see slipping down
    a hallway
The past self you decided not to have anything to do with
    anymore
And it is a more comfortable you, dishonest perhaps,
But alive.

John Ashbery, A Wave

The first readers of 'Burnt Norton' did not know that they were
performing a quartet, or that it might be useful to think of certain
works by Bartok and by Beethoven. Nor did they know that the
poem was the first of a sequence rather than what it appeared to
be, the last poem of the book in hand, *Collected Poems 1909–1935*.
Residents of Gloucestershire might have known that Burnt Norton
was an old manor house, no longer occupied, near Chipping
Campden, and perhaps that the house had a garden, neglected now,
and pools, now dry. Many readers might have thought that Eliot's
career as a poet was finished, and that he had committed himself to
the work of literary, social, political and religious criticism. 'Burnt
Norton' had an air of finality about it; the end of a book of poems
collected, not selected.

    Those readers who knew Greek probably assumed that Eliot,
a poet much given to epigraphs, had left two fragments from
Heraclitus untranslated because no particular translation into English
could encompass the diverse meanings of the Greek *logos*. Readers
who did not know Greek probably assumed that Eliot's English
would give the gist of the Greek matter in its own time. A few

readers may have gone to the bother of translating the Greek somewhat in these terms: (1) although the Word is common to all, most people live as if each had a private intelligence of his own, and (2) the way up and the way down are one and the same. A rebuke, followed by an opacity, directed those readers into a poem which began with its own opacity, four unforthcoming sentences about Time.

Readers in 1936 could not know that those statements, indeed the first fourteen lines of the poem, were originally designed to be spoken by the Second Priest in *Murder in the Cathedral*, to follow Thomas's speech after the departure of the Second Tempter. The passage was cut before the first performance, but Eliot liked it well enough to use it as the opening meditation of a poem he took more seriously, in the event, than anything else in *Collected Poems 1909–1935*.

No reader in 1936 knew that Burnt Norton was a place of emphasized significance for Eliot; that sometime between late August and early September 1935 he had wandered about the garden there in the company of Emily Hale, a woman he might have married if he had not made the mistake of marrying Vivienne Haigh-Wood. By the late summer of 1934 Eliot had started a legal process of separation, but in every spiritual sense he was still married. The emotions he felt in the company of Emily Hale may have included regret for years mainly wasted, and remorse for things ill done, but there was evidently no question of seeking a divorce and starting a new life with Emily Hale or any other woman.

The only advantage we have over the first readers of 'Burnt Norton' is our sense of the significance of the poem's coming between *Murder in the Cathedral* and *The Family Reunion*, two plays in which many feelings barely disclosed in 'Burnt Norton' are more explicitly expressed: notably, an inescapable feeling of self-disgust, a conviction of the meaninglessness of any life closed against divine grace, a sense that the important consideration is not our feelings but the pattern we may make of them. The plays feature the same imagery as 'Burnt Norton'; enchanted gardens, sudden illuminations, gates opened or closed, clouds hiding the sun, children in the foliage, the still point of a turning world; these, and motifs of loss, revulsion, temptation, inner and outer compulsion, and – in the end – an achieved patience, assent to the will of God.

Readers in 1936 knew as much as they needed to know about Eliot's beliefs, or at least about the beliefs which inhabit 'Burnt Norton': they were clearly stated, for instance, in Eliot's 'Introduction' to the *Pensées* of Pascal:

> We cannot quite understand any of the parts, fragmentary as they are, without some understanding of the whole. Capital, for instance, is his analysis of the *three orders*: the order of nature, the order of mind, and the order of charity. These three are *discontinuous*; the higher is not implicit in the lower as in an evolutionary doctrine it would be. In this distinction Pascal offers much about which the modern world would do well to think. And indeed, because of his unique combination and balance of qualities, I know of no religious writer more pertinent to our time. The great mystics, like St. John of the Cross, are primarily for readers with a special determination of purpose; the devotional writers, such as St. François de Sales, are primarily for those who already feel consciously desirous of the love of God; the great theologians are for those interested in theology. But I can think of no Christian writer, not Newman even, more to be commended than Pascal to those who doubt, but who have the mind to conceive, and the sensibility to feel, the disorder, the futility, the meaninglessness, the mystery of life and suffering, and who can only find peace through a satisfaction of the whole being.
>
> (SE, 416)

That passage, available since 1931, gives as much of Eliot's belief, and of his insistence on it, as a reader of 'Burnt Norton' needs to know. Not that even as much as this is necessary, because something approaching it can be deduced from the poem or divined within it. The merit of knowing the nature of Eliot's belief and its particular vocabularies – sufficiently indicated by reference to Augustine, St John of the Cross, Donne, Andrewes, Hooker, Pascal and the English medieval mystics – is that we know what not to expect, the concessions and felicities at the absence of which F.R. Leavis and other readers of 'Burnt Norton' have been affronted to the point of rejecting the main thrust of the poem. There is no need to feel affronted: the poetry does not depend upon the doctrine held but upon the doctrine felt. To read 'Burnt

Norton' it is only necessary to conceive a form of feeling, different from one's own if it has to be, and to imagine what that form means to a mind that holds it or is possessed by it.

The four statements about Time with which the poem begins cannot have won many readers; they sound like a bewildered seminar. Their value consists not in whatever they say about Time but in starting a form of discourse in which the nature of the speaker is the least germane consideration. These sentences are propelled not by a speaker in charge of them but by solemn, impersonal agitations maintained as if without human intervention. Progress from one phrase to the next is made chiefly by repetitions of the emphasized words – time, past, present, future – and the discrimination of conditions in their vicinity; what might have been, what has been. Not that the sentences are otherwise trivial. The first one: 'Time present and time past / Are both perhaps present in time future, / And time future contained in time past' (CPP, 171) implies determinism, since every aspect of time is already inscribed in a future we can't know. The second: 'If all time is eternally present / All time is unredeemable' moves the determinism to the present continuous tense, but doesn't otherwise improve the situation; 'unredeemable' because not open to change. In *The Family Reunion* Harry says, doggedly explaining how he feels for the benefit of the obtuse Charles and Gerald:

> I am the old house
> With the noxious smell and the sorrow before morning,
> In which all past is present, all degradation
> Is unredeemable . . .   (CPP, 294)

and later, to Dr Warburton:

>   Your ordinary murderer
> Regards himself as an innocent victim.
> To himself he is still what he used to be
> Or what he would be. He cannot realise
> That everything is irrevocable,
> The past unredeemable.   (CPP, 315)

The third statement: 'What might have been is an abstraction / Remaining a perpetual possibility / Only in a world of specu-lation' (CPP, 171) posits a world such as Stephen Dedalus's in

Ulysses, where Stephen diverts himself with Aristotelian notions of potentiality and actuality: 'Or was that only possible which came to pass?' In the fourth sentence, not a moment too soon, determinism seems to be set aside: 'What might have been and what has been / Point to one end, which is always present' (CPP, 171), a release effected by letting several possibilities, including hopeful ones, hover upon the hospitably ambiguous 'end'; end as purpose, the ultimate aim, as well as the conclusion. Nothing in this sentence makes forgiveness impossible, or the reception of divine grace, or the reconstitution of one's past life in another pattern.

The direction of this passage, its abstracting style, effects and maintains a distanced relation to events. No impression of immediacy, of an irresistibly punctual convergence of deed and word, experience and the words for it, is allowed to enforce itself. Events will indeed intrude, but only at the one remove of memory. Even then, they are events which didn't happen but might have happened. So while the governing style seems to change from abstract to concrete, from generalizing to narrative, the change is only ostensible, at the double remove of 'memory' and 'echo'.

In Eliot's poetry, birds, not people, urge one to seize the day, and often the listener lives to regret the urging. Or in the presence of birds one is willing to risk immediacies of sense, as in 'Cape Ann': 'O quick quick quick, quick hear the song-sparrow' (CPP, 142). Now, in 'Burnt Norton': 'Quick, said the bird, find them, find them, / Round the corner' (CPP, 171) and even then, if a human intelligence is present, it warns of the 'deception of the thrush'.

Many sources or analogues have been suggested for Eliot's rose garden: *Alice in Wonderland*, Kipling's 'They', Elizabeth Barrett Browning's 'The Lost Bower', Frances Hodgson Burnett's *The Secret Garden*, and a recollection of Eliot's own 'New Hampshire' with its 'Children's voices in the orchard'. All that is required (and nearly any *Kinderscenen* would intimate it) is a sudden, momentary sense of the sublime, of unity sufficient to put one beside oneself or beyond oneself, an otherwise impossible conviction of unity among the constituents of the occasion; human, natural, botanic, meteorological, the complete consort implying perfection of being, its brevity of no damaging account:

Into our first world.
There they were, dignified, invisible,
Moving without pressure, over the dead leaves,
In the autumn heat, through the vibrant air,
And the bird called, in response to
The unheard music hidden in the shrubbery,
And the unseen eyebeam crossed, for the roses
Had the look of flowers that are looked at.

(CPP, 171–2)

The movement of the verse is such as to discourage our asking
who 'they' were; perhaps the quiet-voiced elders who emerge
more clearly in 'East Coker' II. Here they are figures in a ballet
of childhood, called upon to be nothing more than present.
The main direction of the passage gives another instance of the
disjunction between existence and essence; between the actual and
the real; between temporal enchainment and time redeemable.
Here the bird's song is in response to unheard music. As in Keats'
distinction between heard melodies and those unheard, unheard
music is absolute, the essence of sound as distinct from its sensible
existence. The essence of sound, as Kenneth Burke has remarked,
would be soundless, by definition removed from the experience of
sound; just as the unseen eyebeam testifies to the essence of seeing
rather than to its mere existence. That the bird, rather than the
children or the elders, should respond to it is entirely appropriate
– they have fewer distractions – just as the roses seem to be looked
at. The status of these looks and responses is notional, only to be
stabilized – and even then not in mere existence – by memory.

Appropriate, too, that the bird should convey the admonition
– 'human kind / Cannot bear very much reality' (CPP, 172) –
which Thomas has given to the terrified Chorus in *Murder in The
Cathedral*. We can't bear very much reality unless and until we see
it fulfilled as the figure of God's purpose:

Peace, and be at peace with your thoughts and visions.
These things had to come to you and you to accept them.
This is your share of the eternal burden,
The perpetual glory. This is one moment,
But know that another
Shall pierce you with a sudden painful joy

When the figure of God's purpose is made complete.
You shall forget these things, toiling in the household,
You shall remember them, droning by the fire,
When age and forgetfulness sweeten memory
Only like a dream that has often been told
And often been changed in the telling. They will seem unreal.
Human kind cannot bear very much reality.

(CPP, 271)

In 'Burnt Norton' the sublime moment − 'And the lotus rose, quietly, quietly, / The surface glittered out of heart of light' (CPP, 172) − is one in which existence and essence seem to be one and the same. That is what the experience of the sublime comes to, an epiphany, an intuition of divine grace, given lest we despair. In 'Burnt Norton', as in *The Family Reunion*, a black cloud occludes the sun almost before we have apprehended its dazzle and the heart of light from which it issues. In one sense the brevity of the experience doesn't matter; it is an epitome, a sample of the ultimate experience, beatitude, the Heaven of God's presence. In another sense, nothing matters more, because the disjunction between existence and essence renders existence appalling unless we live it in the demanding light of eternity.

It would be absurd to repeat the canard that Eliot hated life and longed only to be rid of it. The poet who wrote, here in 'Burnt Norton' − 'Dry the pool, dry concrete, brown edged, / And the pool was filled with water out of sunlight' (CPP, 172) − felt the ravishments of sense just as keenly as those poets who advertise their possession of such opulence. Asceticism did not come to Eliot more naturally or more easily than to anyone else who practises it. We may wonder why he felt impelled to live among such imageries, but the speculation is null: that was the form his spiritual genius took. It is my prejudice that Eliot was a man of emotional and spiritual violence, living for the most part upon the edge of the rational imagination, compelled by imageries of pain − think of his infatuation with the martyrdom of St Sebastian − and, irregularly but irresistibly, coming upon the other sublimity, of exaltation and joy.

In the second part of 'Burnt Norton' we see the poetic as well as the spiritual form of Eliot's genius. When he read, in 1908, Arthur Symons's *The Symbolist Movement in Literature*, he saw that the modern French form of Symbolism effected yet another disjunction between existence and essence. The motives were secular, chiefly a refusal of the conventions, the positivist syntax, of everyday life. But the otherwise diverse procedures of Baudelaire, Mallarmé, Corbière, and Laforgue could serve a religious end by repudiating current axioms of complacency. The notion that reality could be verified merely by describing its constituents was just as trivial as the commonplace assumptions of evolution and progress. Mallarmé, like Symons and Yeats, deemed it vulgar to deal with objects by describing them: the proper aim of poetry was to replace the object by the essence, the pure idea, it might be accepted as suggesting. Reverie was Yeats's name for the act of consciousness by which the claims of an object are disavowed or transcended and, in their place, nothing is retained but a suggestion of the life they partially exemplify. In 'Crise de vers' Mallarmé has this passage:

> A quoi bon le merveille de transposer un fait de nature en sa presque disparition vibratoire selon le jeu de la parole, cependant; si ce n'est pour qu'en émane, sans la gêne d'un proche ou concret rappel, la notion pure.
>
> Je dis: une fleur! et, hors de l'oubli où ma voix relègue aucun contour, en tant que quelque chose d'autre que les calices sus, musicalement se lève, idée même et suave, l'absente de tous bouquets. (278–9)

It follows that the thing 'to which we grant the character of immediacy and nothing more' makes a sordid claim upon the poet's attention. Description, as in a realistic novel, is the sign that the claim has been met. The poet's motto is: 'pour ne garder de rien que la suggestion.' If the standard relation between speech and the reality of things is merely commercial, then the possibility of a 'pure work' arises antithetically. The first step in this process is to nullify the impression of unity which depends upon the continuity of a speaking voice:

> L'oeuvre pure implique la disparition élocutoire du poète, qui cède l'initiative aux mots, par le heurt de leur inégalité mobilisés; ils s'allument de reflets réciproques comme une virtuelle traînée de feux sur des pierreries, remplaçant la respiration perceptible en l'ancien souffle lyrique ou la direction personelle enthousiaste de la phrase. (276–7)

This programme entails the omission of the author, the speaker, the particular will insofar as it would enforce itself.

The first lines of this second part of the poem sufficiently indicate Eliot's kinship, for the time being, with Mallarmé: 'Garlic and sapphires in the mud / Clot the bedded axle-tree' (CPP, 172). A manuscript draft of 'Lines for an Old Man' has 'Thunder and sapphires . . .', with the thunder scored out and replaced by 'Garlic' (CFQ, 79): the manuscript version is even closer than the final one to Mallarmé's 'M'introduire dans ton histoire' – 'Tonnerre et rubis aux moyeux.' In both versions, there is a further recollection of Mallarmé's 'Le Tombeau de Charles Baudelaire': 'Sépulcrale d'égout bavant boue et rubis.' How garlic got into the line, I have no idea; except that it causes among the words 'the shock of their inequality' to an even greater degree than Mallarmé's 'thunder' does. The axle-tree stayed in Eliot's mind from his first reading of Chapman's *Bussy D'Ambois*: 'fly where men feel the cunning axle-tree . . .' In the typed draft of 'Burnt Norton' and in the American *Complete Poems and Plays 1909–1950*, the last line of 'The trilling wire in the blood / Sings below inveterate scars / Appeasing long forgotten wars' (CPP, 172) appears as 'And reconciles forgotten wars', a worse line if only because the repeated 'reconciles / reconciled' in this section is a rough nudge to an apparently drowsy reader. But in either version we are in the poetic world of Poe, Baudelaire, and Mallarmé, sufficiently glossed by Eliot's 'Note sur Mallarmé et Poe' in its reference to 'un élément d'*incantation*.' With 'Ulalume' and 'Un Coup de Dés' in view, Eliot refers to 'cette incantation, qui insiste sur la puissance primitive du Mot (Fatum).' (526) The addition of 'Fatum' is not at all parenthetical to Eliot's context. The first meaning of *fatum* is a divine utterance, the expressed will of a god, as in Cicero's *fata Sibyllina*. Eliot is claiming for 'la puissance primitive du Mot' in poetry what he has claimed for *logos*, by way of the epigraph from Heraclitus, in theology: the force we cannot put into our words, but which we may find already there. Such force is indeed primitive, and for that reason irrefutable; as Eliot, more insistently than any other modern poet, recognized – memorably in *The Use of Poetry and the Use of Criticism*:

> What I call the 'auditory imagination' is the feeling for syllable and rhythm, penetrating far below the conscious levels of thought and feeling, invigorating every word; sinking to the

most primitive and forgotten, returning to the origin and bringing something back, seeking the beginning and the end. It works through meanings, certainly, or not without meanings in the ordinary sense, and fuses the old and obliterated and the trite, the current, and the new and surprising, the most ancient and the most civilised mentality. (UPUC, 118–19)

The one thing the auditory imagination does not do, apparently, is settle for the swift conversion of syllables into a meaning. Lest we think that Eliot is merely talking gorgeous nonsense, he reverts to the same emphasis in the 'Conclusion' to *The Use of Poetry and the Use of Criticism*, where the context has to do with mysticism, pure poetry, and the Abbé Brémond. Eliot speaks of inspiration, but only to go further and refer to 'this disturbance of our quotidian character which results in an incantation, an outburst of words which we hardly recognise as our own . . .' (UPUC, 145) – a very different thing, Eliot maintains, from mystical illumination:

The latter is a vision which may be accompanied by the realisation that you will never be able to communicate it to anyone else, or even by the realisation that when it is past you will not be able to recall it to yourself; the former is not a vision but a motion terminating in an arrangement of words on paper.
(UPUC, 145)

The opening passage of the second section of 'Burnt Norton' is a motion terminating in words available mostly, if not solely, to divination:

> Garlic and sapphires in the mud
> Clot the bedded axle-tree.
> The trilling wire in the blood
> Sings below inveterate scars
> Appeasing long forgotten wars.
> The dance along the artery
> The circulation of the lymph
> Are figured in the drift of stars
> Ascend to summer in the tree
> We move above the moving tree
> In light upon the figured leaf
> And hear upon the sodden floor
> Below, the boarhound and the boar

Pursue their pattern as before
But reconciled among the stars.   (CPP, 172)

R.P. Blackmur found in these lines the effect of behaviour rising into belief, and made much of the two reconciliations; one as something that happens in the blood under scars, the other as something that happens above among the stars; made much, too, of the superior drift not only of stars in their courses but of the universal course of things. The drift is figured in the rhymed formality of the lines, and in the murmuring of a language which appeases itself in the repetition of 'stars' and 'figured', the rhyme of 'tree' with itself, the drift from 'move' to 'moving'. In this style of incantation 'Ascend to summer in the tree' is joined to 'Are figured in the drift of stars' grammatically, but it is mobile enough to anticipate the 'We' of the line that follows. If the passage shows behaviour rising into belief, the behaviour is a sense of a universal force at work in life, and the belief is as if congenital, given by the gods.

A phrase repeated from 'Coriolan' I, 'At the still point of the turning world', alters the rhythm of 'Burnt Norton' at this point, but not the belief. What follows clears or cures the ground by removing the commonplace possibilities of description. The pattern (neither this nor that) becomes the structural figure of the third section of 'Burnt Norton'. As in the remaining *Quartets*, when a personal voice is heard, it is heard confessing its inability to say exactly what it means or to make enough sense to satisfy the desires it has recognized: 'I can only say, *there* we have been: but I cannot say where. / And I cannot say, how long, for that is to place it in time.' (CPP, 173)

The first consequence of these inabilities, in the next passage, is that the language deploys nine lines and sixty-three words without completing a sentence; intoned phrases explicate one another without sending their vibrations in one direction rather than another. The whole passage sounds as if it were spoken by Thomas à Becket, explaining yet again why humankind cannot bear very much reality:

Yet the enchainment of past and future
Woven in the weakness of the changing body,
Protects mankind from heaven and damnation
Which flesh cannot endure.   (CPP, 173)

Heaven and damnation are both belief, the one above the moving tree and among the stars, the other beneath the inveterate scars. Each involves a scale of values terrifyingly different from those which are gratified by the convergence of our interests upon the daily events that appease them. Because Baudelaire recognized as much, he knew, according to Eliot, that what really matters is Sin and Redemption, and therefore 'he walked secure in this high vocation, that he was capable of a damnation denied to the politicians and the newspaper editors of Paris.' (SE, 429)

The second movement of the poem ends with a resumption of its first style – brooding on time – and with a crucial appeal to the higher perspective of memory. The merit of memory is not otherwise self-evident. Why we remember one episode rather than another is of course interesting, and Eliot often wondered about it, as in *The Use of Poetry and the Use of Criticism*, but the memory he invokes in 'Burnt Norton' is mainly valuable because it is another disjunction between the actual and the real; between the immediacy of an event and the saving grace of distance in which we consider its meaning:

> Time past and time future
> Allow but a little consciousness.
> To be conscious is not to be in time
> But only in time can the moment in the rose-garden,
> The moment in the arbour where the rain beat,
> The moment in the draughty church at smokefall
> Be remembered; involved with past and future.
> Only through time time is conquered.   (CPP, 173)

Smokefall got itself into the *Supplement* to the O.E.D. ('after NIGHTFALL') with an explication by Helen Gardner: 'the moment when the wind drops and smoke that had ascended descends.' The smoke of incense, presumably. In *The Family Reunion* Eliot indulged himself in a lot of snobbery by separating Harry so far from the company at Wishwood – 'You are all people / To whom nothing has happened' (CPP, 293) – even to the extent of saying that an accident followed by concussion can't make much difference to brother John. In 'Burnt Norton' the distinction between those who are conscious and those who aren't isn't drawn: memory is available to anyone who doesn't capitulate to every passing moment. At least the 'strained, time-ridden faces' aren't named; though only a brave reader would claim to be exempt from the condition. 'Conquered' is a gruff word – 'Only through time time is conquered' – when there has been so much talk, in Eliot's early poems and in his essay on Dante, about the redemption of time. It is conquered, presumably, because in the perspective of memory an event can't be peremptory, as it was when it occurred.

It is not necessary to say much about the third section of the poem. I assume that most readers have assented to Hugh Kenner's version of the pattern in process: opposite values, falsely reconciled, and at last truly reconciled. One might add, truly reconciled not by any Hegelian synthesis but by giving a more demanding sense to one of the values. As here: light and darkness are the opposing values, falsely reconciled in the 'flicker' of the third movement, the London Underground episode, then truly reconciled by giving darkness a more profound sense, by recourse to the Dark Night of the Soul in St John of the Cross. The motif of the second movement (neither this nor that) is repeated; neither daylight . . . nor darkness; neither plenitude nor vacancy. But the vacated space is now filled with the flicker of distraction. St John's distinction between the 'night of sense' (available to ordinary penitents) and the 'night of soul' (only for adepts of sanctity) – 'This is the one way, and the other / Is the same, not in movement / But abstention from movement' (CPP, 174) – seems to have suggested itself to Eliot by his remarking the two ways (the stairs and the lift) of getting to the tube at Gloucester Road.

I have been suggesting that the fundamental motive of 'Burnt Norton' is to void the claim of spontaneity; to represent as vulgar any immediate response to an event; to imply a form of life in which the meaning of an event comes long after its mere occurrence and in a light which is not that of punctuality. According to the rhetoric of Eliot's Christian poetry, the only event in which meaning coincides with the act is the Incarnation.

In the fourth movement of 'Burnt Norton', a brief lyric transacts events of the past – 'Time and the bell have buried the day' – the present continuous – 'The black cloud carries the sun away' – lingers upon an entirely hypothetical future:

Will the sunflower turn to us, will the clematis
Stray down, bend to us; tendril and spray
Clutch and cling?
Chill
Fingers of yew be curled
Down on us?   (CPP, 174–5)

and reverts to a present indicative steadied by the repeated 'still'
– 'After the kingfisher's wing / Has answered light to light, and
is silent, the light is still / At the still point of the turning
world.' (CPP, 175) Again the effect of the four questions –
about sunflower, clematis, tendril and spray, and yew – is to
keep the phrases hovering indeterminately above the ground of
our beseeching. The whole passage, one of Eliot's consummate
achievements in language, is at once impersonal, as if the words
were uttering themselves in a ritual to make sense of man's
presence in the natural world; and irresistibly personal in the turns
and trillings of the phrases. The sunflower turns to the sun, but we
do not feel obliged to ask who are the 'us' to whom it may also
turn. An extraordinarily personal presence inhabits the phrases, but
in such a way, and with such unaggressive emphasis, as to remain
within the weavings of word and word; the rhyme of 'turn to us',
'bend to us', and 'curled / Down on us'; the imperative 'Chill'
occupying a whole line of verse without our knowing, at first
reading, whether it is a noun (like the beginnings of its companion
questions; sunflower, clematis, tendril and spray) or the adjective it
turns out to be. The word stays in the air of our minds till it finds
its rhyme, three lines later, in 'still', another word we can't construe
– adjective or adverb – till the last line makes it clear. Hopkins's
kingfisher ('As kingfishers catch fire') made a parable of selving,
the flame of face testifying to the type of individuality; Eliot's
kingfisher speaks of answering light to light, of the silence into
which words after speech reach, and the stillness poised upon the
axle of the turning world.

The fifth and last movement of the poem is its most contentious
part, for reasons I'll try to explain. Much depends on the value
we give to the first three lines: 'Words move, music moves /
Only in time; but that which is only living / Can only die.'
(CPP, 175) It recapitulates the statement about being conscious

and remembering; as if to say that while of course we have to live in time, we are not obliged to live according to its chronometer or in deference to its 'metalled ways'. The distinction between Chronos (Yeats: ' . . . the cracked tune that Chronos sings') and Kairos, the time of meaning and value, is much to the point here. The silence into which words reach is, so far as it is attended to, their meaning, not their defeat:

> Only by the form, the pattern,
> Can words or music reach
> The stillness, as a Chinese jar still
> Moves perpetually in its stillness.
> Not the stillness of the violin, while the note lasts,
> Not that only, but the co-existence,
> Or say that the end precedes the beginning,
> And the end and the beginning were always there
> Before the beginning and after the end.
> And all is always now.   (CPP, 175)

In *The Living Principle* Leavis gives an account of this passage so invidious that it impels him beyond the necessity of his argument into a commentary, finally negative, on Eliot's entire later poetry. It is clear that he reached this position for many complicated reasons; including a radical shift in his scale of values, such that Eliot must be diminished by a revised comparison with Lawrence, a fate that Lawrence, too, suffered by still later comparison with the Tolstoy of *Anna Karenina*. Leavis allowed himself to be scandalized, in his commentary on 'Burnt Norton', by Eliot's insistence – at least it appeared to Leavis to amount to insistence – that 'the really real . . . is the eternal' (177). Except by relation to the ultimately real, which is eternal, human life has no significance: this is what Leavis accused Eliot of believing, on the evidence of 'Burnt Norton'. Eliot, that is, 'insists on the unreality, the unlivingness, of life in time' (179).

I don't find Eliot believing anything of the kind: he couldn't have believed it and still be a communicant of a Church which is founded upon the redemption of time by the Annunciation. How Eliot judged those forms of temporal life which were content to be, in every limiting sense, merely temporal, and to obey the call of punctuality and immediacy, is of course a different matter: on that, the evidence he has left is clear.

In 'Burnt Norton', the words which induced Leavis to pro-
test are those which seem to entail a claim, on Eliot's part,
to know what 'the meaning' is; such words as 'form' and
'pattern', and, from an earlier movement, 'the dance'. 'The
ultimate really real that Eliot seeks in *Four Quartets*', accord-
ing to Leavis, 'is eternal reality, and *that* he can do little,
directly, to characterize' (175). Directly, of course not. Nor is
there any pretence of 'characterizing'. Form, pattern and dance
are merely analogies, ways of putting not 'eternal reality' but
the poet's striving to apprehend it. Form, pattern and dance
denote the point at which an otherwise mere event may be
brought to disclose its meaning; brought, by exerting upon it
the pressure of a more demanding moral and spiritual per-
spective than any judgement entailed in the immediacy of the
event itself.

That the meaning is dynamic is clarified by the 'Chinese jar'
which 'still / Moves perpetually in its stillness' (CPP, 175). Where
Eliot comes a cropper is in his attempt to be more specific than that,
distinguishing between a visible and an audible stillness, and trying
to go beyond the distinction. 'Not that only, but the co-existence':
the co-existence of what? He finds it impossible to say just what
he means; as the passage about the incapacity of words goes on to
confess almost at once.

In the interval between *Murder in the Cathedral* and *The Family
Reunion*, Eliot had temptation much on his mind; the temp-
tation of Thomas à Becket, of Harry's father, of Christ in
the desert and more generally the temptation of silence to
dissolve in chatter. The last lines of this movement are perhaps
melodramatic:

> The Word in the desert
> Is most attacked by voices of temptation,
> The crying shadow in the funeral dance,
> The loud lament of the disconsolate chimera.

> (CPP, 175)

I can't find any particular – or particularly cogent – meaning in the
last two lines: what the shadow is, or who or what the disconsolate
chimera is. Eliot is rattling old bones.

The poem ends more quietly in another attempt to represent the
pattern as dynamic:

>   The detail of the pattern is movement,
>   As in the figure of the ten stairs.
>   Desire itself is movement
>   Not in itself desirable;
>   Love is itself unmoving,
>   Only the cause and end of movement,
>   Timeless, and undesiring
>   Except in the aspect of time
>   Caught in the form of limitation
>   Between un-being and being.
>   Sudden in a shaft of sunlight
>   Even while the dust moves
>   There rises the hidden laughter
>   Of children in the foliage
>   Quick now, here, now, always –
>   Ridiculous the waste sad time
>   Stretching before and after.   (CPP, 176)

Structurally, it is a return to the beginning, a discursive passage about time, love and desire; a passage in which the English language, in this respect like Mallarmé's French, seems to be intoning itself without requiring either a speaker or a listener to be in attendance. As in the first movement, we are released from its monitions to the imagery of gardens, children and laughter. The figure of the ten stairs comes from St John of the Cross and may be left unglossed; it sustains the Heraclitean motif of the way up and the way down. It would be more useful to quote, from the third movement of 'Little Gidding', the passage about the use of memory:

>   This is the use of memory:
>   For liberation – not less of love but expanding
>   Of love beyond desire, and so liberation
>   From the future as well as the past.   (CPP, 195)

This is what 'Burnt Norton', and indeed the other Quartets, are about: starting from the unquestionably rich ground of laughing children in the foliage, how to avoid losing or, worse still, humiliating the promise implicit in the sunshine and the laughter. How to convert the low dream of desire into the high dream of love.

In the chapter on *Alice in Wonderland* in *Some Versions of Pastoral*

William Empson remarks how a certain feeling about children developed in England after the eighteenth-century settlement had come to seem narrow and inescapable; a feeling 'that no way of building up character, no intellectual system, can bring out all that is inherent in the human spirit, and therefore that there is more in the child than any man has been able to keep' (260–1). This idea of the child, 'that it is in the right relation to Nature, not dividing what should be unified, that its intuitive judgment contains what poetry and philosophy must spend their time labouring to recover, was accepted by Dodgson and a main part of his feeling' (261). 'Burnt Norton' is full of this feeling, along with a doomed conviction that it can't be recovered, and that the only thing possible is to invoke the plenitude of one's memory of such unity, and start again from there under better, because more exacting, auspices.

The success of 'Burnt Norton' is still in dispute. The reason is, I think, that none of the critical procedures developed and employed in the fifty years since the publication of the poem has been responsive to the kind of poetry we find in 'Burnt Norton'. I can put this briefly by saying: nobody, not even Leavis, took up where D.W. Harding's account of the poem left off. Most of the critical procedures which have been used with success in the analysis of poems have concentrated upon one or another of a limited set of terms: image, symbol and structure. No critical method has arisen which proposes to show the poetic character and potentiality of discourse. It is still an effort to take the harm out of the word 'discursive'; as reviews of John Ashbery's poems sufficiently indicate.

Harding's 1936 review of 'Burnt Norton', reprinted in his *Experience Into Words* (1963), is the place to begin:

> Ordinarily our abstract ideas are over-comprehensive and include too wide a range of feeling to be of much use by themselves. If our words 'regret' and 'eternity' were exact bits of mosaic with which to build patterns, much of 'Burnt Norton' would not have had to be written. . . . One could say, perhaps, that the poem takes the place of the ideas of 'regret' and 'eternity'. Where in ordinary speech we should have to use those words, and hope by conversational trial-and-error to obviate the grosser misunderstandings, this poem is a newly created concept, equally

abstract but vastly more exact and rich in meaning. It makes no statement. It is no more 'about' anything than an abstract term like 'love' is about anything: it is a linguistic creation. And the creation of a new concept, with all the assimilation and communication of experience that that involves, is perhaps the greatest of linguistic achievements. (109)

Harding goes on to indicate, too briefly perhaps, how Eliot's methods in 'Burnt Norton' differ from ordinary attempts 'to state the meaning by taking existing abstract ideas and piecing them together in the ordinary way' (110). It might have been expected, especially after the publication of Stevens' *Notes Toward a Supreme Fiction*, that a critical method sensitive to poetry as a work in the creation of new concepts might have been developed. It has not happened. Readers are still encouraged to believe that a poem is an action (or a structure) of words chiefly concerned with the development of the resources of imagery and symbolism within the fiction of a dramatic monologue. The discrimination of concepts (not this precisely . . . or even that) is regarded as fit matter for an essay, but not for a poem. We have not yet devised a poetics of discourse in any way comparable to the several poetics of image, symbol and structure. The result is that we don't quite know what to do with such passages as the first lines of 'Burnt Norton'. The problem differs from that of 'argufying in poetry' – Empson's programme – because such argufying is content to take concepts as they come, and to engage in conversation with them. Quite a different matter. What Harding tried to describe, in relation to 'Burnt Norton', is unfinished business, I am embarrassed to have to say.

References

Eliot, T.S., 'Note sur Mallarmé et Poe', *La Nouvelle Revue Française*, Paris, XIV 158 (1 November 1926), [524]–526, trans. Ramon Fernandez (English text not published).

Empson, William, *Some Versions of Pastoral*, London, Chatto & Windus, 1935.

Harding, D.W., *Experience Into Words*, Harmondsworth, Penguin, 1974 (rpt).

Leavis, F.R., *The Living Principle: 'English' as a Discipline of Thought*, London, Chatto & Windus, 1975.

Mallarmé, Stephane, *Oeuvres*, ed. Yves-Alain Favre, Paris, Garnier, 1985.

2

Limitation and Transcendence in 'East Coker'
Edward Lobb

T.S. Eliot apparently began 'East Coker' early in 1940. In February of that year, John Hayward wrote to Frank Morley that the first two sections had been drafted; the poem was completed later that month, and first appeared in the *New English Weekly* for March 21 (CFQ, 16–17). We cannot assume that 'East Coker' was an 'unwilled' poem, but the speed with which it was composed does suggest that the material had been in suspension in Eliot's mind, and needed only a seed to precipitate it. Eliot speaks in *The Use of Poetry* of the visual experience of a child, which 'might lie dormant in his mind for twenty years, and re-appear transformed in some verse-context charged with great imaginative pressure' (UPUC, 79). Poems written as quickly as 'East Coker' was – the later *Duino Elegies*, for example – often reveal not only transformed personal experience but the continuing, half-conscious use of a body of images which goes back to the poet's first work.

To read the later poem with that body of images in mind is to see both the unity of a career and the diversity which even a small number of images makes possible. One could, for example, write a complete study of Yeats based on his use of a few images: bird, tree, tower, stair, sun and moon. A similar study of Eliot might well begin with the image of the closed room, which, in various forms, is central to Eliot's entire poetic career and particularly to the themes and orchestration of 'East Coker'.

I

In order to understand why this image is crucial to understanding 'East Coker' and its place in the *Quartets*, it is necessary to look at the development of the closed-room motif from the beginning of Eliot's career.[1] The image tends to take two distinct forms in Eliot's early poetry. The first evokes the loneliness of individuals in separate rooms:

> With the other masquerades
> That time resumes,
> One thinks of all the hands
> That are raising dingy shades
> In a thousand furnished rooms.
>
> ('Preludes' II; CPP, 22)

Prufrock has seen 'lonely men in shirt-sleeves, leaning out of windows', and the speaker of 'Rhapsody on a Windy Night' thinks of 'female smells in shuttered rooms' (CPP, 15, 25). Gerontion remembers Mr Silvero, 'Who walked all night in the next room' (CPP, 37). But the rooms suggest more than loneliness and melancholy; they function also as images of limited or solipsistic consciousness. In 'The Love Song of J. Alfred Prufrock' particularly, they are reinforced by other, analogous images of isolation. The etherized patient and the sleeping fog-cat are unaware of anything outside the self; the 'ragged claws', with their protective exoskeleton, are likewise wholly self-enclosed, and the 'silent seas' in which they move reflect Prufrock's sense that he can communicate neither with other people nor with the universe (CPP, 13, 15).

Gerontion's situation is similar. His isolation is presented in physical terms – he is blind and his other senses are failing – but it is essentially metaphysical since, like Prufrock, he is too sceptical or too fearful to commit himself to any belief. His 'decayed house' (dwelling, dynasty, body, mind) is in effect a closed room, and his world is one in which even Christ is a baby 'unable to speak a word' or a mute tiger (CPP, 37). The walls between people are unbreached and apparently unbreachable. It is easy to see why Eliot originally intended to use 'Gerontion' as a sort of prologue to *The Waste Land*, where the same sense of isolation is pervasive and the closed room becomes explicitly a prison:

> I have heard the key
> Turn in the door once and turn once only
> We think of the key, each in his prison
> Thinking of the key, each confirms a prison.
>
> (CPP, 74)

Eliot's footnote on this passage refers the reader to Ugolino's tower in *Inferno* XXXIII and Bradley's *Appearance and Reality*, but this information – like most of the material in Eliot's alternately pedantic and whimsical footnotes – adds almost nothing to the image itself, which encapsulates all of the themes of *The Waste Land* and Eliot's poetry generally. On the emotional level, it suggests loneliness, *ennui, cafard*; on the intellectual level, that fear of solipsism which, as A.D. Nuttall has shown, has haunted western literature since the eighteenth century. What if all our ideas are merely private fantasias, projections on the walls of our private cells? What if the universe is wholly unknowable? The emotional and intellectual aspects of the image are of course closely related. Prufrock, Gerontion and most of the characters in *The Waste Land* have immediate worries which are sexual and personal, and ultimate concerns which are metaphysical: many readers see the two themes as a form of ironic counterpoint – the trivial juxtaposed with the cosmic – but the two are finally aspects of the same thing: a desire to get beyond the self.

The second form of the closed-room image is slightly more complex, but still essentially straightforward. Here the room is shared by two or more people, and conversation may occur, but no communication takes place. Prufrock notes twice that 'In the room the women come and go / Talking of Michelangelo' (CPP, 13–14), and we assume that their talk is trivial – not because they are women, but because everything else in the poem suggests the failure of communication. Prufrock and his silent companion (if he is in fact talking to someone other than himself) are also in that room, but he forestalls his companion's questions ('Oh, do not ask "What is it?"') and tells us that 'It is impossible to say just what I mean!' (CPP, 13, 16). Enclosed in his carapace of collar, necktie and morning coat – the equivalent of the crab's exoskeleton, a room within a room – he can neither express himself nor be sure of understanding others. His great fear is that 'one, settling a pillow by her head, / Should say: "That is not what I meant at all. / That is not it, at all."' (CPP, 16)

In 'Portrait of a Lady', the male speaker notes the sepulchral atmosphere of his woman friend's room:

> And four wax candles in the darkened room,
> Four rings of light upon the ceiling overhead,
> An atmosphere of Juliet's tomb
> Prepared for all the things to be said, or left unsaid.

(CPP, 18)

But what is said might as well be unsaid, for the male speaker is detached and self-conscious, the lady self-absorbed, throughout. The darkened room represents both his claustrophobia and the failure of what should be shared experience; the poem traces, through four seasons, a relationship which never develops. Madame de Tornquist in 'Gerontion', 'in the dark room / Shifting the candles' (CPP, 37) is involved in a similar charade, and parallel scenes occur in *The Waste Land*. The most notable is obviously the bedroom scene in 'A Game of Chess'. Here a husband and wife engage in nervous, febrile conversation, but the scene is a study of two solitudes: nothing can touch the wife's neurosis or the husband's detachment. This room is echoed thematically by the typist's bedsitter in the next section of the poem. The single room in which she lives, cooks, eats and sleeps is a metaphor of enclosed consciousness; she is 'hardly aware' of her lover after he leaves, or indeed while he is there. The house-agent's clerk also inhabits a private world. He misreads the typist's silence, making 'a welcome of indifference', and – a final comment on his egoism – gropes blindly down the unlit stairs afterwards (CPP, 68–9).

It is surely significant that, in the age of gas or electric light, three of these rooms are lit by candles:

> And four wax candles in the darkened room,
> Four rings of light upon the ceiling overhead
> > ('Portrait of a Lady'; CPP, 18)

> Madame de Tornquist, in the dark room
> Shifting the candles
> > ('Gerontion'; CPP, 37)

> these [odours] ascended
> In fattening the prolonged candle-flames,
> Flung their smoke into the laquearia
> > (*The Waste Land* II; CPP, 64)

The candles, particularly when associated with smoke and darkness, are the equivalent of the fire in the cave in Plato's *Republic*, and reinforce the association of the rooms with the false or limited consciousness discussed by Plato.

As if to underline the point, some of the rooms contain mirrors. In the wealthy woman's bedroom, Eliot draws attention to 'the glass / Held up by standards wrought with fruited vines / From which a golden Cupidon peeped out' (CPP, 64). The mirror is implicitly contrasted with the pictures or tapestries in the room. The latter are unlooked-at, and consequently mere 'withered stumps of time', but they represent the past and the world, a world of action and real emotion prompted by external objects; the mirror, on the other hand, merely reflects the closed room, from which the inhabitants will escape only to 'a closed car' (CPP, 65). The typist, an even more extreme case, 'turns and looks a moment in the glass,' her self-absorption intact (CPP, 69).

II

All of these closed-room images are consistent with the Bradley passage referred to in Eliot's note to the '*Dayadhvam*' passage, and that note has predictably been used to summarize the theme of solipsistic consciousness in the poem and in Eliot's early work generally. Such explanations tend to be genetic: even when they do not assert explicitly that the poem is developing a philosophical idea which existed before the poem, they assume the priority of philosophical explanation by using its terminology. The implicit assertion is that the poetic complexities of a passage are 'really' philosophical complexities, or that a poem dramatizes issues which are best explained in philosophical terms.

But Eliot was not a philosopher. The current prominence of linguistic philosophy in criticism, and Eliot's initial seriousness about a philosophical career, occasionally overshadow important facts. We know from Lyndall Gordon's excellent account of Eliot's early life that philosophy was simply one manifestation of that interest in subject and object which informs his poetry, his criticism and the dissertation. Philosophy was not the *fons et origo*; it was a symptom, not a cause (EEY, 15–64). Eliot was primarily a poet, and poetry is not just a means of epistemological inquiry: when it does deal with knowledge, it does so in specifically poetic ways. Questions which are in essence extremely simple – questions like 'Can I trust my knowledge of the external world?' – become complicated as philosophers discuss their implications in technical and often abstract language; they become complicated in a different and far more concrete way in poetry.

As obvious as these facts are, it is necessary to re-emphasize them, and to remind ourselves that Eliot had little use for philosophical poetry, or, in fact, for ideas of any kind in poetry. He believed that a 'creation of art' should not embody a philosophy, but should '*replace* a philosophy' (SW, 66). The celebrated sneer at Tennyson and Browning, who 'ruminated' (SE, 288), and the praise of Henry James's mind, 'so fine that no idea could violate it' (SP, 151), are in the same mould. If we accept the idea that Eliot's poetry is a valid form of discourse in itself, we can begin to understand how issues are addressed and finally resolved in poetic terms.

The image of the closed room represents – or 'replaces' – the idea of limited and possibly solipsistic knowledge; if we follow that image through Eliot's later poetry, it will show us a way out of the dilemma in its own terms. The resolution is poetically and emotionally complex, but intellectually simple: if we are confined to our individual consciousnesses, we must simply accept the fact. Thus in the first part of *Ash-Wednesday*, the abandonment of hope becomes, paradoxically, the only hope; the speaker prays to leave ratiocination behind, to forget 'These matters that with myself I too much discuss / Too much explain' (CPP, 89). In one sense this simply re-enacts the recognition, in *The Waste Land*, that consciousness is not the answer but the problem: 'each in his prison / Thinking of the key, each confirms a prison'. But Eliot's post-conversion poetry reveals – not surprisingly – a new attitude towards the prison of the self and consciousness. In part III of the poem, the speaker is confined, like many of Eliot's earlier characters, to a room (in this case a tower much like Ugolino's) but finds 'strength beyond hope and despair / Climbing the third stair' (CPP, 93); he is no longer trying to escape from the tower or even thinking about doing so.

What the speaker has attained is humility, a proper sense of one's limits as a creature. The Christian knows that he is incapable of attaining grace or salvation (or knowledge of God) through his own efforts: these things come, if they come at all, as gifts from God. So the speaker continues to climb, but his actions are not to be seen as a form of work or effort: the climbing is simply a visual representation of movement in time, of ongoing life and a growing detachment from created things. The transcendence of hope and despair, outside a religious context, would be mere stoicism; here, however, it clearly signals an acceptance of the idea that what matters is not the speaker's own progress but the will of God. In his criticism, Eliot quoted Dante's '*la sua volontade è nostra pace*' more than once, and he paraphrases it in part VI of *Ash-Wednesday*: 'Our peace in His will' (CPP, 98).

It is particularly important to recognize the state of mind that lies behind *Ash-Wednesday* because the *Quartets* begin where *Ash-Wednesday* ends, and continue the same speaker's spiritual autobiography. The *Quartets* describe a deliberate withdrawal to the dark world of individual consciousness – to the closed room in one or another of its forms. In 'Burnt Norton' it is the enclosed, flickering world of the tube train (another echo of Plato's cave); in 'East Coker' it is 'the deep lane / Shuttered with branches, dark in the afternoon' (CPP, 177) and later the darkening theatre; in 'Little Gidding' it is the cold church, 'the world's end' (CPP, 192). The difference between these 'rooms' and the earlier ones is that these are accepted – even embraced – as the only possible arena of discourse. The speaker recognizes the ultimate futility of thought, and that recognition is the key to his freedom.

> There is, it seems to us,
> At best, only a limited value
> In the knowledge derived from experience.
> The knowledge imposes a pattern, and falsifies . . .
>
> The only wisdom we can hope to acquire
> Is the wisdom of humility: humility is endless.
>
> (CPP, 179)

Eliot here alludes to the title of his dissertation (*Knowledge and Experience in the Philosophy of F.H. Bradley*), and thereby to its scepticism about the possibility of knowledge. What is more interesting is the way in which humility – the acceptance of limitations – enables one to go beyond limitation: knowledge is limited, but humility is *endless*.

This, I would argue, is the central drama of the *Quartets* generally, and of 'East Coker' in particular. In theological terms, the recognition of our powerlessness enables us to accept grace and transcend our limitations; we cannot free ourselves by 'thinking of the key' (CPP, 74), but we can be freed, like St Peter from his prison, when we acknowledge a higher power.[2] Thus the enclosed and dark places in three of the *Four Quartets* become places of purgation, as in mystical literature, and lead to enlightenment; the closed rooms open into visionary experience which is not finally undercut by doubt, despite the poems' acknowledgment of the problematic nature of all perception. Nor is the closed room, by this point, simply an image of limited or self-reflexive knowledge. It stands for all kinds of limitation, but I shall focus on three forms which are especially prominent in 'East Coker': time, ascetic discipline, and poetic form.

III

The first of these is the most obvious. 'East Coker' is the most time-ridden of the *Quartets*. In contrast to 'Burnt Norton', with its lotus-vision of our 'first world' and the still point beyond time, 'East Coker' presents an antithetical vision of our bondage to time, a vision of ceaseless and apparently purposeless activity.

> In succession
> Houses rise and fall, crumble, are extended,
> Are removed, destroyed, restored, or in their place
> Is an open field, or a factory, or a by-pass.
>
> (CPP, 177)

The wonderful flatness of these lines achieves its own kind of eloquence, but what is most important in the opening of 'East Coker' – and least discussed – is the question of tone. Readers of Eliot's earlier poetry can hardly help hearing in these lines the jadedness of Tiresias or Prufrock's 'I have known them all already'. The whole passage owes a good deal, I suspect, to the vision of 'the timekept City' in *The Rock*:

> In the land of lobelias and tennis flannels
> The rabbit shall burrow and the thorn revisit,
> The nettle shall flourish on the gravel court,
> And the wind shall say: 'Here were decent godless people:
> Their only monument the asphalt road
> And a thousand lost golf-balls.'   (CPP, 155)

If the opening of 'East Coker' simply duplicates this dark irony, we are inclined to read the whole poem as black comedy, a Beckettian vision of 'dung and death'. On the other hand, the echoes of Ecclesiastes later in the passage ('there is a time for building / And a time for living and for generation') seem to imply a divine context for human activities, and the consequent possibility of their being meaningful.

This tension in the opening verse-paragraph may simply be Eliot's way of maintaining, as he often does in the *Quartets*, a double focus. The next verse-paragraph repeats the opening line of the poem ('In my beginning is my end') and thus seems to enact the cyclical repetition which has already been described. But the lines following offer a way of reconciling irony and vision, time and eternity:

> Now the light falls
> Across the open field, leaving the deep lane
> Shuttered with branches, dark in the afternoon,
> Where you lean against a bank while a van passes,
> And the deep lane insists on the direction
> Into the village, in the electric heat
> Hypnotised.   (CPP, 177)

The lane's insistence on the direction into the village is of course an illusion: if you were facing the other way, it would insist just as firmly on the direction away. That insistence is the false certainty of all linear systems – time, logic, visual perspective – which are either inherent in our minds or built into them by education. Even outdoors, we inhabit a 'shuttered' closed room.

But in Eliot's post-conversion perspective, the limitations of human perception are now accepted as part of the discipline of humility: with the recognition that our own perspective is limited comes the recognition that the two views of human activity in the first verse-paragraph – the ironist's and Ecclesiastes' – are perhaps not incompatible. Irony and vision can be reconciled. This reconciliation can also be seen in the 'summer midnight' scene. Just as St Peter's prison walls dissolve, the shuttered lane opens into visionary experience, but the vision is itself ironic, a glimpse of human frailty in the fire of time. The peasants who dance 'round and round the fire' are Plato's cave dwellers again.

Ideally, we are supposed to keep the previous parts of the *Quartets* in mind as we read, so 'East Coker' is always, in theory, balanced by the vision of 'Burnt Norton'. But the ideal reader who experiences the sequence spatially as well as temporally has never been more than an ideal fiction, and Eliot was aware of this. In fact, we read 'East Coker' discretely, but with a general sense of Eliot's method which is likely to include, if only at the subconscious level, an awareness of Eliot's use of the closed-room motif. The emphasis of 'East Coker' on time, change and decay seems less bleak when we realize that Eliot has come to terms with limitation. Even the elegiac opening of part III ('O dark dark dark'), which might easily have become ghoulish or morbid or – worse – grotesquely funny, is characterized rather by a sense of the dignity, finality and pathos of human experience.

From it emerges another instance of the closed room, one which illustrates Eliot's method perfectly:

> I said to my soul, be still, and let the dark come upon you
> Which shall be the darkness of God. As, in a theatre,
> The lights are extinguished, for the scene to be changed
> With a hollow rumble of wings, with a movement of darkness
>   on darkness,
> And we know that the hills and the trees, the distant panorama
> And the bold imposing façade are all being rolled away –
>
>   (CPP, 180)

This is immediately effective because it evokes an experience which every reader has had, but the image works on many levels. It echoes the experience which Eliot had around the time of his graduation from Harvard: 'while walking one day in Boston, he saw the streets suddenly shrink and divide' (EEY, 15). The experience left him with an abiding sense of the unreality of 'real' life which is shared by many of his personae, from Prufrock to Lord Harry in *The Family Reunion* ('You have gone through life in sleep, / Never woken to the nightmare.' [CPP, 293]).

In 'East Coker' this sense of unreality is brilliantly caught in the image of the theatre, explicitly a place of illusion. This is succeeded by the tube train stopped between stations: 'And you see behind every face the mental emptiness deepen / Leaving only the growing terror of nothing to think about; / Or when, under ether, the mind is conscious but conscious of nothing –' (CPP, 180). This sequence of images (theatre, tube train, etherised patient) encapsulates in reverse order the whole history of Eliot's closed rooms from the opening lines of 'Prufrock' to the tube train's first appearance in 'Burnt Norton' III. His former claustrophobia has become, as I have suggested, an acceptance of limitations: the human experience of time in 'East Coker' is a synecdoche for all the forms of limitation and inadequate perception which are inherent in our status as creatures. Humility enables us to accept our limitations, but humility – represented in *Ash-Wednesday* by acceptance of the tower – is merely the first stage of a long process.

This brings us to the second form of limitation in 'East Coker', that of ascetic discipline. The recognition and acceptance of limitations is succeeded by the willing of further self-limitation: in the terms we have been using, we strive to make the closed room smaller than nature herself makes it. In 'East Coker' this process is first implied by forms of absence (darkness, silence, emptiness, 'nothing'), then described directly in the words of St John of the Cross, which introduce further negations – ignorance, dispossession, and 'the way in which you are not'. The *via negativa* is a means of emptying the self in preparation for the mystical illumination we are past desiring.

The details of the process are not described in the poem for obvious reasons. Eliot never saw poetry as a means of explanation, and any interested reader can look up the relevant texts, particularly *The Ascent of Mount Carmel.* Eliot is concerned here rather with connections, and the connections show the consistency and subtlety of his metaphors. The darkness of the tube train in 'Burnt Norton' III, with its evocation of human limitations, physical and mental, is not dark enough; we must 'Descend lower' to find the 'Internal darkness'. This pattern is repeated precisely in 'East Coker' as the darkness of the deep lane gives way, via Dante's 'dark wood' (II) and Milton's 'dark dark dark' (III), to the darker paradoxes of St John. In each case, the same image is used to show how human limitations can become the means of their own transcendence: if time can only be conquered through time ('Burnt Norton' II), other forms of limitation can only be conquered through limitation. The literary references in 'East Coker' make the point unobtrusively. Dante must descend in order to rise and experience the beatific vision; Milton's Samson must experience a narrowing of ordinary human capacities in order to 'see'. 'Dark amid the blaze of noon', his situation parallels exactly that of the speaker in the deep lane shuttered with branches and that of the pilgrim of the *via negativa.*

Post-war readers of 'East Coker' – particularly non-religious ones – are apt to view the poem as gloomy, and I have already mentioned that it is the most time-ridden of the *Quartets.* But it is important to see the poem historically, as a product, in part, of wartime; in this context it becomes, paradoxically, almost cheerful. Unlike 'Little Gidding', 'East Coker' refers only covertly to the war, but the poem's first readers got the point. Rationing was a form of asceticism, and evacuation was a form of 'dispossession': Eliot was suggesting, among other things, that the hardships of war could be put to spiritual use. This helps to make sense of his remark – otherwise rather puzzling – that the last three *Quartets* are primarily patriotic poems. Lyndall Gordon remarks, justly, that 'for all its rigour, "East Coker" is the most optimistic of the *Quartets*' (ENL, 110); Helen Gardner comments on its impact during the darkest period of the war (CFQ, 17).

The third form of limitation in 'East Coker' is one which is not discussed or even alluded to in the language of the poem. It is the limitation of poetic form, and it is dealt with, appropriately, through the form of the poem itself. The relation of this topic to the other forms of limitation I have been discussing will become clear, I hope, within a few pages; the subject is as important, and as consciously (if silently) addressed, as any in 'East Coker'.

It was during the composition of 'East Coker' that Eliot first conceived of a group or suite of poems with 'Burnt Norton' at their head, and settled on some unifying devices. As he wrote in 1949 to William Matchett, an undergraduate at Swarthmore, 'Certainly by the time ['East Coker'] was finished I envisaged the whole work as having four parts which gradually began to assume, perhaps only for convenience sake, a relation to the four seasons and the four elements.' (CFQ, 18) At some point during the writing of 'East Coker' he also decided to duplicate the five-part structure of 'Burnt Norton'. The surviving drafts of 'East Coker' are late ones and consequently not helpful in establishing how or why Eliot decided to repeat the form. From our knowledge of his working methods, however, it is possible to infer probable causes.

C.K. Stead has established that Eliot usually wrote short passages very quickly, then revised and arranged them into larger wholes. This process of inspiration and collage, or vision and revision, is one which Stead traces in the evolution of several of Eliot's early poems, notably 'The Hollow Men' (167–70); it is the basis of his contention that Eliot's theory of composition was essentially Romantic. Stead's conclusions, controversial when Eliot's classicism was taken at face value, are now generally accepted.

It seems likely, then, that as Eliot began 'East Coker' he wrote a

number of short passages – some 'poetic', others more colloquial –
and that the two styles suggested the possibility of juxtaposing them
as he had in 'Burnt Norton'. Whatever the reason, the similarities
in style and form are striking. As in 'Burnt Norton', the first part
of 'East Coker' begins abstractly and moves to a specific scene;
the second part begins with a lyric and continues prosaically; the
fourth part is brief and transitional; the fifth includes a meditation
on language. Eliot was to employ the same pattern in the remaining
two quartets, with variations (particularly in 'The Dry Salvages')
which have been the subject of debate in themselves.

Eliot's use of a repeated form has been criticized. Stead sees the
structure as imposed and mechanical, allowing too little room for
'the unwilled creative moment' (176). Ronald Bush faults Eliot
for 'acceptance of a set poetic structure of the kind he had
always struggled to avoid' (222) and finds the middle quartets
inauthentic, even dishonest. Like all literary judgements, these
are of course subjective: I refer to them because they reflect a
common post-Romantic assumption that inspiration and genuine
poetry are incompatible with 'fixed' forms – even ones as elastic as
those of the *Quartets*.

This is obviously not the way Eliot himself thought of form.
Despite his Romantic inheritance (aspects of which have been
analysed by Kermode, Bornstein and myself [1981]), Eliot was
always aware of the liberating aspects of form. When *vers libre*
became free to the point of slackness, Eliot looked to Gautier and
wrote quatrain poems like 'Sweeney Among the Nightingales'. In
'The Possibility of a Poetic Drama' (1920), he argued that real
form is never arbitrary: 'To create a form is not merely to invent
a shape, a rhyme or rhythm. It is also the realization of the whole
appropriate content of that rhyme or rhythm' (SW, 63). It is not
enough, however, to suggest that Eliot found the form of 'Burnt
Norton' a suitable realization of the content of the succeeding
quartets: we must ask *why* he found it so, and why critics like
Stead and Bush do not.

The beginnings of an answer lie, I think, at the very beginning of
the *Quartets*. 'Burnt Norton' I reminds us that any act or choice is
two-edged: it closes off certain alternative possibilities just as surely
as it realizes the one settled upon. Any choice – including the
choice of a form – is therefore a kind of limitation. I have already
outlined some of the ways in which 'East Coker' is concerned with

limitation and transcendence of limitation: I would suggest that the form of the poem is the largest and most dramatized (in that it is performed, not commented on) instance of choice and limitation in the *Quartets*.

The Irish poet Austin Clarke once defined his poetics by saying that he loaded himself with chains, then tried to get out of them. Within the strictures of a repeated form, Eliot creates or discovers freedom, largely through his use of the two dominant and contrasting styles already mentioned – one characterized by figurative language and elevated ('poetic') style, the second close (occasionally too close) to prose. These two styles are not there primarily to provide variety within the poems, nor to facilitate ironic cross-fire ('That was a way of putting it – not very satisfactory'). Each represents a cluster of associated characteristics and values which we can summarize roughly as follows:

high	low
lyric	prosaic
subjective	objective
visionary	quotidian
religious	sceptical

– or, to use the terms we employed in discussing point of view, Ecclesiastes and the ironist. The presence of the two styles, and the fact that neither overcomes the other, suggest that the final aim is reconciliation of what they represent – a recognition that they are not alternative but complementary visions of reality.

That reconciliation is accomplished within each quartet through a dialogue of styles, and reinforced by each succeeding quartet, which accomplishes a similar work of reconciliation at the level of form. Each quartet duplicates the five-part structure of the preceding quartet and repeats the dominant themes of the sequence as a whole, but also introduces new settings, incidents and ideas; each quartet is the same, but different, and reconciles sameness and difference in its use of a repeated form. The dialectic of reconciliation therefore goes on at three levels: verbally, through alternation of styles; formally, through repetition of the quartet form with variation; and poetically, in the orchestration and final harmonizing of all the poem's images of conflict. In the ideal reader's mind the diachronic experience of reading the

Quartets becomes finally a synchronic or spatial vision of the whole consort, a poetic reinforcement of the *Quartets' terminus ad quem* – the perception that the fire and the rose are one, the way down is the way up, the closed room opens into freedom.

My point is simply that the exhilaration of that perception is made possible largely by Eliot's choice of a restricted form which enacts rather than simply contains the theme, and which reflects and subsumes the other forms of limitation discussed or implied in the poem. In Eliot's own terms, cited earlier, the creation of art replaces the philosophy. This account at least defines a specific function for the repeated form of the *Quartets*. Critics like Stead and Bush, who attack that form, blame it for what they see as the shortcomings of the whole sequence, but cannot do so very convincingly. Stead is really bothered by Eliot's later style, with its abstractions and discursiveness; the finest passages of the *Quartets* are, in his reading, those which are 'permitted to rest for a moment in the physical world', but we have only his assertion that these 'run counter to the planned intention of the poem' (180). It seems more likely that what Stead sees as conflict between plan and feeling is in fact a conscious dialectic of the kind I have been describing.

Bush pursues a personal and psychological line, accusing Eliot of evading his own guilt and anger, and choosing 'a form that would not let him face his demons honestly' (226). He is obliged, however, to acknowledge the honesty and power of the visionary encounter in 'Little Gidding', and therefore equates this honesty with the breaking of form. But 'Little Gidding' follows the five-part structure of the *Quartets* in most of its details, and the evidence Bush quotes of Eliot's anxiety about repeating himself deals with Eliot's sense that he has exhausted his personal material, not the form (227). Bush's real quarrel, then, is not with the form of the *Quartets* at all, but with aspects of Eliot's personality and religion which he finds distasteful: he quotes with apparent approval E.M. Forster's judgement that 'Little Gidding' is an 'homage to pain'.

All of this may appear to have brought us a long way from 'East Coker', but – especially with the *Quartets* – consideration of the part often involves examination of the whole. We can begin to see by this point a series of oppositions which may appear programmatic in summary, but are subtly invoked in the narration and meditation that make up 'East Coker': the lower elements in the diagram (forms of constriction or limitation) become the entrance to or the very means of their own transcendence.

freedom	illumination	eternity	sanctity	art, freedom
closed	consciousness	time	asceticism	poetic or
room				other form

Other pairs of opposed terms could obviously be added: I have not discussed the theme of the limits of language, for example, because it is so overtly developed in three of the four *Quartets*. The primary symbol of limitation in Eliot's poetry generally, as I suggested earlier, is the closed room, which remains closed as long as we 'think of the key' but opens (if it is going to open at all) when effort ceases. The liberation into a larger sphere of thought or being may or may not occur: the important thing is to accept limitation, not simply as an act of humility but because life itself is limitation. Critics who find Eliot's Christianity unacceptable because it 'rejects life' (the later Leavis is the obvious example) have, I think, missed the point; the *Quartets* constitute a complex act of acceptance which embraces the whole of experience, including its apparently malign aspects. It is the self-proclaimed humanist Forster who cannot accept the reality of pain, and imagines that anyone who can is a masochist. (Forster was, of course, an admirer of the world-embracing Whitman, who accepted pain and death as part of the cosmic process: it is presumably Eliot's Christianity that Forster cannot stomach.)

It should be apparent that I disagree with the strictures of Stead and Bush, but I am not attempting to defend 'East Coker' or *Four Quartets* against all comers. The poems certainly have flaws: what is most remarkable about them is that, given what they set out to do, they succeed as often as they do.

> Bringt doch der Wanderer auch vom Hange des Bergrands
> nicht eine Hand voll Erde ins Tal, die allen unsägliche, sondern
> ein erworbenes Wort, reines, den gelben und blaun
> Enzian. Sind wir vielleicht hier, um zu sagen: Haus,
> Brücke, Brunnen, Tor, Krug, Obstbaum, Fenster, –
> höchstens: Säule, Turm . . .
>
> (Rilke, *Duino Elegies* IX)

For the traveller brings from the mountainside to the valley
not a handful of untranslatable earth, but rather
some word he has found, a pure word, the yellow and blue
gentian. Are we perhaps here just to say: house,
bridge, fountain, gate, jug, fruit-tree, window –
or, at most: column, tower?

(my translation)

Like other great meditative poems of our century – Valéry's
Cimetière Marin, Rilke's *Duino Elegies*, Stevens' *Esthétique du Mal*
– the *Quartets* are written in an idiom which resists paraphrase
and reveals personality only in very indirect ways. But as one
reads and re-reads them, the poems' obliquities become more
and more personal; what is not revealed directly comes through
in the choice of subjects and phrasings until the poems seem as
subtly personal as any lyric. For me, the most moving part of 'East
Coker' is not the *confessio* that opens part V, but Eliot's scepticism
about the wisdom of old men, his sense that 'As we grow older /
The world becomes stranger'. 'East Coker' ends with movement
into 'the dark cold and the empty desolation, / The wave cry, the
wind cry, the vast waters / Of the petrel and the porpoise' (CPP,
183). It is Eliot's last rewriting of Tennyson's 'Ulysses', and moving
evidence of the poem's openness to experience, its refusal to rest
in any comforting formulae, including those which the *Quartets*
themselves have proposed.

Notes

1 This section of the essay is an abbreviated version of an argument
  developed more fully in my 1990 article 'Chamber Music: Eliot's
  Closed Rooms and Difficult Women' (see *References*).
2 As Eliot wrote in 1935, 'To me, the notion of *liberty* is meaningless
  without the further notion of *liberation*. One lives, not to be free, but
  to be freed' (88). I am indebted to Ronald Schuchard for drawing my
  attention to this passage.

References

Bornstein, George, *Transformations of Romanticism in Yeats, Eliot, and
  Stevens*, Chicago, University of Chicago Press, 1976.
Bush, Ronald, *T.S. Eliot: A Study in Character and Style*, New York,
  Oxford University Press, 1983.
Eliot, T.S. 'Notes on the Way', *Time and Tide*, 16:3 (19 January
  1935), 88–90.

Kermode, Frank, *Romantic Image*, London and Boston, Routledge & Kegan Paul, 1957.

Lobb, Edward, *T.S. Eliot and the Romantic Critical Tradition*, London and Boston, Routledge & Kegan Paul, 1981.

————, 'Chamber Music: Eliot's Closed Rooms and Difficult Women' in Laura Cowan, ed., *T.S. Eliot: Man and Poet*, (Orono, Maine, National Poetry Foundation, 1990), 167–79.

A.D. Nuttall, *A Common Sky: Philosophy and the Literary Imagination*, Berkeley, University of California Press, 1974.

Stead, C.K., *The New Poetic: Yeats to Eliot*, London, Hutchinson, 1964.

3

The American Eliot and 'The Dry Salvages'
Lyndall Gordon

In his last years Eliot returned more often to his native country, and in the last important interview, the *Paris Review* interview of 1959, stressed the American origins of his poetry: '. . . in its sources, in its emotional springs, it comes from America.'

He was born in St Louis in 1888, to a New England family that was highly conscious of its descent from the Puritan settlers of the seventeenth century. The Mississippi River and the childhood summers on Cape Ann, Massachusetts, were later to provide some 'essential moments' (CFQ, 183) of his poetry. In 'The Dry Salvages' (1941), Eliot took up the challenge of autobiography. To do this, he sank back into the past to extract the defining scenes: the childhood on the longest river; the youth sailing his precarious course through the granite teeth of the rocks offshore from Cape Ann – in particular the treacherous Dry Salvages, rocks which are hidden at high tide. The name, it is said, derived from the fact that the dangerous, partly-hidden rocks reminded settlers of the red men – the 'savages'. In a fog, Eliot and his Harvard classmate, Harold Peters, would hear the 'groaner' (a whistling buoy) east of Thatcher Island, scene of a famous shipwreck in the seventeenth century. Once Eliot and Peters rounded Mount Desert Rock in a fog and heavy sea, and had to take refuge on Duck Island and, after a rough night, with a gale still blowing, made it to the little harbour at Somesville, Maine. The logbook had a sketch of Eliot unmooring in the wind with the caption: 'Heroic work by the swab'.

Later, Eliot was to draw on sailing memories for 'The Dry Salvages' which is, in part, about the frontiers of action where a significant life is made. A man like Eliot becomes significant precisely because he conceives a shape to his life, which he defines through the visionary moments which formed the dominant figure in the carpet of his existence. (Eliot said, after completing 'The Dry Salvages', 'We look, in a poet as well as in a novelist, for what

Henry James called the Figure in the Carpet.' [OPP, 235]) These transforming moments lay 'unattended' beneath the usual clutter of biographic trivia. In a draft of 'Little Gidding' he recalls the essential moments of his own history, especially the emotional quickening that came to him as a young man as he sailed from Massachusetts to Maine:

Remember rather the essential moments
   That were the times of birth and death and change
   The agony and solitary vigil.
Remember also . . .
The fresh new season's rope, the smell of varnish
   On the clean oar, the drying of the sails,
Such things as seem of least and most importance.
So, as you circumscribe this dreary round,
   Shall your life pass from you

(CFQ, 183)

After a year in Paris (1910–11), Eliot returned to Harvard to study philosophy. In 1914 he went abroad again to complete his dissertation at Oxford. He seemed destined for an academic career, but it was in this year, 1914–15, that he met Ezra Pound. Pound urged him to stay in London and become a poet and, soon after, at the end of Trinity term 1915, Eliot made his impulsive marriage to an Englishwoman, Vivienne Haigh-Wood. She declined to cross the Atlantic in wartime, so Eliot settled in London, to the dismay of his family. His uncle Charles William Eliot (President of Harvard, 1870–1909) wrote a stiff letter, urging Eliot not to stay abroad and ruin his art like Henry James (L1, 322–3).

Eliot's move from America to England gave him a peculiar detachment from all environments, a universal foreignness which was the obverse to his strong feeling for certain locales, like Gloucester, Massachusetts. As he shed his American youth, he cultivated the front of an Englishman – and yet sudden American allegiances would surface. He delighted to upset a solemn board meeting at Faber and Faber by setting off a firecracker, on 4 July, under Geoffrey Faber's chair. In old age, he wrote fan letters to Groucho Marx. An English friend, Hope Mirrlees (at whose mother's house, Shamley Green, Eliot lived during the Blitz) said categorically, 'He wasn't a bit like an Englishman,' though he could feel 'most violently English,' as when he sported a white rose in his lapel on the anniversary of the defeat of Richard III in 1485 on Bosworth Field. 'I once said to him: "You know there is this indestructible American strain in you." And he was pleased. He said: "Oh yes, there is. I'm glad you realized it. There is."'

What aspects of America were 'indestructible' in Eliot? He once said that he felt at home in America as it had been before about 1830. What that date meant to him must be a guess. It was soon after that his grandfather left Boston for the frontier. It was then, too, that the civilized élite of the Eastern seaboard lost its power in the bitter election of 1828, when John Quincy Adams fell before the ruder, less cultivated Andrew Jackson. Was Eliot still resisting the impact of Jacksonian democracy – more Western, more individualistic – a hundred years on?[1] Or did 1830 represent some subtler change – the fading of the last traces of Calvinist piety before the cheery optimism of a new age of self-reliance? For Emerson, the very advocate of self-reliance, that old, demanding piety remained a lingering force through his memory of his Calvinist aunt, Mary Moody Emerson: 'What a debt is ours to that old religion which, in the childhood of most of us, still dwelt like a sabbath morning in the country of New England, teaching privation, self-denial, and sorrow!' (130)

What distinguished the old religion of the New England Puritans from their English brethren was their unique demand, in the words of Increase Mather, 'That persons should make a Relation of the work of Gods Spirit upon their hearts' (Morgan, 91). Eliot set down such a relation from 'The Hollow Men' (1925) to the confession of the Elder Statesman in his last play (1958). In his second play, *The Family Reunion* (1939), Harry's testimony, with its emphasis on sin, conforms to the set pattern of these old New England 'Relations'. There, persons wishing to join a church had to relate publicly the story of their salvation. These narratives were often anxious and open-ended, for success lay not so much in formal measurement of sin but in the quality of penitence: it had to be desperate and uncertain enough to prove genuine abasement. Formal confession in the Anglican church was, for Eliot, too mild a ritual. His scrupulousness demanded more unflinching introspection, severer chastisement.[2] In any case, public confession was well beyond the requirements of entry into the tolerant Anglican church of which Eliot actually had little immediate knowledge at the time of his conversion in 1927. It was conversion itself that drew him: through that experience, he could revive the strenuousness of the New England divines for whom it was not enough to profess faith. For Eliot, too, it was not enough to try to repeat 'For Thine is the Kingdom'. These words must pierce the prospective convert, must annihilate his rotten self. In Puritan New England grace must come unsought to a soul wrestling with sin, as Eliot wrestled with the devil of the stairs.

In this piece, I don't wish to explore Eliot's use of American locale in some later poems – notably three of his 'Landscapes' ('Virginia', 'New Hampshire' and 'Cape Ann') – but to look for something recurrent in the American imagination of which Eliot partakes: the dream of self-transformation. For many, this is projected through imagery of the frontier; for Eliot, it is the first frontier, the Atlantic ocean and Massachusetts' shore, as experienced by the first settlers, his ancestors in the seventeenth century. Eliot's writings suggest that he actually became more attached to his dream of the American past *after* he relinquished his nationality in 1927. It might, in fact, be said that he relinquished present-day America to retrieve a dream of the fresh green breast of the New World. The nostalgia came through in the poetry of 1927–30 and again, more personally, in two lines which Eliot cut from a draft of *The Elder Statesman* on the exile who must exchange 'The loneliness of home among foreign strange people / For the loneliness of home which is only memories.' (Browne, 320)

Eliot's youth was interred in another land, its shadow moving with the shades behind the grey rocks of the New England shore. Eliot's poems of 1927–30, *Ash-Wednesday* and 'Marina', move towards the New England shore to recover not a geographical place but its meaning, its moral ideal: 'the unread vision in the higher dream'. In 'Marina' (1930), this higher dream comes as a call through the New England fog. The poem revives the ancestral voyage, the 'Bowsprit cracked with ice', the weak rigging, the rotten canvas, the leak and the seams that need 'caulking' in the same detail as Bradford's history of the voyage of the Pilgrim Fathers, written between 1630 and 1650: 'the shipe was shroudly shaken, and her upper works made very leakie; and one of the main beames in the midd ships was bowed and craked, which put them in some fear that the shipe could not be able to performe the voiage' (Miller, 98–9). Some wished to return, but others heartened them: 'And as for the decks and uper workes they

would calke them as well as they could. . . . So they commited
them selves to the will of God, and resolved to proseede.' For they
were convinced, as another early New England historian, Edward
Johnson, put it, that they were destined for 'the place where the
Lord will create a new Heaven, and a new Earth in, new Churches,
and a new Common-wealth together.' (Miller, 145) In the same
way, Eliot's voyage points to a new life. In a draft of 'Marina' in
the Bodleian Library, the old forms re-form in a New World.

What stimulated this imaginative moving across the sea was a
renewed relationship with a Bostonian, Emily Hale, Eliot's first
love. Having parted in 1914, they began corresponding from about
1927, some time after Eliot had sent her *Ara Vos Prec* in 1923 with
a suggestive Dantean inscription: 'SIETI RACOMMENDATO /
IL MIO TESORO / NELLO QUAL VIVO ANCOR / E NON
PIU CHIEGGIO.' – 'May my Treasure be entrusted to you, my
Treasure in which I am still living. And I do not ask more than this.'
(Horowitz). Emily Hale came to England in 1930, and from then
until his second marriage, Eliot wrote her about a thousand letters.
It is possible that she was the source of the life-giving Lady in
Ash-Wednesday. In the final section of that poem, the higher dream
locates itself on the New England shore. The poet's wings, which
were collapsed in the opening section, and then strengthened by
the Lady, now fly seaward, and his memory stirs of sailing off
Cape Ann, a scene always associated with divine intimations.
Across space and time, he hears the whisper of ancestral voices
of New England divines who spoke the Lord's Word. Eliot sees
these family figures not as individuals, but collectively as shades
who beckon the poet to the exalted state for which he is destined.
Then he must return to his own time, where he must live, as he
puts it, in 'exile' from the promised land that he sees is still, after
all, his imaginative inheritance.

Exile's dreams bring back the granite rocks of the shore, the
bent golden-rod and the salt smell. Once more he hears the
distant call of ghostly forebears as they drift back into the fastness
of their own time and, with that, his resolve hardens. He too
must speak the Word everlasting. And over this resolve presides
the blessed woman, nameless, faceless, known only in a series of
subordinate clauses beginning with 'who': who walks with the
'new years', who restores his power to write 'new verse', who
gives the all-important sign that the Word would come (perhaps

an answer to Gerontion's hopeless cry in 1919: 'We would see a sign!'). The spirit of his creative fount, she alone can bring him back to the New World. In 'Marina', written in July 1930 and published in September, while Emily Hale was still in England, Eliot effected this imaginative crossing. The speaker – the voyager – resigns his present stale life for 'the new ships' as he homes in hope, lips parted, towards a pure woman. The lone voyager battered, almost broken, as he crosses from one life to another, comes at last to a haven of love – but it is not ordinary love, and the woman is not human in the ordinary sense. She appears to be the embodiment of a divine call, an emblem of a 'new Heaven' in the New World.

In *Four Quartets* another voyage begins at the end of the second poem, 'East Coker'. East Coker is the village in Somerset from which Andrew Eliot set out for America in 1669. His voyage, as Eliot imagines it, takes him from the Old World community of couples, merry-makers, destined solely for 'dung and death'. This dark judgement comes like a shot, a stern voice of denial like that of the Puritan killjoy in Hawthorne's tale, who rebukes and breaks up the nuptial frolics in 'The Maypole of Merry Mount'. The moral fire of the American lurks invisible but dominant on the edge of the English scene. 'East Coker' is a poem about family origins that links the American progenitor with his English roots: a way for Eliot to resolve his own dual allegiance.

Eliot first went to East Coker in June 1936 (on foot from Yeovil) where he examined a stained-glass window with the family arms, put in that year by an American cousin.[3] In August 1937 he went to stay with Sir Matthew Nathan at a manor house in West Coker, Somerset, and from there explored, again, his family village. The poem retraces his approach that late summer day, looking down the lane in the haze of heat. The present seems to dissolve in a dream of the past: ancient ancestors with clumsy, loam-clogged feet dancing in a ring. Eliot will not keep time. He maintains a spectatorial distance that is not only a distance in time, but a refusal of the rounds of the temporal life. What alerts him is the dawn wind that beckons the emigrant to the New World. At this point, Eliot joins in: 'I am here,' he says suddenly: 'In my beginning.' He must renew the ancestral state of mind: venturesomeness ('Home,' he says, 'is where one starts from').

Eliot switches back and forth from English to American perspectives. *Four Quartets* is thought of as an English work with some

reference to America, but the reverse may be true. The very
notion of an Old World implies a New-World perspective from
which the Old World may be seen, made explicit. The sequence
of poems, as it evolved at an early stage (in January–February 1940,
when it was to conclude with the third quartet), had at this point
a plot that was essentially American, a recoil from civilization to
expose oneself to the wilderness, in this case the sea. The 'three
quatuors'[4] would move from the civilized enclosures of the English
garden with its box hedge, straight walk, and concrete pool, to the
wild ocean; from the predictable routines of the English village to
encounter 'Through the dark cold and the empty desolation, / The
wave cry, the wind cry, the vast waters / Of the petrel and the
porpoise.' (CPP, 183)

The waterway beckons the American – Ishmael, Huck, Arthur
Gordon Pym – as a mysterious and terrible power. Eliot's sea is
strewn with treacherous rocks and drowned men; his Mississippi
in spring flood carries its usual 'cargo' of Negro bodies and chicken
coops. This nature is not English. It is not the nurse, the guide, the
guardian. It is alien to man; he cannot interfuse with its moods. He
might pit himself against it, like Ahab or the Gloucester fishermen
who had been Eliot's boyhood heroes. He might beat obedient to
the sea's control, as at the end of *The Waste Land*. Ideally, he must
'fare forward', a refrain that echoes Whitman, and through him
Columbus – pioneers with inextinguishable visions in their heads.
'Sail forth,' urges Whitman in 'Passage to India', 'bound where
mariner has not yet dared go.' Like the voyaging in 'Marina' and
'The Dry Salvages', it is a metaphor for the spiritual frontier. Poetry
must explore the frontiers of the spirit, Eliot said on 27 April 1939,
'but these frontiers are not the surveys of geographical explorers,
conquered once for all and settled' (27). He imagines a perpetual
frontier, a perpetual mystery on the borders of the known world.

It is not before the world but out of sight 'between the rocks'
(CPP, 97) that a convert must test the reach of his faith. And
farther out, in the lap of creation, where there is nothing but the
ground swell that is and was from the beginning – no personal,
no intellectual distraction – is some naked confrontation of which
Eliot can speak only indirectly. His venture is always to confront
'reality', his word for what lies beyond the Unreal City. He
believes reality exists – it comes to him in the silence that
obliterates the twittering world – but he can't be sure he can

meet it. Eliot despised a watered-down Christianity of sweet comforts. He looked to the spring of 'Christ the tiger' (CPP, 37) or the havoc of the sea with its wrecks of those who did not survive the encounter with the timeless element.

Eliot first rehearsed this voyage in a long narrative which Pound cut in its entirety from the *Waste Land* manuscript. The hardy Gloucester fishermen sail through winter seas to the Grand Banks, and their journey, terrible as it is, does turn its back on the urban waste. Eliot did, at one stage, counter London, the 'Unreal City', with the venturing nerve of his native tradition. The draft was like a scene from Melville or, more likely, Poe's 'Narrative of Arthur Gordon Pym' in its visionary horrors and approach to the ice. This was the 'indestructible' strain that remained part of Eliot in all the strange journeys in his poetry that find a final expression in 'The Dry Salvages'.

In the 1921 manuscript the ship strikes an iceberg and goes down. In 1940–1 another of Eliot's voyagers braves the sea, conscious of the menace to all who venture from their natural habitat. We see a drifting boat at the mercy of winds and current. The sheer daring of 'The Dry Salvages' recovers the heady recklessness of Whitman: 'And we will risk the ship, ourselves and all' seeking 'You, strew'd with the wrecks of skeletons, that, living, never reach'd you' (421, 420). Eliot, too, has seen the bone on the beach. Appalled by the destruction of life, he asks an overwhelming question: 'Where is there an end of it?' and has to surrender to a reality he cannot fathom, beyond momentary intimations of a sustaining divinity.

The Waste Land concludes with a dramatic progression into the mountains. There are no such peaks of attainment in *Four Quartets*, no thunderous message. Eliot owns that for him, as for others, the most to be looked for is the odd hint or guess when he drifts into the interface between time and the timeless. Part of the exercise in humility was not to play up, or even expect, progression. The later *Quartets* are a corrective to the self-absorbed heroics of Harry when he exits from family drama to follow the bright angels. Drama is now a consolation that the poet has refused. Not for him the lifetime burning in every moment, he insists, as he sinks into massive repose, content to lie near his ancestors in St Michael's Church, East Coker.

Yet the timeless horizon of 'The Dry Salvages', that farthest reach of the *Quartets*, remains in view. Eliot's most elusive self who disappears across the sea is not, he says, the same person who disembarks. The cosy Eliot of Shamley Green and the public Eliot of many masks are superfluous to the invisible poet, not to be known outside his work, and even there vanishing into silence. He is inchoate, carried along by the rhythm of the poem itself, always in the making, suspended between the flawed and the perfect life like a traveller who has left one shore and has not yet reached the other as he crosses the space of his lifespan. It is impossible to fix him through his flawed past or even through the saintly life of his ideal future. After this venture across the horizon of the timeless, he must reconcile himself to a continual suspension in time, on the verge of 'hints and guesses'.

To keep the verge open is to retain the native posture of the American, the openness implied by the persistent 'Fare forward'. He is urged on by a disembodied voice, like the alien pulse that beats in the arm of the voyager in 'Marina'. The voice descants in the rigging, like the eerie quickening of the strings in the finale of Beethoven's A minor quartet, composed when he was deaf and which, Eliot said, had a sort of heavenly gaiety (Spender, 54). The voice descants 'not to the ear' but to the spirit. It speaks 'not in any language', in the way Eliot himself wished to get *'beyond poetry'* as Beethoven in his later works strove to get *'beyond music'* (Matthiessen, 90). Out at sea, at the farthest verge of time, there is a renewed intimation of immortality that was to bring him, in the final quartet, into unison with the timeless poets of the past.

Dante, Eliot said, was the most *'European'* of writers, and this was his own insistent image. It might appear a simple repudiation of America, but for Eliot, the notion of the 'European' was not a matter of locale but a state of mind that overpassed all frontiers. It actually had a native connotation which he explained in his 1918 essay 'In Memory of Henry James': 'It is the final perfection, the consummation of an American to become, not an Englishman, but a European – something which no born European, no person of any European nationality, can become' (44). The benefit of transplantation was to have a horizon beyond St Louis, Boston, or London. Wherever Eliot stood, part of him was not there – he had something in reserve. His detachment took on the authority of a Modernist position, but this was not the end in itself because he was also detached in time. From that vantage point he saw, like a prophet, the destruction of corrupt societies.

Eliot's declaration in 1959 that his poetry came from America has been overlooked because of the prestige of his internationalism and understandable ignorance (since so much of Eliot's criticism remains buried) of the American implications of his stance as 'European'. Only Edmund Wilson, reviewing *Poems 1909–1925*, perceived at that time that Eliot's 'real significance is less that of a prophet of European disintegration than of a poet of the American Puritan temperament' (Grant, 239–40). He went on to align Eliot with Marcher, Strether and Hawthorne. Eliot himself provides a further clue to these affinities when he finds in James and Hawthorne a 'peculiarly American' sense of the past (1918, 50). For them, as for Eliot, the present becomes pressing just as the past dominates with its ghostly presences. Eliot wrote this in 1918: it foretells the visitations of the hyacinth girl, the ghosts of the rose garden, the Furies, and the guilty past of the Elder Statesman. The settings are English, but the disturbed and haunted sense of the past is, by implication, American – connected, perhaps, with that drive to fare forward that would seem to leave the past behind.

Eliot said in 1936 that 'the American writing in English does not write English poetry' (881). The difference did not lie fundamentally in local subject matter but in 'the different rhythm in the blood' which made it impossible for him to enjoy the kind of English verse that fell into 'an ecstatic contemplation of peaceful landscape.' (882) In the 1855 'Preface' to *Leaves of Grass*, Whitman defined the American poet as a seer: not just an arguer, he is judgement itself. 'High up out of reach he stands turning a concentrated light . . . he turns the pivot with his finger.' (715) And behind Whitman stands the Emerson of 'Self-Reliance', saying 'Let us affront and reprimand the smooth mediocrity and squalid contentment of the times.' (267) He stands in the same New England tradition of moral earnestness as Eliot's forebears: the Reverend Andrew Eliot in the eighteenth century who (as T.S. Eliot liked to recall) preached to Boston society on 'a generation of vipers', meaning his audience; and, in the nineteenth century, William Greenleaf Eliot, the admired grandfather, of whom a classmate at Harvard Divinity School said, 'His eye is single. . . . There is something awful about such conscientiousness. One feels rebuked in his presence.'[5]

The grandson's own 'CRY' ('Coriolan' II) was the imminent decline and fall of civilization. This sounds like the American Jeremiad, the sermon developed by settlers in the seventeenth century in order to repossess their dream of perfectability. 'I speak as a New Englander,' Eliot told his Virginia audience in 1933, and as such tried to re-introduce terms like 'heresy', 'original sin' and 'the diabolic' into modern discourse (ASG, 16). He prophesied a time 'of scourges and lamentation': only the saints would prevail, holding to 'the ultimate vision' (CPP, 105).

In 'American Literature and the American Language' (1953), Eliot recalled the stimulus of what a man said 'long ago or in another language' which 'corresponds' to what he himself wanted to say (TCC, 56). I want to propose an unorthodox idea: that Eliot was finding prestigious European parallels for what mattered to him in his native tradition, with the result that, in his early years, when he was making his reputation as an international writer, he obscured this tradition. He looked to Dante for extremities of sin and vision, instead of his own Puritan heritage. He looked to the Jansenism of Pascal which, as Eliot himself described it, was 'morally a Puritan movement within the Church' (SE, 404). He looked to Baudelaire for psychic decadence rather than to Poe, Baudelaire's actual source of inspiration. He remarked on the influence of the style of F.H. Bradley, the English idealist philosopher on whom Eliot wrote his dissertation, yet in an obscure piece of 1924, we find that Bradley's style corresponds, for Eliot, to that of Henry James, whose prose 'pulsates with the agony of the spiritual life' (29). Bradley believed that what we observe are fragments of a greater reality: this idea, central to the structure of Eliot's early poetry, actually corresponds to the Transcendentalism of Emerson, who wrote in his journal that 'fractions are worth more to me because corresponding fractions are waiting . . . that shall be made integers by their addition' (119). Finally, Eliot's use of quatrain form in his second volume, *Poems* (1920), was said to derive from the mid-nineteenth-century French poet Gautier, but it also derived, Pound noted, from the Bay State Hymn Book of the colonial settlers of Massachusetts. Later, when Eliot's international reputation was unassailable, he could acknowledge the centrality of his American origins.

Auden once remarked that no genuine European could have made Eliot's celebrated statement that tradition is not inherited but acquired by great labour. It has been assumed that Eliot's acquired tradition is to be found in the literary and historical parallels by which he attempted to universalize private (and sometimes idiosyncratic) states of mind. But is there an inherited tradition nonetheless? Did his American forebears, the many divines or Judge Blood, who made himself conspicuous in the punishment of witches, leave no residue? Hawthorne was prepared to recognize that 'strong traits of their [Puritan] nature have intertwined themselves with mine'. The obsessive introspection of the Reverend Arthur Dimmesdale in *The Scarlet Letter* seems to prefigure something of Eliot's temperament, the insistent agonizing of a sinner of high spiritual gifts, gazing absorbed into the mirror of election with its associated dangers of pride and despair:

> To their high mountain peaks of faith and sanctity he would have climbed, had not the tendency been thwarted by the burden, whatever it might be, of crime or anguish, beneath which it was his doom to totter. It kept him down, on a level with the lowest; him, the man of ethereal attributes. (103)

Yet it is this same secret burden that gives to the minister the power to move others through his persuasive eloquence.

The American aspect of Eliot is still neglected, but the dominant forms of early American writing, soul history and sermon, give a curious backing to Eliot's impenetrability. For he shares with Emerson, Thoreau, Whitman and Dickinson a guarded mode of confession. Unlike St Augustine or Rousseau, who draw us into intimacy, these Americans throw the onus of introspection back into the lap of the reader. Their confessions, like *The Waste Land*, are fragmentary and, left so deliberately incomplete, demand a reciprocal effort. The point lies not in their content so much as in the act of self-discovery and judgement. Its ultimate purpose is not to expose the speaker but to create the reader. In short, it is a form of sermon: a call to awaken.

Eliot hailed in Wordsworth 'a profound spiritual revival'. Once again, a European writer is used in a way that 'corresponds' neatly with American tradition, the revolt against deadness in a pattern of religious revivals: in the 1740s the Great Awakening, led by Jonathan Edwards; in the next century, the secular revivals of Emerson, Thoreau and Whitman; and in the next – *The Waste Land*. From *The Waste Land* (1922) to *The Elder Statesman* (1958),

Eliot became an expert on spiritual revival. Like the New England divines, the ancestors who shook off the Old World and, with it, the temporal existence, no one knew better than Eliot the stages and signs of salvation. But he had limited spiritual gifts. He did have diagnostic self-insight, strength of will, endurance and a readiness to recognize the reality of the unseen. But he had not a great gift of vision. He craved a lifetime burning in every moment, but had to accept, in 'The Dry Salvages', a lesser course of 'trying'.

Eliot was too self-conscious to be a saint. Yet his struggle to subdue intellectual pride, his almost savage intolerance, proved the fertile matter of his mature poetry. There remains the paradox of a man who wished to be saint above poet, but who became all the greater as poet for his failure to attain sainthood. He fell back on another goal, to be God's agent, and as public spokesman achieved an extraordinary authority. His pronouncements are still repeated as truths from on high. The prophetic role, like the Puritan rigour of introspection, came most directly from America, as did the challenge of a terrifying Nature where man measures himself in the face of an immeasurable power that is and was from the beginning.

Eliot's career circled back so that the sources of his own life, the Mississippi River and Cape Ann, came to stand for the source of all life. Despite his adaptation to England, his adoption of English religion, manners and clothes, and despite marriages to English women, his poetry led him back to 'the source of the longest river', and to the silence the child heard between two waves of the sea.

Notes

1 The Eliots are distantly related to the Adams family. In a letter to Pound (1 January 1931), praising the American *Cantos*, Eliot referred jokingly to 'Uncle John' (John Adams, the second president and father of John Quincy Adams). Letter in Beinecke Library, Yale.

2 Letters to William Force Stead, Osborn Collection, Beinecke Library, Yale.

3 Information from a recently discovered letter from Eliot to Mrs Polly Tandy (18 June 1936; British Library). In Yeovil, he stayed at an inn called the Three Choughs and complained of its expensiveness.

4 Writing to Frank Morley, John Hayward refers to 'East Coker' as 'the second of three quatuors' in No. XI of Tarantula's Special News Service (February 1940; King's College Library). See CFQ, 16.

5 Eliot mentioned his admiration to Mary Trevelyan in a letter (26

January 1948) quoted in her unpublished memoir of Eliot, 'The Pope of Russell Square' (privately owned). W.G. Eliot's classmate was James Freeman Clarke, writing in his journal, May 1839; quoted in his obituary (Hayward Bequest, King's College Library).

References

Browne, E. Martin, *The Making of T.S. Eliot's Plays*, Cambridge, Cambridge University Press, 1969.

Eliot, T.S., 'In Memory of Henry James' and 'The Hawthorne Aspect', *Little Review* 5.4 (August 1918), 44–53.

———, 'A Prediction in Regard to Three English Authors, Writers Who, though Masters of Thought, Are likewise Masters of Art', *Vanity Fair* 21.6 (February 1924), 29, 98.

———, 'Tradition and the Practice of Poetry' (January 1936), ed. with an introduction and afterword by A. Walton Litz, *The Southern Review* 21.4 (Autumn 1985), 873–88.

———, 'A Commentary: That Poetry Is Made with Words', *New English Weekly* XV.2 (27 April 1939), 27–8.

Emerson, Ralph Waldo, *Essays and Lectures*, ed. Joel Porte, New York, Library of America, 1983.

———, *Emerson in His Journals*, ed. Joel Porte, Cambridge, Mass., Belknap Press, 1982.

Grant, Michael, ed., *T.S. Eliot: The Critical Heritage*, vol. 1, London and Boston, Routledge & Kegan Paul, 1982.

Hall, Donald, 'T.S. Eliot' in George Plimpton, ed., *Writers at Work: The Paris Review Interviews, Second Series*, New York, Viking, 1963, 91–110.

Hawthorne, Nathaniel, *The Scarlet Letter*, ed. Sculley Bradley, Richmond Croom Beatty and E. Hudson Long, New York, Norton, 1962.

Horowitz, Glenn (bookseller), *Catalogue 22: T.S. Eliot*, New York, 1990.

Matthiessen, F.O., *The Achievement of T.S. Eliot: An Essay on the Nature of Poetry*, 3rd ed., New York, Oxford University Press, 1959.

Miller, Perry, and Thomas H. Johnson, eds, *The Puritans: A Sourcebook of Their Writings*, rev. ed., vol. 1, New York, Harper & Row, 1963.

Morgan, Edmund S., *Visible Saints: The History of a Puritan Idea*, Ithaca, NY, Cornell University Press, 1965.

Spender, Stephen, 'Remembering Eliot' in Allen Tate, ed., *T.S. Eliot: The Man and His Work*, London, Chatto & Windus, 1966. 38–64.

Whitman, Walt, *Leaves of Grass*, ed. Sculley Bradley and Harold W. Blodgett, New York, Norton, 1973.

4

'If I think, again, of this place': Eliot, Herbert and the Way to 'Little Gidding'
Ronald Schuchard

I

T.S. Eliot did not just happen upon Little Gidding; it was a symbolic place of mind long before his pilgrimage to the chapel in 1936, well before he began to write the poem in 1941. Even as he wrote the renunciatory fragments of *Ash-Wednesday*, a prelude to his conversion, his mind was fixed on the Anglican example of Nicholas Ferrar, whose stark renunciation of worldly preferments and whose friendships with George Herbert and Richard Crashaw had struck Eliot's imagination. Early in the 1920s he was familiar with Walton's portrayal of the devotional community in his *Life of Herbert*. When he read Mario Praz's account in *Secentismo e Marinismo in Inghilterra* (1925) of Crashaw's relation to Ferrar and his remarkable niece, Mary Collett, he was moved to write: 'The section of Signor Praz's book which deals with . . . Crashaw's connexion with the retreat of Little Gidding and with the misfortunes of Peterhouse makes extremely good reading' (1925, 878). If he was not as yet familiar with J.H. Shorthouse's detailed description of religious life at Little Gidding in *John Inglesant* (1881), he was soon to be so, for he added the 1927 edition to his library. By the time of his baptism and confirmation in that year, Eliot already saw Little Gidding as a distant paradigm of the contemplative life, founded as it was on a mystical devotional spirit which he would embrace with increasing intensity. During the next decade, as he prepared for his fated visit, he did indeed think again and again of 'this place' and its people. Eliot, like Herbert, was touched and led to Little Gidding by the 'genius' of Ferrar, but the drama of the pentecostal journey to both place and poem lies in Eliot's rediscovery of Herbert in the 1930s.

The thrust of this study emerges from the neglected fact that Herbert became a crucial figure to Eliot in an intense personal drama – the collapse of his marriage to Vivienne Eliot and the resumption of his relationship with Emily Hale. This tension in his personal life was further complicated by austere religious commitments – including a vow of celibacy – made in the aftermath of his conversion, but in Herbert (and in St John of the Cross) Eliot found a way of working out the conflict between personal and religious emotion in a new mode of contemplative poetry – *Four Quartets*. Further, it was through Herbert that Eliot rediscovered the English mystical tradition, and in making that tradition an integral part of his own contemplative life he made Herbert and the fourteenth-century English mystics the guiding spirits of 'Little Gidding'. As new biographical and bibliographical material reveals, and as a fresh reading of the poem confirms, Herbert did indeed show Eliot the way to 'Little Gidding'. For the rest of his life Eliot continued to acknowledge the impact of *The Temple* on his poetic consciousness and to include Herbert among the final handful of poets to whom he paid his greatest homage.

II

Throughout the 1920s Herbert remained a 'devotional poet' of minor interest to Eliot in comparison to Donne and Crashaw, who were the primary objects of his inquiry into the relation of thought and feeling. At the end of the decade Eliot still looked upon Herbert as a mild-mannered poet of the domestic vicarage, and though his admiration of Donne's verse was still intact he had become sharply critical of Crashaw's religious wandering. However much he admired the devotional verse of the seventeenth century, at the time of his conversion in 1927 Eliot had not found a patron poet in Herbert or in any other poet of the Anglican communion; he had to look to the Continent, to Baudelaire, to find the nature of his spiritual struggle exemplified in poetry. In May, the month before his baptism in Finstock Church, he wrote that Baudelaire, in his isolated discovery of Christianity, 'was alone in the solitude which is only known to great saints. To him the notion of Original Sin came spontaneously, and the need for prayer. . . . And Baudelaire came to attain the greatest, the most difficult, of the Christian virtues, the virtue of humility' (1927, 420–1). Eliot had himself come the purgative way of John of the Cross, whom he chose as his spiritual patron, and of Baudelaire – a way based on the reality of sin, the necessity of prayer, and the achievement of humility. For the next three years Eliot would praise the spiritual heroism of Baudelaire's attitude toward life, writing in 'Baudelaire' (1930) that 'such suffering as Baudelaire's implies the possibility of a positive state of beatitude' (SE, 423). The concomitant importance of St John to Eliot's spiritual life, and the depth of Eliot's immersion in *The Ascent of Mount Carmel*, were only hinted at in the epigraph to 'Fragment of a Prologue', the first section of *Sweeney Agonistes*: 'Hence the soul cannot be possessed of the divine union, until it has divested itself of the love of created beings' (CPP, 115). Accompanied to the Anglo-Catholic Church by a French poet and a Spanish mystic, Eliot had nonetheless begun his search for their counterparts on English soil.

When Eliot resumed his comparative study of Donne, Crashaw and Herbert in 'The Devotional Poets of the Seventeenth Century' (1930), he appeared not to have altered his estimation of Crashaw and Herbert as devotional poets. The religious feeling in Herbert's poetry, he observed, 'is easy for the English mind, whether Anglican or Dissenting', whereas in Crashaw 'we encounter a fine English poet who is at the same time a little alien' (553). Donne remains the superior poet, and in comparing the two Eliot was moved to remark that Walton 'perhaps overdoes it' in portraying Herbert's reputation for saintliness. Herbert would seem to be completely divorced from Eliot's critical consciousness, and yet a complexity in the poet had begun to intrigue him, evidenced in his unexpected reassessment of the 'simplicity' of Herbert's verse. He discussed Herbert's 'Prayer (I)', ostensibly to show Donne's influence on the conceits, but primarily to point to Herbert's genius for simplifying intense emotion in his devotional verse. 'There remains his personal quality', he concluded, 'and the necessity for saturating oneself in his verse to get it' (553).

During the next two years Eliot's immersion in Herbert's verse led to a dramatic transformation, indeed reversal, of his previous attitude toward Herbert as an Anglican poet and priest. In 'George Herbert', published as part of a series in the *Spectator* entitled 'Studies in Sanctity', he criticized not only the 'false setting' in which Herbert has been represented in anthologies and popular editions, but his own participation in the conventional view. Having moved beyond the anthology pieces himself, and having read industriously in *The Temple*, Eliot expressed his astonishment at the 'spiritual stamina' of the work, at its extraordinary sincerity, at the inextricability of Herbert's religious vocation from his poetic talent. 'Throughout there is brain work', he wrote with conviction, 'and a very high level of intensity; his poetry is definitely an *oeuvre*, to be studied entire. And our gradual appreciation of the poetry gives us a new impression of the man.' (361)

In penetrating the complex architecture of *The Temple*, Eliot had discovered the 'personal quality' that had eluded him – Herbert's unique consciousness of sin, prayer and humility and his profound sense of purgation in the pursuit of beatitude. In his newfound recognition of the intensity of Herbert's spiritual struggle, Eliot cautiously associated him with St John of the Cross, not to compare Herbert's spiritual accomplishment but to suggest that 'no lower theme could have evoked his genius'. Herbert's balance of emotion and intellect led Eliot to describe him as 'an anatomist of feeling and a trained theologian', and he quoted from 'The Pearl' to show that Herbert's mind 'is working continually both on the mysteries of faith and the motives of the heart': 'I know the wayes of Learning', Herbert begins his address to the Holy Spirit, and yet in spite of his knowledge of the human ways of Learning, Honour and Pleasure, achieved by attributes that lead only to prideful separation from the Holy Spirit, he cries in each refrain, finally aware that the 'silk twist' of grace is the only requirement for divine union, 'And yet I love thee'. Eliot's essay was thus more than a retraction and correction of old attitudes; it was a proclamation of his spiritual identity with Herbert as penitent and poet. Herbert's poetry, he wrote, 'expresses the slow, sometimes almost despairing and always agonizing toil of the proud and passionate man of the world toward spiritual life; a toil and agony which must always be the same, for the similar temperament, to the end of the world'. Herbert not only displaced Baudelaire at the side of St John; he displaced Donne at the centre of Eliot's consciousness. It was a remarkable admission and conclusion: 'I never feel that the great Dean of St Paul's, with his mastery of the spoken word, his success and applause to the end, quite conquered his natural pride of mind; Herbert, the vicar of Bemerton, in his shorter life went much farther on the road of humility' (361).

Eliot had come to view Herbert's poems as Herbert humbly described them when, on his deathbed, he sent the unpublished manuscript to Ferrar, as 'a picture of the many spiritual conflicts

that have passed betwixt God and my soul, before I could subject
mine to the will of Jesus my Master: in whose service I have now
found perfect freedom' (Walton, 417). The week after his essay on
Herbert appeared, Eliot revealed in a BBC talk the essentials of his
spiritual life. They read like a litany of the Christian values that had
inspired both Ferrar and Herbert, 'values which I must maintain
or perish', he declared, 'the belief, for instance, in holy living and
holy dying, in sanctity, chastity, humility, austerity' (1932b, 383).
Thus, Eliot must have been delighted as editor to receive T.O.
Beachcroft's study, 'Nicholas Ferrar and George Herbert', which
he would publish in the *Criterion* for October.

Beachcroft's article was a timely confirmation and extension of
Eliot's own reading of Herbert. Tracing Ferrar's influence on the
personal life and religious poetry of Herbert, Beachcroft argued the
complexity of Herbert's verse, asserting that his so-called saintliness
and simplicity constituted 'a protracted struggle of the intellect
and will' (40). The essay was an invitation to the further study
of Herbert's mystical faculty, which Eliot was later to apprehend
in English mystics of the fourteenth century.

Just as Beachcroft's essay appeared, Eliot sailed to America for
the academic year at Harvard, leaving behind his estranged wife
Vivienne, in what would become a permanent separation. As
Lyndall Gordon has movingly shown, Eliot was on the threshold
of 'the gravest moral crisis of his life' (ENL, 52). In March 1928,
after bringing Vivienne back to London from the Sanitorium de
la Malmaison in Paris, he had taken a vow of celibacy. That act of
detachment had become a significant aspect of his spiritual progress;
it freed him to make a total commitment to the Holy Spirit. In
1930, however, that commitment was greatly complicated by the
renewal of his relationship with Emily Hale, his first love, whom
he had left behind in America sixteen years earlier. He would soon
see her again in America, and yet again after his return to England.
The clash of his determined drive for purity and the unexpected
renewal of an old desire brought on an intense personal and moral
dilemma – greatly aggravated by his impending separation from
Vivienne. Ever since he learned of, or intuited, her affair with
Bertrand Russell from 1917 to 1919 (see Bell), he had found
her morally repugnant. On 14 March 1933 he wrote to Ottoline
Morrell from Harvard about the permanent separation: 'For my
part, I should prefer never to see her again; for hers, I do not

believe that it can be good for any woman to live with a man to whom she is morally, in the larger sense, unpleasant, as well as physically indifferent' (HRHRC, Texas).

It is not yet known how long after the Russell affair Eliot entered into correspondence with Emily Hale, but by 1923 he was sending her copies of his books with telling inscriptions of his hellish situation. On 5 September 1923 he inscribed to her a copy of *Ara Vos Prec* (1919): 'For Emily Hale with the author's humble compliments' (Horowitz, 4). After his signature and the date he boldly added a dramatic passage from *Inferno* XV – Brunetto Latini's departing words about his work, *Il Tesoro*, as he makes his poignant turn to catch his wretched troop: 'SIETI RACOMMENDATO / IL MIO TESORO / NELLO QUAL VIVO ANCOR / E NON PIU CHIEGGIO / POI SI REVOLSE' ('"Let my 'Treasure,' in which I still live, be commended to thee; and more I ask not." Then he turned back'). From 1927 to 1930, during the composition of the *Ash-Wednesday* fragments, Eliot sent numerous inscribed copies of his works to her, including 'Journey of the Magi' (1927), inscribed less than a month after his conversion (Baker, 433). Gordon has argued that Emily Hale had already 'replaced Vivienne as Eliot's muse in *Ash-Wednesday*' (ENL, 15), which was ironically dedicated 'To My Wife'. Their eventual reunion in the summer of 1930 clearly revitalized Eliot's emotional life, but he had nonetheless committed himself to the purgative way. The persistent theme of regret, always coloured by the presence of imaginary children in the garden, was struck in part I of 'Landscapes' – 'New Hampshire', an autobiographical poem written after their visit together in June 1933, twenty years after their love began: 'Children's voices in the orchard . . . Twenty years and the spring is over; / To-day grieves, to-morrow grieves, / Cover me over, light-in-leaves' (CPP, 138). In part III of this sequence, 'Usk', a poem that looks forward to 'Little Gidding', Eliot would reveal the conflicting voice of his spirit as he contemplated a ruined chapel in the Welsh landscape: 'Seek only there / Where the grey light meets the green air / The hermit's chapel, the pilgrim's prayer' (CPP, 140).

After he returned to England, and in the midst of this growing crisis, Eliot immersed himself in Herbert once again. When he visited Pikes Farm in the winter of 1934 his friend Frank Morley recorded: 'I recall one crisp wintry night . . . when, out of doors, we happened to be talking about Herbert. It made me think, erroneously, he might be thinking of an essay, and I asked him. "Not yet," said Tom, or something to the effect that he had marked many passages in Herbert but, or so I gathered, had not felt ready to write about him' (Tate, 107).[1] But Eliot had already written his essay; he was now thinking of Herbert's treatment of 'the mysteries of the faith and the motives of the heart', the subject of a poem that would be precipitated by his visit to Burnt Norton with Emily Hale in September 1934.

The dilemma posed by his love for Emily Hale – to find happiness in a new marriage or in a kind of spiritual martyrdom, in attachment or detachment – had been irrevocably resolved in Eliot's mind months before he began to write 'Burnt Norton'. Shortly after beginning *Murder in the Cathedral* in December 1934, he contributed to *Time and Tide* an untitled essay on 'Liberty' under the weekly heading 'Notes On the Way'. In the course of the essay he moved from political liberty to moral liberty, from the meaning of liberty to 'a paradox of liberty', as stated by St John of the Cross in a passage that was now at the centre of Eliot's spiritual consciousness:

> *To follow Christ is to deny self; this is not that other course which is nothing but to seek oneself in God, which is the very opposite of love. For to seek self in God is to seek for comfort and refreshment from God. But to seek God in Himself is not only to be willing to be deprived of this thing and of that for God, but to incline ourselves to will and choose for Christ's sake whatever is most disagreeable, whether proceeding from God or from this world; this is to love God.* (1935, 89–90) [*The Ascent of Mount Carmel*, Book 2, ch. 7, para. 4]

Eliot moved from liberty to liberation, and from liberation to the 'last word' on free will, as stated by Dante in the *Paradiso* (III: 85) and translated by Eliot at the end of *Ash-Wednesday*: '*la sua volontade è nostra pace*' ('Our peace in His will'). Ultimately concerned with the individual's freedom to choose his own salvation or damnation, he wrote out of his concern with the small amount of 'real freedom' in the lives of most people. It moved him to a startling assertion: 'Our obligation, certainly, is to *love* – to love *without desire* (for the latter is to seek oneself in the beloved object, see St John of the Cross quoted above) – or I might say to love beyond desire – for such love is not effected by the mere quenching of desire' (90).

Here, before the first quartet was composed, is an almost verbatim statement in prose of the primary theme of detachment in part III of 'Little Gidding': 'liberation – not less of love but expanding / Of love beyond desire, and so liberation / From the future as well as the past' (CPP, 195). Again, he rested the rationale of his statement on the words of St John:

> *The soul, by resigning itself to the divine light, that is, by removing every spot and stain of the creature, which is to keep the will perfectly united to the will of God – for to love Him is to labour to detach ourselves from, and to divest ourselves of, everything which is not God's for God's sake – becomes immediately enlightened by, and transformed in, God.* (90) [*The Ascent of Mount Carmel*, Book 2, ch. 5, para. 7]

Eliot's essay on liberty was determined by his own resolve to sublimate human love in divine contemplation. Thus, 'Burnt Norton' possessed from the beginning what he felt 'Little Gidding' was lacking in its first draft, 'some acute personal reminiscence (never to be explicated, of course, but to give power from well below the surface)' (CFQ, 67). From that substratum the opening of 'Burnt Norton' expresses a deeply personal conversation with Emily Hale; it reads as a love poem of great regret, expressed with an emotional resignation that is relieved only by a timeless intersection in the rose garden. It is a poem of painful human loss – of what might have been, of the laughter of hidden children, of 'the waste sad time / Stretching before and after' (CPP, 176) – all this in conflict with a greater call toward the possibility of beatitude through deprivation and solitude.

During this period of moral struggle and poetic formulation, Eliot associated himself with the Society of the Sacred Mission at Kelham, an Anglican religious community. Visiting the Society periodically from 1931 to the outbreak of war, he became not a saint but an advanced student of contemplative life through study, devotion and solitude. Kelham was a place of spiritual retreat for Eliot, and it became, in effect, his Little Gidding. There he befriended Brother George Every, himself a poet and playwright, and early in 1936 Every asked Eliot to criticize the manuscript of his verse-play, *Stalemate – The King at Little Gidding* (unpublished). The play focuses on Charles I's third visit to Little Gidding in May of 1646 when, in the company of his chaplain, he sought refuge in the dark of night after the battle of Naseby –

the 'king at nightfall' in Eliot's poem. On 13 March Eliot wrote to Every about the merits and faults of the play, criticizing the lack of action and the uneven verse but encouraging him to persevere (Spurr, 30). Helen Gardner suggests that 'it was Mr. Every's play that linked fire with Little Gidding in his mind' (CFQ, 63), but the fire in Eliot's mind came from his pentecostal experience there, and from the poetry of George Herbert.

Eliot's long-delayed pilgrimage to Little Gidding had now become imperative, and so arrangements were made. On Saturday, 23 May 1936, he went up to Cambridge to spend the weekend with John Maynard Keynes, who took him to guest night at King's College and to lunch on Sunday. On Monday afternoon, the 25th, after participating in a viva that morning, Eliot motored over to Little Gidding in the company of the eminent Pascal scholar, the Rev Hugh Fraser Stewart, and his wife Jessie. It had been a miserably wet May, and though the white may blossoms were in full bloom on the hawthorns, the forecast was for more unsettled weather, cloudy and cold with occasional rain. However, when Eliot later mentioned his visit in a letter to Emily Hale's aunt, Mrs Edith Perkins, he described it as the 'only really lovely day' in May that he could remember (CFQ, 35). It was, indeed, a day of 'Midwinter spring'.

The symbolic coincidence that his visit took place in the week leading to Whitsunday would not have escaped him as he stood before the 'dull facade' of the restored chapel and the weathered tomb of Nicholas Ferrar. He knew from Walton and others that it was on Whitsun eve of 1625, during the plague, that Ferrar persuaded his family to leave London for Little Gidding; he knew that during the week before Whitsun of 1626 Ferrar fasted and prayed, waiting for the descent of the Holy Spirit, before going to Archbishop Laud on Trinity Sunday to take the deacon's orders that would enable him to conduct services for his community. Over the entrance to the chapel is the stone slab from the original front, chiselled with words chosen by Ferrar: 'THIS IS NONE OTHER BUT THE HOUSE OF GOD AND THE GATE OF HEAVEN'. Eliot's pentecostal poem, when it came, would record not only the private 'glow' that he experienced there, but his communication in prayer with the dead of Little Gidding.

Similar moments of illumination occurred in swift succession – at the Dry Salvages in the late summer of 1936 and at East Coker in August 1937. Meanwhile, in the years before the composition of the last three quartets, a wealth of new information appeared on Little Gidding. When Bernard Blackstone's 'Discord at Little Gidding' appeared in the *TLS* (1 August 1936, 628), the public learned of the strident personality and 'singularly unpleasant' behaviour of John Ferrar's wife, Bathsheba, who would make her way into Eliot's poem among those 'not wholly commendable'. When A.L. Maycock, the Cambridge author and librarian, published his *Nicholas Ferrar of Little Gidding* (1938), Eliot had Blackstone review it for the *Criterion* in October. Maycock's book, wrote Blackstone, erases myths and distorted views of Ferrar and lays the groundwork for a much-needed scholarly study. Later in the year, Blackstone brought out the materials for such a study in *The Ferrar Papers* (1938), declaring Ferrar to be 'in singleness of vision and completeness of achievement . . . the most original genius in the church during the vital period of her post-Reformation history' [xi]. Eliot had the volume reviewed by another Kelham friend, the Rev Charles Smyth, who praised Blackstone's sense of the spiritual complexity of Ferrar's writings: 'we should not wish to quarrel with the statement that "the restraint, the quiet dignity, and the objectivity of Ferrar's writings proceed rather from a continuous inner tension than from habitual serenity"' (369). Eliot thus encouraged and witnessed in his own periodical a critical elevation of Ferrar similar to Beachcroft's earlier revaluation of Herbert. Elaborations of his own knowledge and experience of Little Gidding were appearing at every turn, and when his friend Charles Williams published *The Descent of the Dove: A Short History of the Holy Spirit in the Church* (1939), Eliot expressed relief in his review that Williams had given St John of the Cross 'his due place' (1939, 866). But he would have found further satisfaction in the special importance that Williams gave to the *via negativa* of the fourteenth-century English mystics, particularly Dame Julian of Norwich and the anonymous author of *The Cloud of Unknowing*, authors who had become integral to Eliot's study of Herbert.

Eliot had not found such satisfaction in the recent writings of his friend Paul Elmer More, who had made his own way into the Anglican Church concurrently with Eliot. In fact, when More traced the stages of his spiritual progress in 'Marginalia' (1936), in which he describes at length 'how deeply my own philosophy of life was moulded . . . by *John Inglesant*' (7), Eliot wrote to More on 11 January 1937 that his spiritual biography was 'oddly, even grotesquely, more like my own, so far as I can see, than that of any human being I have known' (Princeton). Earlier in their correspondence, however, Eliot had been frankly critical of More's view of St John of the Cross in *The Catholic Faith* (1931). Writing on 17 February 1932, he argued that 'you are over-bold in your criticism of one who is crowned with so much authority' (Princeton). When, shortly before More's death, Eliot wrote an article on him for the *Princeton Alumni Weekly*, he renewed the criticism: More 'seems to me to fail to appreciate the greatness of St John of the Cross' (1937, 373). But in More's *Anglicanism* (1935) Eliot had come to see a more significant failing: 'he seems to me more Anglican than the Anglicans, and to write as if the English Church began with Hooker. . . . He does not give recognition to the probable importance of the mystics of the fourteenth century – of Richard Rolle and Julian of Norwich for instance – as late as the time of Lancelot Andrewes and George Herbert' (373).

Eliot had first studied the English mystics at Harvard in Evelyn Underhill's *Mysticism* (1911), in which she discussed Rolle, Dame Julian, Walter Hilton and the author of *The Cloud of Unknowing*. As he renewed his reading of them in the 1930s, he had Beachcroft review F.M.M. Comper's *Life and Lyrics of Richard Rolle* in the *Criterion* (January 1934). They were all so much in his consciousness when writing *The Family Reunion* (1939) that he had Agatha say to Harry, as he goes off to follow the Eumenides, 'Accident is design / And design is accident / In a cloud of unknowing' (CPP, 337). Eliot believed with Underhill and others that Andrewes, Herbert and Ferrar were steeped in the *via negativa* of these mystics and that a knowledge of their works was necessary to penetrate much seventeenth-century theology. Eliot steeped himself in their manuals of contemplative life, and when the first draft of 'Little Gidding' stalled in 1941 it was these English mystics whom Eliot summoned for help.

In consciously linking himself to them through the seventeenth century, he became the direct descendant of the English devotional tradition. Of greater consequence, in identifying himself with them through St John and Herbert, he placed himself specifically in a more ancient tradition that he wished to revive – that of the contemplative poet. In this tradition lay the foundation of what Eliot had described to the Rev William Force Stead in a letter of 9 August 1930 (Osborn Collection, Yale) as 'a theory I have nourished for a long time, that between the usual subjects of poetry and 'devotional' verse there is a very important field still very unexplored by modern poets – the experience of man in search of God, and trying to explain to himself his intenser human feelings in terms of the divine goal. I have tried to do something of that in *Ash-Wednesday*.' This was his aim in *Four Quartets* as well, and his models for the undertaking were Herbert, St John and the English mystics.

Prior to composing his last three quartets Eliot wrote a lecture on George Herbert that has escaped most eyes. On 25 May 1938, at the behest of the Dean of Salisbury, the Rev E.L. Henderson, Eliot addressed the Friends of the Cathedral in the Chapter House on 'George Herbert'. The body of the 'Brilliant Lecture' on 'A Tough Man in a Tough Age', a by-line taken from the text, was printed in the report of the local paper, the *Salisbury and Winchester Journal* (27 May 1938, 12). After his introductory remarks on Herbert's local associations, Eliot told the audience that his greater familiarity with Herbert's works and his greater maturity of mind and sensibility had led him 'to concede to Herbert as a religious poet a pre-eminence among his contemporaries and followers. I am, therefore, at the stage of asking for a revision of his reputation; feeling, as I do, that he has been not so much critically as implicitly underrated'.

In the address Eliot describes Herbert variously as 'the most intellectual of all our religious poets', as 'a man of his time, for whom sin was very real, and the promises of death very terrible', and as a man who 'happened to be something very near a saint'. He affirms Herbert's superiority not only to Donne, in whom 'something of the particular and private sinner . . . remains, as a kind of sediment, even in his most religious verse', but to Vaughan and Traherne, whose occasional 'mystical flashes' cannot stand up to Herbert's 'steady intellectual light'. Writing without his earlier caution in comparison, Eliot now asserts that 'the only poetry I can think of which belongs to quite the same class as Herbert – as expression of purity and intensity of religious feeling, and . . . for literary excellence – is St John of the Cross'. With this association of the poet and the contemplative now significantly in place, he goes on to characterize the presence of Herbert's personal voice in his impersonal poems:

What impresses me as the peculiar quality of Herbert's poetry is that while familiarity with it makes us feel that we have got to know a particular, unique man, we know him only in his poetry and not through his poetry. We cannot, as with Donne, read his poetry as a kind of cypher which will yield clues to a peculiarly interesting personality behind poetry [sic]. What is relevant is all there, and we do not ask to know more of him than what is conveyed in his utterance of his meditations on the highest spiritual mysteries. Within his limits, therefore, he achieves the greatest universality in his art; he remains as the human soul contemplating the divine.

In urging his listeners to return to Herbert's text, Eliot asks them to see him as 'a man of great intellectual gifts and great psychological insight: and to regard devotional verse like his, not as a pleasant by-path of poetry, but as the highest, if not the most comprehensive that a poet can attempt.' Eliot's praise of Herbert in this 1938 lecture confirms what his 1932 essay had strongly suggested, that Herbert's achievement as a meditative poet in *The Temple* had become Eliot's aim in *Four Quartets*. Lecturing coincidentally on the second anniversary of his visit to Little Gidding, Eliot concluded with a reading of Herbert's 'Whitsunday', chosen, he says, 'for its sublimity of content and its technical mastery':

> Listen sweet Dove unto my song,
> And spread thy golden wings in me;
> Hatching my tender heart so long,
> Till it get wing, and flie away with thee.
>
> Where is that fire which once descended
> On thy Apostles? thou didst then
> Keep open house, richly attended,
> Feasting all comers by twelve chosen men. . . .
>
> Lord, though we change, thou art the same;
> The same sweet God of love and light:
> Restore this day, for thy great name,
> Unto his ancient and miraculous right.

Herbert's invocation of the descending fire had become a permanent image in Eliot's imagination, an image enriched by the sublimity of his own pentecostal experience at Little Gidding. And yet the worldly fires remained: in July 1938, after Emily Hale had returned for her annual summer visit, Vivienne was certified and committed to an asylum. This event would only compound Eliot's desire to atone for abandoning her. Emily returned the following summer, but the onset of war was not only to hasten her departure; it was to bring years of separation and despondency. As Lyndall Gordon observes, 'At some point she must have come to terms with the fact that, so long as Vivienne lived, Eliot would not marry' (ENL, 166). After her late-summer departure in 1939, Eliot, sharing a flat with the Rev Eric Cheetham, Vicar of St Stephen's Church, enrolled at the Air-Raid Wardens' Post in Kensington and returned not only to a life of disciplined prayer, but to the *Quartets*.

III

Even as Eliot wrote and published 'East Coker' and 'The Dry Salvages', the Cambridge critic Muriel Bradbrook had sensed the presence of Herbert in Eliot's later poetry, and even before the appearance of 'Little Gidding' she had published 'The Liturgical Tradition in English Verse: Herbert and Eliot' (1942). Bradbrook argued astutely that 'Herbert's successes throw light on Eliot's difficulties and help to an understanding of what he has achieved' (13). Eliot himself felt the anxiety of influence as he composed the poems, writing to Anne Ridler on 10 March 1941, as he turned to the first draft of 'Little Gidding', that his intention in part IV of 'East Coker' had been 'to avoid a pastiche of George Herbert or Crashaw – it would be folly to try' (CFQ, 109). In the fifty years since the publication of *Four Quartets*, however, critics have hardly touched what a few have occasionally intuited. David Ward asserts that 'One is reminded strongly of the devotional poems of George Herbert', but concludes that Eliot's technique 'is radically different from Herbert's practice' and that 'Eliot lacks Herbert's confidence' (283–4). Derek Traversi remarks only in passing that 'the spirit of Herbert is indeed present in the poem' (183); only Ronald Bush hints that Eliot 'anticipated' 'Little Gidding' in his remarks on Herbert (224).

Though it is beyond the scope of this essay to initiate a comparative study of their verse techniques, a reconsideration of 'Little Gidding' does show how pervasively the 'spirit' of Herbert informs the poem. That spirit, however, guides as much as it informs, for in his fusion of the personal and the mystical Herbert served Eliot immeasurably as a spiritual architect of *Four Quartets*. His poetry inspired in Eliot a modern form of devotional verse and showed him how to explore personal emotions in terms of the divine goal. Shortly after the publication of *Four Quartets*, Eliot took pains, in 'What Is Minor Poetry?' (1944), to characterize *The Temple* 'as something more than a number of religious poems by one author', describing the work in terms that characterize *Four Quartets* in general and 'Little Gidding' in particular:

> What has at first the appearance of a succession of beautiful but separate lyrics, comes to reveal itself as a continued religious meditation with an intellectual framework; and the book as a whole discloses to us the Anglican devotional spirit of the first half of the seventeenth century. What is more, we get to understand Herbert better, and feel rewarded for the trouble, if we know something about . . . the English mystical writers of the fourteenth century . . . (OPP, 45–6)

In 'Little Gidding', where the pressure of sin on Eliot's own devotional spirit emerges as a primary theme, Herbert and the English mystics join Nicholas Ferrar and St John of the Cross as the presiding spirits of the poem. Behind them stand the shadowy figures of Emily Hale and Vivienne Eliot.

'Winter scene. May', wrote Eliot in his preliminary sketch of the poem (CFQ, 157). How familiarly and appropriately his eventual portrayal of that 'Midwinter spring' draws on Herbert's 'The Flower', which Eliot later described as a poem in which 'we hear the note of serenity, almost of beatitude, and of thankfulness for God's blessings' (1962, 25). Herbert likens the Lord's visitation to his 'shrivel'd heart' to that sudden moment in May when the 'late-past frosts' humbly pay tribute to the freshly budding flowers, and he compares his spiritual transformation to the physical change in nature: 'Grief melts away / Like snow in May, / As if there were no such cold thing.' Though sin and pride have brought God's wrath ('What frost to that?') and the death of previous springtime rebirths, the poem celebrates the return, once again, of the Holy Spirit to the penitent-poet:

And now in age I bud again,
After so many deaths I live and write;
  I once more smell the dew and rain,
And relish versing: O my onely light,
    It cannot be
    That I am he
On whom thy tempests fell all night.

'I cannot resist the thought', Eliot later wrote, 'that in this . . . stanza – itself a miracle of phrasing – the imagery, so apposite to express the achievement of faith which it records, is taken from the experience of the man of delicate physical health who had known much illness. It is on this note of joy in convalescence of the spirit in surrender to God, that the life of discipline of this haughty and irascible Herbert finds conclusion: *In His will is our peace*' (1962, 26). But Herbert's joy significantly gives way to humility before the 'Lord of love', to the recognition that 'we are but flowers that glide' between deaths, that we are dependent upon grace, that those who would be any greater 'Forfeit their Paradise by their pride'.

Eliot's poem, too, analogically portrays a divine visitation to his dormant, darkened soul at Little Gidding through the silent transition from winter to spring. Like the soul, the frost-frozen landscape creates an illusion of perpetual suspension, only to become 'sodden' with the day's slow thawing. The solar fire that flames the ice and creates a blinding glare suddenly becomes a pentecostal fire, an intense 'glow' that rekindles the 'dumb spirit' and warms the 'soul's sap'. At that moment of beatitude the natural world of Little Gidding is wholly transformed by the supernatural: poet and hedgerow are lifted out of sense and time; for 'an hour', flower blossoms revert to snow blossoms in an unfading world free from the progressive 'scheme of generation'. If this intense glow occurs at zero spring, the astounded poet is moved to ask in an extension of the season-soul analogy, 'Where is the summer, the unimaginable / Zero summer?' (CPP, 191) Where is the full inward fire, the blinding glare, of the Holy Spirit? That terrifying, 'incandescent' descent is richly imagined in part IV of the poem.

The lyrical re-creation of his visionary experience at Little Gidding leads the poet to a subjunctive and impersonal meditation on the sameness of the experience for all contemplatives who gravitate toward this holy place, past the pigsty and other mundane objects to the 'dull facade' of the chapel and Ferrar's tombstone. 'For wherever a saint has dwelt', Eliot had written in *Murder in the Cathedral*, as though he were thinking of Little Gidding, 'There is holy ground, and the sanctity shall not depart from it / Though armies trample over it, though sightseers come with guide-books looking over it' (CPP, 281–2). In the second and third verse paragraphs of part I Eliot does indeed celebrate the place, the discipline and the prayer of 'the Protestant-Saint', Nicholas Ferrar. There are 'other places' of other saints, named by Eliot elsewhere and alluded to in *Murder in the Cathedral* and in earlier quartets – those 'at the sea jaws', St Columba at Iona and St Cuthbert at Lindisfarne; 'over a dark lake', St Kevin at Glendalough; 'in a desert', the Egyptian St Anthony and the hermits of Thebes; 'or a city', St Anthony at Padua – but Ferrar's Little Gidding, 'the nearest', affirms the promise of Pentecost: the presence and accessibility of the Holy Spirit in the world, 'Now and in England' (CPP, 192).

As Eliot evokes the present and the past of Little Gidding, he remains wrapped in the subjunctive contemplation of a future communicant: 'If you came this way, / . . . It would always be the same: you would have to put off sense and notion' (CPP, 192). At whatever time or season, for whatever refuge, each penitent must follow the purgative way to Little Gidding, must arrive in humility and without expectation to engage in the mystery of prayer: like Ferrar, who came in renunciation; like Charles, who came as a 'broken king'; like Herbert, who came continuously in spirit, counselling Ferrar on his nightly prayer vigils, or 'night-watches', and trying in vain to exchange his parish in Bemerton for a smaller one near Little Gidding before he died; like Crashaw, who attended Ferrar's night-watches and continued them in the chapel at Peterhouse; like Eliot, who came three centuries later just before Pentecost.

Suddenly the narrative shifts from the subjunctive to the indicative mood, as if the poet were impatient of the communicant's sense of purpose: 'You are not here to verify', he is instructed, 'You are here to kneel / Where prayer has been valid' (CPP, 192). The achievement of humility, the poet implies, is inextricable from the efficacy of prayer, both of which are the hallmarks of Little Gidding. His declaration of the power of prayer on this hallowed ground, and his attempt to suggest the complexity of prayer as 'more / Than an order of words', reverberate with Herbert's 'Prayer (I)', in which nothing less than a string of conceits can suggest the range and reach of prayer for 'something understood', and with 'Prayer (II)', in which prayer has become not only 'an easie quick accesse' to the Lord and a weapon against the destructive power of sin but the one human necessity:

> I value prayer so,
> That were I to leave all but one,
> Wealth, fame, endowments, vertues, all should go;
> I and deare prayer would together dwell,
> And quickly gain, for each inch lost, an ell.

Eliot's meditation on Little Gidding as a personal and historical place of 'the intersection of the timeless moment' is governed by a realization in 'The Dry Salvages' that after the 'hints and guesses' of a timeless world 'the rest / Is prayer, observance, discipline, thought and action' (CPP, 190). The discipline of contemplative prayer, the fixing of the human upon the divine will, is 'right action', a way to divine communion. In that communion the Holy Spirit bestows upon the poet, as upon the Apostles at Pentecost, the tongues of flame of the dead, who speak in fire the language of redemption – purgation, prayer and purification. The tongues here unfolded remain persistent voices in the poem.

In each quartet the eternal stillness of a divine pattern of reality is set against the endless movement of a temporal pattern, a pattern characterized by action and appetency, desire and knowledge, hope and despair, and, in 'Little Gidding', sin and error. At the beginning of part II Eliot turns from the intersection of the timeless at Little Gidding to its movement in time, bounded as it is by earth, air, fire and water. Eliot reportedly told a friend that this section of the poem 'came out of' his fire-watching experience during the Blitz, that the bombing debris 'would slowly descend and cover one's sleeves and coat with a fine white ash' (Levy, 14–15). Even allowing that description, however, the fragmented London scene is no more than a projection upon Little Gidding, for the lyric is built upon Eliot's rich familiarity with the history and place of Little Gidding. The succession of images in the first stanza – roses, story, house, wall, wainscot and mouse – allude to both the manor house and the chapel as they were first restored and inhabited by the Ferrars: the abundant rose gardens, trellises and cut flowers that beautified them; the oak wainscoting deftly installed in them; the story books read in the great chamber of the house by members of the 'Little Academy', the family study circle that met daily to read stories and dialogues based on the lives of saints. In depicting the continuous dissolution of Little Gidding, the dust of its objects now 'suspended' and 'inbreathed', Eliot draws on Herbert's heavy consciousness of dust, perhaps directly on what he called the 'striking effect' (1962, 28) of lines in Herbert's 'The Church Floore': 'Sometimes Death, puffing at the door, / Blows all the dust about the floore'.

Eliot's lyric begins and ends with allusions to the 'burnt roses' and the 'marred foundations' of the chapel, which was plundered, wrecked and partially burned by a Puritan soldiery in 1646, leaving Ferrar's faithful brother, John, an aging man, standing in the ashes to record the destruction. In time, the objects of Little Gidding – its roses, readers, house and chapel – become, like the objects of London in the Blitz, ash of fire, dust of air, particles of earth and water, substances that mock human pride and the illusion that time can be conquered without grace. 'Where is there an end of it?' the poet had asked of the 'soundless wailing' and the 'silent withering' in 'The Dry Salvages' (CPP, 185). 'There is no end of it', he answers there and here, no end to the pattern of hope and despair until the death of air, no end to the 'vanity of toil' until the death of earth and water and fire (CPP, 193).

The allusions to the pillaging of Little Gidding during the Civil War thus precipitate the poet's psychological dislocation to Kensington during the Blitz. His removal from the place of beatitude to the 'three districts' of bombardment is governed by a series of ironic declensions: vision becomes hallucination; Ferrar's night-watches become Eliot's fire-watches; the descent of the Dove in tongues of flame becomes the destructive dive of 'the dark dove with the flickering tongue'; the auditory communion with the dead of Little Gidding becomes an automatized dialogue with the compound ghost of masterful writers – the central figure of whom we know to be Yeats. Eliot's intention, as he later explained, 'was the same as with my allusions to Dante in *The Waste Land*: to present to the mind of the reader a parallel, by means of contrast, between the Inferno and the Purgatorio which Dante visited and a hallucinated scene after an air-raid' (TCC, 128).

The phantasmal encounter of the poet and his composite master is based on a fusion of *Inferno* XV, where Dante meets the shade of Brunetto Latini, and *Purgatorio* XXVI, where he encounters the shades of Guido Cavalcanti and Arnaut Daniel. But, as Eliot explained to John Hayward, 'I wished the effect of the whole to be Purgatorial which is much more appropriate' (CFQ, 175). The parallel between Dante's and Eliot's encounters with their dead masters lies in the purgatorial realization that the poet cannot seek redemption or immortality in art, and in the further recognition of the evanescence of poetic fame. 'You taught me how man makes himself eternal', Dante says to Brunetto, but Brunetto, damned for his lust, answers about his writing: 'I am prepared for Fortune as she wills . . . He listens well who notes it.' So the shade of Yeats, who to Eliot became the greatest writer of the century but who also followed the religion of art, now urges that they be forgiven their 'thought and theory' and admonishes his companion about the illusion of poetic permanence: 'last year's words belong to last year's language / And next year's words await another voice' (CPP, 194). The composite voice speaks, like Guido and Arnaut, from the refining fire, and as Eliot explained the parallel to Hayward, 'the people who talk to him [Dante] at that point are represented as not wanting to waste time in conversation but wishing to dive back into the fire to accomplish their expiation' (CFQ, 196). Dante swears his lasting devotion to his poetic father, Guido, and proclaims the sublimity and permanence of his art: 'Your sweet ditties, which so long as modern use shall last, will make their very ink precious'. But Guido, mindful of the transience of literary glory, quickly points to 'a better craftsman', Arnaut Daniel, and before disappearing into the fire he petitions not Dante's praise but his prayers for those in a world 'where power to sin is no more ours'.

Dante would make for Arnaut 'a grateful place for his name', but the thankful Arnaut replies, before he returns to the refining fire, 'be mindful in due time of my pain'. Eliot's ghostly poet, momentarily removed from the purgatorial flames, is similarly mindful not of their common art but of the poet's mortal decline from that art. He recounts only 'the gifts reserved for age', the ironic 'crown' of the poet's kingly effort in language – expiration of sense, impotence of rage, laceration of laughter, shame of motives, consciousness of harm inflicted, persistence of humiliation. Before he fades like Hamlet's ghost, Eliot's ghost, aware that neither art nor fame lends peace to the artist, echoes Arnaut's awareness of the necessity of purgation: 'From wrong to wrong the exasperated spirit / Proceeds, unless restored by that refining fire / Where you must move in measure like a dancer' (CPP, 195). It is a timely admonition for a poet engaged, like Herbert and St John, in the poetic contemplation of divine love.

It is the more ironic that the most discernible voice of the shade is that of Yeats, whom Eliot had criticized severely during his lifetime for his romantic, self-redemptive view of art and reality. But as Yeats' and Dante's shades testify, art provides no protection from sin and error, no possible means of redemption, and all suffer remorse for their intellectual pride. The insistent voice of the encounter, that the poet must achieve humility in his art as in his life, is strongly informed by the voice and verse of Herbert, who in such a poem as 'Jordan (II)' describes how he 'bustled' in fascination with 'my lines of heav'nly joyes', how in pride 'did I weave my self into the sense', only to hear an imagined friend 'Whisper, *How wide is all this long pretence!*' After the war, when Emily Hale asked Eliot to speak 'On Poetry' to the 1947 class of Concord Academy, he said it again in prose: 'I am sure that for a poet humility is the most essential virtue' (9).

The poet departs the disfigured streets of Kensington and returns in part III to the mental locale of Little Gidding, where he turns over three 'conditions' of mind like multiple flowers in a hedgerow. Here the poem moves toward a dramatic moment as the poet brings his 'intenser human feelings' to bear on his divine goal. In the early drafts Eliot had sought to infuse an 'acute personal reminiscence' into part II, but his attempts to do so were cancelled. That reminiscence occurs here, in the spiritual liberation of the desiring self from painful memories which are expressed obliquely as abstract states of mind, 'never to be explicated': his attachment to Emily Hale and his human love for her; his detachment from her in contemplation of the Holy Spirit; and, 'growing between them', his indifference to Vivienne. This is the triangular complex, the tormenting matrix of memory, that underrides the *Four Quartets*. But now comes the dramatic declaration that the memory, which imprisons the self in its fixation on things and persons, may be transformed in contemplative prayer from a human to a spiritual knowledge of things and persons. 'This is the use of memory', he declares in affirmation of that primary faculty of the soul described by the English mystics and by St John, who chart the purging and purification of memory in advancement towards divine union: 'For liberation − not less of love but expanding of love beyond desire, and so liberation / From the future as well as the past' (CPP, 195). 'See', he points in climactic release at the moment of transformation, 'now they vanish, / The faces and places, with the self which, as it could, loved them, / To become renewed, transfigured, in another pattern' (CPP, 195).

The 'unflowering', death-in-life condition of indifference is not to be slighted in the poet's personal search for spiritual liberation. Detachment from desire is painful in itself and demands disciplined self-denial; simultaneous detachment from indifference, from a total absence of feeling toward another object whose reality is as intense as its opposite, disturbs and hinders the mind in concentration. Thus the doubly difficult aim of the contemplative poet is to transcend desire on the one hand and indifference on the other through spiritual knowledge of both objects. The spiritual man, explains St John, 'attains to liberty of spirit' in detachment. 'He acquires also in this detachment from creatures a clear comprehension of them, so as to understand perfectly the truths that relate to them, both naturally and supernaturally. For this reason his joy in them is widely different from his who is attached to them, and far nobler' (298). As St John makes clear, detachment from the beloved object leads not to indifference but to serene exaltation ('Detachment & attachment only a hair's width apart' Eliot wrote on a draft of part III [CFQ, 197]). Eliot thus employs a political analogue to distinguish states of detachment and indifference: a patriot, in the ordinary process of mature detachment from self-interest, may in time find his 'own field of action' to be 'of little importance', but he is 'never indifferent', never so acutely removed from his object. For Eliot, unflowering indifference is a motive for, not a result of, liberation.

The juxtaposition of spiritual liberation and political liberty prompts a momentary reflection that anticipates the redefinition of history in part V: 'History may be servitude, / History may be freedom' (CPP, 195). Whatever the historical extremes of political being, there is no individual liberty without the liberation of the soul. It was a central theme of his earlier essay on liberty:

To me, the notion of *liberty* is meaningless without the further
notion of *liberation*. One lives, not to be free, but to be freed.
And to be *freed from* is meaningless unless one has some notion of
what one is to be *freed for*. . . . If human souls are not ultimately
important, or if they are not equally important, then liberty
does not matter . . . I do not think that the political idea of
liberty can subsist quite apart from the religious idea of *liberation*.
Mere political liberty cannot be permanently interesting; unless
we have some notion of the purpose and destination of the
individual, which makes it necessary that he should be free to
fulfill this purpose and destination. (1935, 88–9)

For Eliot, who in part III meditates his spiritual liberation between
the historical fluctuations of servitude and freedom, the only
human liberty consists in the salvation of the individual soul, in
liberation from sin in contemplative prayer.

As the mind moves over the painful footfalls and spiritual
ecstasies of the memory, a Voice obtrudes, as once it did upon
a predecessor in prayer, the anchoress of Norwich, Dame Julian,
who in asking the Lord of the reality of sin heard from Him
the necessity of sin: 'Sin is Behovable'. This Voice from her
fourteenth 'shewing', assuring her that 'all shall be well' through
prayer and the grace of the Holy Spirit, frames the poet's return
to the personages of Little Gidding. It was a late but significant
addition to the draft, as was the allusion to *The Cloud of Unknowing*
in part V. As Eliot wrote to Hayward on 2 September 1942, he
wanted to 'give greater historical depth to the poem by allusions
to the other great period, i.e. the 14th century' (CFQ, 70). Though
he remarked that he 'might have dragged in Richard Rolle and
Walter Hilton' if he knew them better and if he did not think that
he would be 'overdoing it', their mystical presence is nonetheless
felt in the contemplative reach for what they both call 'the fire of
love'. As Eliot reaches deeper into history – deeper into the English
mystical tradition – for moments of revelation in solitude, those
lifted moments become continuous with Eliot's present, 'Now and
in England'. 'It seems, as one becomes older,' he had written in
'The Dry Salvages', 'That the past has another pattern, and ceases
to be a mere sequence' (CPP, 186). In 'Little Gidding' that
other pattern of timeless moments prevails; it collapses historical
sequence and binds Dame Julian and Ferrar and Herbert and Eliot

together on another plane of reality as he begins to think, 'again, of this place'.

Eliot recalls the inhabitants and visitants of Little Gidding before and after the Civil War – including those of a 'peculiar genius', the Anglican poet Herbert, dead before the war, and the Royalist poet Crashaw, Anglican turned Catholic – all of whom were touched by the spiritual genius of Ferrar and by a 'common genius' for prayer and devotion. He thinks again of the encirclement of Little Gidding by Puritan forces, of Charles' final visit, of his execution with Laud, Strafford and others, and even of Milton, who, though he died 'blind and quiet' after justifying the ways of God to men, had gone blind writing tracts in defence of the execution. Poet and politician, deacon and penitent, Puritan and Royalist, victor and defeated, all are removed in the communality of death from their impure fields of action. In recollection of these separate struggles for political and religious liberty, the poet is driven to ask, 'Why should we celebrate / These dead men more than the dying?' (CPP, 196). What is celebrated is not the divided group of dead men but the symbolic place of the defeated men, Little Gidding, a place where motives have been purified in prayer, a place where grace has been bestowed. Desecrated as it was during the bitter religious conflict of the Civil War, Little Gidding remains, in war-torn England, a symbol of liberation in the loss of liberty, of salvation in the midst of defeat. At one with Eliot's voice is the Voice from Dame Julian:

> And all shall be well and
> All manner of thing shall be well
> By the purification of the motive
> In the ground of our beseeching.   (CPP, 196)

The purpose of repeating Lady Julian's shewing, he wrote, was 'to escape any suggestion of historical sentimentality about the seventeenth century by this reiterated reference to the fourteenth century and therefore to get more bearing on the present than would be possible if the relation was merely between the present and one particular period of the past' (quoted in Matthiessen, 195n). The bearing on the present is the immediacy of her belief that the reality and necessity of sin are made well by the reality and necessity of prayer. 'Beseeching', she writes of contemplative prayer, 'is a true, gracious, lasting will of the soul, oned and fastened into the will of our Lord by the sweet inward work of the Holy Ghost' (85).

Tormented by the irreconcilable conflict between human desire and divine love, the poet envisions in part IV the awesome moment, the 'Zero summer' of the Holy Spirit's pentecostal descent before the Apostles, the blinding fire striking spiritual terror as the tongues of flame speak the language of redemption and declare that grace is 'the one discharge from sin and error' (CPP, 196). In the temporal world of desire and movement, of hope and despair, the 'only hope' lies in redemption from the consuming fire of desire by the consuming fire of the Holy Spirit.

Dame Julian, who sought 'oftentimes to learn what was our Lord's meaning', was answered in 'ghostly understanding' in her sixteenth revelation: *'Learn it well: Love was His meaning. Who shewed it thee? Love. What shewed He thee? Love'* (202). The poet, seeking to understand the involuntary persistence of desire, also hears that ghostly Voice: 'Who then devised the torment? Love.' 'Desire itself is movement', he had written in 'Burnt Norton', 'Not in itself desirable; / Love is itself unmoving, / Only the cause and end of movement' (CPP, 175). Like Hercules upon his self-made pyre – his great strength useless to remove the 'intolerable shirt of flame', his mortal body burned to release his soul to Olympus – the poet would mount the pyre of purgation in great relief from the pyre of desire.

Dame Julian concludes her *Revelations* with a meditation on beginning and ending: 'In our making we had beginning; but the love wherein He made us was in Him from without beginning. And all this shall we see in God, without end' (203). Eliot draws upon her ending to consider the nature of 'any action,' including poetry. Like contemplative poets before him, particularly Herbert in numerous poems, Eliot turns to reflect upon his craft of words in relation to his quest for the Word. Indeed, it would appear that Herbert's lyrics on the relation of poetic language and divine love determined this recurring pattern of the quartets. Eliot's words and lines, like all human actions, are in constant movement, beginning and ending, and as every poem becomes 'an epitaph' to an action, so every action ends beneath 'an illegible stone' – the words of all epitaphs erased in time (CPP, 197). Humble in his 'devotional' poetry, and caught up as he is among the paradoxes of beginnings and endings, the poet moves assertively toward the final paradox of belief: the end 'is where we start from', he had said in opening the section, but death 'is where we start'.

The relation of the dying (that is, the living) and the dead takes command of the poet's consciousness as he suddenly reverts to the visionary moment of part III, where he had pointed ('See, now they vanish') only to the transformation of personal memory and self in a timeless pattern of reality. Uttering the same soft imperatives, he points once again to the rebirth of the dying and the dead in an expanded vision of redemption and eternal union: 'See, they depart, and we go with them. . . . See, they return, and bring us with them' (CPP, 197). Eliot's visionary moment is one with a pattern of timeless moments in time, moments of eternal life symbolized in the rose and the yew-tree. His moment 'in a secluded chapel', gradually unfolded in the poem, unites him with hermit and anchoress, poet and saint, beloved and estranged, in an eternal present. For the poet, liberated at that moment from what he had called in 'Gerontion' the 'contrived corridors' of history, 'History is now and England'. The voice of one contemplative, the author of *The Cloud of Unknowing*, speaks to all who would answer the call to the difficult life of the spirit. His last resounding phrase closes this moment of beatitude: 'What weary wretched heart and sleeping in sloth, is that, the which is not wakened with the drawing of this love and the voice of this calling?' (1924, 9). For Eliot, the calling was irresistible.

The spiritual and historical transformation of self and its objects at Little Gidding leads to the momentary serenity and reconciliation of the poet's final address. On an abstract level he speaks for a universal 'We', but on a personal level for an intimate 'we', the 'we' at the beginning of 'Burnt Norton'. In 'A Note on War Poetry', published a month after the appearance of 'Little Gidding', Eliot concluded in a throwaway afterthought to his major poem that 'the abstract conception / Of private experience at its greatest intensity / Becoming universal, which we call 'poetry', / May be affirmed in verse' (CPP, 202). At the close of 'Little Gidding', the pressure of intense experience releases the poem from abstraction, releases a succession of private images recalled from earlier poems – the 'remembered gate'; the 'voice of the hidden waterfall', which was meant, Eliot wrote to Hayward, 'to tie up New Hampshire and Burnt Norton' (CFQ, 29); the recurring image of imaginary 'children in the apple-tree'; the 'stillness' in which the children were 'half-heard' between waves at the Dry Salvages; a line repeated from the rose garden in 'Burnt Norton' – 'Quick now, here, now, always'. But in this extraordinary poem of prayer, love and transcendence – Eliot's *Vita Nuova* – the poet speaks to his beloved beyond desire, in detached love, all too aware that the 'condition of complete simplicity' demanded of him has in human terms cost 'not less than everything' (CPP, 198). His voice thus gives way yet again to the consoling Voice that spoke to Dame Julian in prayer, 'And all shall be well and / All manner of thing shall be well'. Renunciation of desire, assures the author of *The Cloud of Unknowing*, 'will at the last help thee to knit a ghostly knot of burning love betwixt thee and thy God in ghostly onehead and accordance of will' (112). Whatever the visionary source of 'the crowned knot of fire', for Eliot too the knot is knit through continuous self-denial and purgation. At the poem's end the relentless 'tongues of flame' are not yet in-folded, and the fire of desire and the rose of divine love are not yet one. Like the ubiquitous figure of his art, Arnaut, who sees with joy the day for which he hopes before him, Eliot turns away, back into that fire which refines them: 'sovegna vos a temps de ma dolor'.

IV

As each quartet was published, Eliot sent an inscribed copy to Emily Hale, and he continued to send her inscribed copies of his work as late as 1959 (Baker, 436), but detachment was never to descend to attachment, even after Vivienne's death in 1947. When they met in America later that year, Eliot convinced Emily that he loved her, 'but', as she wrote, 'apparently not in the way usual to men less gifted i.e. with complete love thro' a married relationship' (ENL, 170). Had he tried to say as much in 'Little Gidding'? Prior to speaking to her in 1947, he had joined A.L. Maycock in founding the 'Friends of Little Gidding'. That symbolic and practical act was meant to reawaken interest in Little Gidding as a place of holiness three hundred years after the Puritan plundering, but it also renewed his commitment to 'the voice of this Calling'. Meanwhile, in admiration of a poetry that explores the mysteries of faith and the motives of the heart, Eliot had again turned his attention to the correction of Herbert's status as a 'minor' poet.

On 26 September 1944, several weeks before the publication of *Four Quartets* in England, Eliot delivered his address 'What is Minor Poetry?' Using Herbert as his primary poet for comparison, and defining a major poet as 'one the whole of whose work we ought to read, in order fully to appreciate any part of it', he argues that in *The Temple* 'there is something that we get from the whole book, which is more than a sum of its parts. . . . So in the end, I, for one, cannot admit that Herbert can be called a "minor" poet: for it is not of a few favourite poems that I am reminded when I think of him, but of the whole work' (OPP, 45–6). Fully saturated in what he had earlier called the 'personal element' and the 'spiritual stamina' of Herbert's work, Eliot had become Herbert's champion in his criticism. At one point in the mid–1930s, when he curiously labelled Herbert a minor poet in 'Religion and Literature' (1935), he had been shy of revealing Herbert's importance to his own work. But when he included that essay in the second American and third English editions of *Selected Essays* (1950 and 1951), he added a note to his earlier remarks, reaffirming his judgement in 'What is Minor Poetry?': 'I stated with some emphasis that Herbert is a major, not a minor poet. I agree with my later opinion' (SE, 391).

In succeeding years Herbert grew in stature from a major poet to a great poet in Eliot's mind, one of a shrinking number in his reading life. 'I turn more often the pages of . . . George Herbert than those of Donne', he wrote in 'To Criticize the Critic' (1961): 'what has best responded to my need in middle and later age is different from the nourishment I needed in my youth' (TCC, 22–3). In that same year, at a luncheon given by Bonamy Dobrée for Herbert Read and Frank Morley, Dobrée mentioned that Eliot had promised him an unspecified essay for the British Council pamphlets. 'I suggested', Morley recalled, 'try him on George Herbert. Read's electrometer woke. "Would he do it?" asked Bonamy. "Try him," suggested Read. Bonamy tried him, and by then Tom felt ready' (Tate, 107).

Eliot's pamphlet, *George Herbert* (1962), is in part a synthesis of his uncollected and unpublished essays on Herbert during the previous thirty years, a formal act of homage to the poet who led him through the 1930s to the quartets and whose poetry had been a mainstay of his later years. Though he quotes extensively from individual poems in praise of their technical mastery and metrical virtuosity, and though he praises Herbert for 'a resourcefulness of invention which seems inexhaustible, and for which I know no parallel in English poetry' (1962, 31), his emphasis is on 'the *content* of the poems which make up *The Temple*' (1962, 19). In 'The Collar' and other poems, writes Eliot in definition of his affinity for Herbert, 'we can find ample evidence of his spiritual struggles, of self-examination and self-criticism, and of the cost at which he acquired god-liness' (1962, 13). As in his earlier essays, he describes *The Temple* as if he were describing *Four Quartets*, 'as a coher-ent sequence of poems setting down the fluctuations of emo-tion between despair and bliss, between agitation and serenity, and the discipline of suffering which leads to peace of spirit' (1962, 23). Appropriately, he concludes the essay by quoting in full the poem with which Herbert concluded *The Temple*, 'Love III'. In the poem, which to Eliot 'indicates the serenity finally attained by this proud and humble man' (1962, 34), Love repeatedly summons the hungry poet, who is hesitant in his unworthiness, 'Guiltie of dust and sinne'. The final lines could serve as an epigraph for 'Little Gidding': 'You must sit down, sayes Love, and taste my meat: / So I did sit and eat'.

   George Herbert, published in November 1962, was to be his last major essay. On 29 May 1963, following the fiftieth-anniversary commemorative performance of *Le Sacre du Printemps* in Lon-don, Igor Stravinsky visited Eliot and his wife Valerie, who in 1957 brought Eliot the human love and happiness that he had long denied himself, and who later revealed that 'sometimes he thought of himself as a minor George Herbert' (Appleyard, 35). At this meeting Eliot told Stravinsky 'that the best parts of his new essay on George Herbert were the quotations, and he regretted that he had not had a "sense of his audience" while writing it . . . "Herbert is a great poet," he went on, "and one of a very few I can read again and again"' (Stravinsky, 92). Stravinsky, whose *Le Sacre du Printemps* had influenced the composition of *The Waste Land*, had recently completed his setting of part IV of 'Little Gidding', entitled *Anthem (The dove descending breaks the air) for Chorus a cappella* (1962). Less than two years later, at the memorial service for Eliot on 4 February 1965, the Westminster Abbey Choir filled the church with Eliot's lyrics and Stravinsky's music. As Eliot would have approved, and as his wife, who shared his love of Herbert, arranged, the congregation then stood and joined the choir in singing one of Eliot's favorite hymns, Herbert's 'Praise (II)', one that Eliot thought was, 'like all the rest of his work, personal' (1962, 33):

> King of glory, King of peace,
>   I will love thee:
> And that love may never cease,
>   I will move thee.
> Thou hast granted my request,
>   Thou hast heard me;
> Thou didst note my working breast,
>   Thou hast spared me.
>
> Wherefore with my utmost art
>   I will sing thee,
> And the cream of all my heart
>   I will bring thee.
> Though my sins against me cried,
>   Thou didst clear me;
> And alone, when they replied,
>   Thou didst hear me.
>
> Seven whole days, not one in seven,
>   I will praise thee;
> In my heart, though not in heaven,
>   I can raise thee;
> Small it is, in this poor sort
>   To enrol thee:
> E'en eternity's too short
>   To extol thee.

(*The English Hymnal*, #424)

Notes

1 Eliot's marked copy (private) of *The Poems of George Herbert*, with an introduction by Arthur Waugh, was in The World's Classics series (London, New York and Toronto: Oxford, 1907).

82   *Words in Time*

References

Anonymous, *The Cloud of Unknowing*, ed. Dom Justin McCann, London, Burns, Oates, & Washbourne, 1924.

Appleyard, Bryan, 'Interview: A Poet's Wife and Letters', *The Times* (17 September 1988), 35.

Baker, William, 'T.S. Eliot and Emily Hale: Some Fresh Evidence', *English Studies*, 66 (1985), 432–6.

Beachcroft, T.O., 'Nicholas Ferrar and George Herbert', *Criterion* 12 (1932), 24–42.

Bell, Robert H., 'Bertrand Russell and the Eliots', *American Scholar*, 52 (1983), 309–25.

Blackstone, Bernard, *The Ferrar Papers*, Cambridge, Cambridge University Press, 1938.

Bradbrook, Muriel C., 'The Liturgical Tradition in English Verse: Herbert and Eliot', *Theology* 44 (1942), 13–23.

Bush, Ronald, *T.S. Eliot: A Study in Character and Style*, New York, Oxford University Press, 1984.

Eliot, T.S., 'An Italian Critic on Donne and Crashaw', *TLS* 1248 (17 December 1925), 878.

———, 'Poet and Saint . . .' *Dial* 82 (1927), 424–31.

———, 'The Devotional Poets of the Seventeenth Century', *Listener* 3 (1930), 552–3.

———, 'George Herbert', *Spectator* 148 (1932a), 360–1.

———, 'Christianity and Communism', *Listener* 7 (1932b), 382–3.

———, 'Notes on the Way', *Time and Tide* 16:3 (19 January 1935), 88–90.

———, 'Paul Elmer More', *Princeton Alumni Weekly* 37 (1937), 373–4.

———, 'George Herbert', *Salisbury and Winchester Journal* (27 May 1938), 12.

———, 'A Lay Theologian', *New Statesman and Nation* 18 (1939), 864, 866.

———, *On Poetry*, Concord, Mass., Concord Academy, 1947.

———, *George Herbert*, London, Longmans, Green, 1962.

Horowitz, Glenn, Bookseller, *Catalogue 22: T.S. Eliot*, New York, 1990.

Julian of Norwich, *Revelations of Divine Love*, 13th edn, London, Methuen, 1952.

Levy, William Turner, and Victor Scherle, *Affectionately, T.S. Eliot*, Philadelphia, Lippincott, 1968.

Matthiessen, F.O., *The Achievement of T.S. Eliot*, 3rd edn, New York, Oxford University Press, 1958.

More, Paul Elmer, 'Marginalia', *American Review* 8 (1936), 1–30.

St John of the Cross, *The Ascent of Mount Carmel*, trans. David Lewis, London, Thomas Baker, 1906.

Smyth, Charles, Untitled review of *The Ferrar Papers, Criterion* 18 (1939), 366–71.

Spurr, Barry, 'The Genesis of "Little Gidding"', *Yeats–Eliot Review* 6 (1979), 29–30.

Stravinsky, Igor, 'Memories of T.S. Eliot', *Esquire* 64 (1965), 92–3.

Tate, Allen, ed., *T.S. Eliot: The Man and His Work*, London, Chatto & Windus, 1966.

Traversi, Derek, *T.S. Eliot: The Longer Poems*, New York, Harcourt Brace Jovanovich, 1976.

Walton, Izaak, *The Complete Angler & The Lives of Donne, Wotton, Hooker, Herbert & Sanderson*, London, Macmillan, 1906.

Ward, David, *T.S. Eliot Between Two Worlds*, London, Routledge & Kegan Paul, 1973.

5

From The Waste Land to Four Quartets: Evolution of a Method
Jewel Spears Brooker

The poems of T.S. Eliot can be thought of as a series of experiments by a scrupulous artist searching for form in a formless age. Major moments in his quest can be measured by the form realized in such works as 'The Love Song of J. Alfred Prufrock', 'Preludes', 'Sweeney Among the Nightingales', *The Waste Land*, *Ash-Wednesday*, and *Four Quartets*. His struggle to achieve form in art reached its apogee in *Four Quartets*. I will approach the poem comparatively, or, to use the poet's own language, I will examine it as a new start, a new attempt to address the old problem of form. After a review of the aesthetic challenge to which Eliot's work is in precise ways a response, I will discuss briefly the poet's 'solution' in *The Waste Land*, namely, his method of recollecting fragments and re-constructing wholes by use of a Darwinian reference-point myth from Frazer. In the main part of this paper, I will argue that Eliot's method in *Four Quartets* is based on repetition and relation-in-itself rather than on juxtaposition and re-construction, and that he uses a key pattern instead of a key myth. In changing from a linear mythic model to a diachronic/synchronic, musical/mythic model, he anticipates in striking ways the work of Lévi-Strauss.

I

> The notion of a structure lacking any centre represents the unthinkable.
>
> Jacques Derrida

The notion that the creation or perception of order is dependent on the existence of a reference point (or centre) is crucial in understanding form in art. This notion was a given in Western art before the twentieth century, and its problematization is part of the crisis of modernism. The herculean effort to cope with the loss of a shared reference point, involving ingenious attempts to retrieve or discover or create substitutes, characterizes modernism in all of the arts. The modernist preoccupation with form should be seen in the context of dispensationalism, the view that history can be best understood if analysed into several giant blocks, each of which is identified with some overarching idea or assumption about fundamentals. Mallarmé, Yeats, Eliot and Pound are profoundly dispensationalist; Spengler, Kuhn, McLuhan and Foucault also work from a dispensationalist analysis of history. The most influential contemporary dispensationalist is Derrida. In *Writing and Difference*, he divides Western intellectual history into two giant eras, each characterized by an assumption about Being or presence. His first dispensation includes the entire history of Western thought before (roughly) the twentieth century, which he claims was erected on an acceptance of 'Being as presence in all senses of this word' and must be thought of as 'a series of substitutions of centre for centre.' In the late nineteenth century, he continues, a 'rupture' occurred in the history of thought. Derrida associates the rupture with the 'Nietzschean critique of metaphysics', the 'Freudian critique of self-presence', and the 'Heideggerian destruction of metaphysics'. After these destructive discourses, 'it was necessary to begin thinking that there was no centre' (278–80).

Major writers responded in different ways to the collapse or disappearance of what Derrida calls the centre. Yeats in *A Vision* made up a mythology to serve as a reference point for his poetry, and Joyce in *Ulysses* retrieved a Homeric reference point. Stevens creates a reference point by the simple act of introducing difference, as when, in 'Anecdote of the Jar', he transforms a 'slovenly wilderness' into an orderly kingdom by the simple act of placing an artifact on the hill. The jar, totally *other*, facilitates definition by creating difference and at the same time creates order by serving as a focal point. The jar was not made for the use to which Stevens puts it; it was at hand, however, and in a pinch it sufficed. This 1923 poem shows Stevens playing *bricoleur*, to borrow the term Lévi-Strauss used for mythmakers in *The Savage Mind*. A *bricoleur*, in the translator's gloss, is a kind of professional do-it-yourself man who works with whatever he has around the house, tools and materials which were not designed for the use to which he puts them, but which, through cleverness and trial-and-error, can be adapted for his purpose.

Eliot typically analyses the modernist crisis in terms of a mythic *absence* in contemporary life. 'The present situation is radically different from any in which poetry has been produced in the past: namely, . . . now there is nothing in which to believe, . . . Belief itself is dead' (UPUC, 130). Most of his poems from 'The Love Song of J. Alfred Prufrock' through *Four Quartets* are conscious experiments in achieving form apart from dependence on a fixed centre. His solution is different in each case, although his achievements in each poem become platforms for beginning again. His most strenuous effort, perhaps, came in *The Waste Land* with the use of what he called the 'mythical method'. Because the form which unfolded in the *Quartets* has many traces of this often misrepresented method, I will describe it briefly before taking up form in the *Quartets*.

II

These fragments I have shored against my ruins.

The Waste Land

In his 1923 review of Joyce's *Ulysses*, Eliot addresses himself in specific terms to the problem of creating order in the absence of a centre or reference point. He says that the greatest challenge facing the modern artist is finding 'a way of controlling, of ordering, of giving a shape and a significance to the immense panorama of futility and anarchy which is contemporary history' (SP, 177). Joyce met this challenge by retrieving a reference point and by forcing the reader to use it. In attempting to clarify Joyce's achievement, Eliot draws a clear distinction between an artist's 'material' and his 'method'. The material is 'actual life', that of the artist (including his emotional life) and of his moment in history. The method is how he deals with it. Eliot goes on to maintain that an artist is not responsible for his material, which is given, but for his method, which must be discovered or invented. In 'Four Elizabethan Dramatists' (1924), he again distinguishes between material and method and goes on to claim that the modern malaise is a result of the fact that artists and audiences share no abstractions, no mental constructs in which to anchor their material (SE, 109-17).

Joyce's significance for Eliot is that, in the absence of a shared abstraction, he arbitrarily selected one and built it into the text of his novel. Joyce overcame his obstacles by 'using a myth . . . manipulating a continuous parallel between contemporaneity and antiquity' (SP, 177).

Eliot insists that the mythical method was made possible by breakthroughs in the social sciences. 'Psychology . . ., ethnology, and *The Golden Bough* have concurred to make possible what was impossible even a few years ago. Instead of narrative method, we may now use the mythical method' (SP, 177). The fact that most critics dismiss or misinterpret this statement makes it necessary to explain it briefly. Frazer was one of those scientists who extended Darwin's thesis (evolution) and Darwin's method (comparative study of fragments) into the social sciences. As Darwin had attempted to discover the origin of species and chart the descent of man, Frazer and his contemporaries tried to discover the origin of religion and chart the descent of gods. They wished to show a single evolutionary sequence in the development of religion from primitive to modern, and as Darwin had postulated a common ancestor for human beings, they postulated a common ancestor for all religions. They believed in the original unity of human consciousness and in the continuous evolution of that consciousness from prehistory to the present. And they believed that although the common ancient myth had broken up in prehistoric times, it could be reconstructed through a comparison of its remaining fragments.

The Golden Bough began as an attempt to explain a single myth. This myth is evocatively narrated on the first page of the first volume, and through twelve volumes of data it never passes from Frazer's one-track mind. His work may seem to be a hodgepodge of primitive customs, but it is a thoroughly systematic attempt to explain the myth of the golden bough. He tracked this myth by collecting innumerable analogies and by carefully comparing them. He found no analogies to the myth as a whole, but he did find analogies to parts of it. So he dissected the myth into small pieces and collected analogies to each part. Through comparison and analysis of thousands of pieces of myths, he was able to construct ever more comprehensive myths. He then used these consciously constructed abstractions as reference points for understanding the fragments with which he had begun. In this way, he moved backward toward primitive unity.

Frazer's conclusion, consistent with his Darwinian beginnings, is that all myths, including the myth of the golden bough, derive from a parent myth, which he tries to reconstruct. His method, which I have discussed in detail (1984), involves privileging a single myth and keeping it constantly in mind as a reference point. The omnipresence of one myth enabled him to manipulate comparisons between contemporaneity and antiquity, and, through continuous comparison and contrast, to generate the parent myths which contain and unify both the reference-point myth and the assembled fragments. By focusing on the myth of the golden bough, Frazer was able to shape and control his material, the fragments of futility and anarchy littering human history.

Frazer's method, then, more or less duplicates Darwin's. It is *scientific*, not mythical. Frazer used the inductive method; that is, he collected samples and then generalized from them; he then used the generalizations as a means of understanding the samples with which he had begun. A careful reading of the *Ulysses* review shows that Eliot was using 'mythical' in his own way, as a near-synonym for scientific or comparative or inductive, or at least as a term for the scientific method as transformed by its application in the arts. Other scientists were quick to use Frazer's method of generating abstractions through the comparative study of fragments. Jessie Weston used it in *From Ritual to Romance* to construct a parent myth behind the Grail legends. In the notes to *The Waste Land*, Eliot acknowledges his debts to both Frazer and Weston.

In the *Ulysses* review, Eliot argues that Joyce's method 'makes the modern world possible for art' (SP, 178) by allowing the artist to be true to both chaos and order. On the surface, Joyce in *Ulysses* and Eliot in *The Waste Land* pay their respects to contemporary history and to their personal lives – that is, to their 'material'. But, like Frazer, these artists anchor their material in carefully chosen abstractions. Frazer brings his pet myth and takes special care to keep it always in his reader's mind. He names his work – all twelve volumes – *The Golden Bough*, and in the first few paragraphs he explains the myth and tells what he wants to discover about it. He proceeds to his thesis by constantly comparing and contrasting his fragments with each other and with his reference-point myth, and by constructing abstractions suggested by this process.

Similarly, in *Ulysses* and *The Waste Land*, unity derives from reference to an abstraction brought by the artist: in Joyce, the

Ulysses legend; in Eliot, the waste land myth. As in Frazer, the reference-point myth is kept in the reader's mind throughout the work. In *Ulysses*, the myth is suggested by the title and kept in the reader's mind by the presence of parallel actions and characters. In *The Waste Land*, the myth is suggested by the title and the notes, and is reinforced by fragments of the myth within the poem. The artist does not bring the reference-point myth in its entirety; rather he brings pieces of it and the necessary hints for reconstructing it. In *Ulysses*, it exists as a whole and may be recovered by reading the *Odyssey* in a good translation. In *The Waste Land*, the myth is more elusive. The monomyths of Weston and of Frazer exist only as reconstructions generated by using the comparative method, and Eliot's background myth is only loosely theirs. Eliot assumes a reader who is willing to take the fragments on the surface of his poem and re-collect them (both remember where they came from and gather them up again). Each reader of *The Waste Land* will construct a variant of Frazer's monomyth, a variant which will be composed anew with every reading.

III

> Except for the point, the still point,
> There would be no dance, and there is only the dance.
> 'Burnt Norton' II

The question of form in *Four Quartets* can only be addressed with reference to Eliot's concern with the case of the missing abstraction. Between 1922 and 1934–42, the concern is evident not only in the poet's evolving convictions about art, but in the larger convictions shaping his life. Two personal events (complementary in some ways) are particularly relevant to his continuing quest for order in life and in art. The first is the disintegration of his marriage and the second is his entry into the Church of England. In accepting the Christian position, he willed to believe that there really is a Centre, a shared Centre, whether it is named or unnamed, recognized or unrecognized, acknowledged or ignored. His focus changes from reconstructing a shared reference point to glimpsing a universal pattern.

Three aspects of structure in the earlier poem can be traced in the later one. The first has to do with the method of creating order,

of finding a reference point. The basic principle of structure in
The Waste Land is the juxtaposition of fragments which can be
(re)collected and organized by reference to a privileged myth.
The basic principle in *Four Quartets* is repetition, the function of
which is to permit the emergence of a common pattern beneath
particulars. The second aspect of structure represents a more radical
departure from *The Waste Land*. In his earlier masterpiece, Eliot
focuses on fragments and on the reconstructions which they
make possible; in *Four Quartets*, he focuses not on fragments
or experiences or ideas, but rather on relations between them,
on the gaps opened by intersection and difference. Thus, in the
Quartets, a focus on betweenness, on what is absent or 'not there',
causes relation-in-itself to emerge as the most important presence
of the sequence. The final aspect of structure has to do with the
identification of a reference point. In *The Waste Land*, Eliot solved
the case of the missing abstraction by leading his readers to refer his
fragments to a single myth borrowed from Frazer and his colleagues
in comparative religion. In *Four Quartets*, Eliot anchors his texts not
in a myth, but in a pattern, a pattern archetypally presented in the
Christian doctrine of the Incarnation.

IV

> You say I am repeating
Something I have said before. I shall say it again.
>
> 'East Coker' III

> The function of repetition is to render the structure of myth
> apparent.
>
> Claude Lévi-Strauss

The reader opening *Four Quartets*, like the reader opening *The
Waste Land*, is immediately confronted with fragments. But the
fragments differ greatly in content and in the way they are to
function in the overall structure of the poem. The fragment from
the *Satyricon* is one of many bits and pieces of an ancient original
– a myth once present, now absent, and forever lost in the dark
backward abysm of time. The Sibylline shard is the first of many
fragments of this Ur-myth, a rough and abstract approximation of
which can be constructed by the reader. The fragments introducing
'Burnt Norton' (and thus *Four Quartets*) are philosophical principles

attributed to the pre-Socratic thinker Heraclitus. The first can be translated as 'Though there is but one Centre, most people live in centres of their own'; the second as 'The way up and the way down are one and the same.' These fragments are not morsels of myth or shreds of a story, but philosophic principles having integrity in themselves. The first refers to a common point of stillness and the second to a common pattern of movement. In the experience of reading and re-reading Eliot's poem, they will come to be understood as imperfect realizations of a complex encompassing both, as part of an ever-present but usually imperceptible pattern. In *Four Quartets*, the missing abstraction is not something to be constructed, but something to be experienced in miniature, to be half-heard, or half-glimpsed. The pattern emerges through repetition.

Repetition is the most important structural principle in *Four Quartets*. Eliot seems to have discovered the principle *qua* principle while he was working on 'East Coker', which was begun as a new poem 'in succession to "Burnt Norton"' (CFQ, 16). In Book X of *The Republic*, Plato reveals what happens when one begins a sequel. 'God . . . made one bed in nature and one only; two or more such beds neither ever have been nor ever will be made by God.' The reason is that 'even if he had made but two, a third would still appear behind them of which they again both possessed the form, and that would be the real bed and not the two others.' In beginning 'East Coker', Eliot intended to write a two-poem sequence. But as Plato's explanation of why God could have made only one bed indicates, it is impossible to duplicate something without causing a third to arise above the two. In writing a sequel to 'Burnt Norton', the poet generated an abstraction encompassing both the first poem and its sequel, an abstraction to which each individual poem could be compared and by which each could be judged. This abstraction arising from the two works assumes a life of its own, a life which is in certain ways superior to the individuals which generated it. Eliot discusses Elizabethan drama in similar terms by arguing that all of Shakespeare's plays are one play. When critics write of Shakespearean tragedy, of course, they are generally referring to the abstraction in the mind of the reader/spectator who knows all of the individual plays.

Repetition carries the risk of becoming *mere* repetition. 'It ['East Coker'] may be quite worthless,' Eliot confided to John Hayward, 'because most of it looks to me like an imitation of myself' (CFQ, 16–17). Nevertheless he persisted, and as he worked on 'East Coker' he came to think in terms of a four-part sequence.

> The idea of the whole sequence emerged gradually. I should say during the composition of 'East Coker'. Certainly by the time that poem was finished I envisaged the whole work as having four parts which gradually began to assume, perhaps only for convenience sake, a relation to the four seasons and the four elements. (CFQ, 18).

At first 'East Coker' takes its shape from an abstraction arising above 'Burnt Norton', but increasingly this abstraction is balanced by a second one, an 'idea of the whole', an imaginative construct comprehending and accommodating four poems, two of which were not much more than vague requirements emerging from the poet's sense of symmetry. Relating each poem to one of the four seasons and one of the four elements became a poetic convenience, a part of the frame for his four meditations and also part of the justification for seeing them as one poem. The idea of the whole, constantly being revised and refined as he worked, became a still but always moving reference point. In one sense, he had solved the case of the missing abstraction by forcing the work itself to generate the abstraction by which it was to be guided, understood and finally judged.

As the first poem in the sequence and retrospectively the model for the other three, 'Burnt Norton' is not related in any direct sense to a previous work; nor is there any 'idea of the whole' to which it could have been related. In Lyndall Gordon's view, the main reference point in 'Burnt Norton' is the idea of a perfect life, generated by Eliot's attempt to understand the troubles in his personal life at the same time that he was working on *Murder in the Cathedral*, a play about a martyr and a saint. The actual text of the poem originated from lines cut from the play, lines in which Becket is confronted by a tempter who suggests a return to the past as a way to escape the dangerous present: 'The Chancellorship that you resigned / When you were made Archbishop – that was a mistake / On your part – still may be regained.' (CPP, 248) In this scene, which requires a re-examination of the whole of one's life in the light of the present moment, a priest originally responded with the following words:

> Time present and time past
> Are both perhaps present in the future.
> Time future is contained in time past. . . .
> What might have been is a conjecture
> Remaining a permanent possibility
> Only in a world of speculation. . . .
> Footfalls echo in the memory
> Down the passage which we did not take
> Into the rose-garden.   (CFQ, 82)

These beautiful lines, only slightly modified, now form the open-
ing paragraph of 'Burnt Norton'.

Eliot visited Burnt Norton, a country house in Gloucestershire,
in 1934, just as he was emerging from the long night of his first
marriage. Emily Hale, a woman with whom he had once been in
love and perhaps intended to marry, was with him. It seems likely
that on this summer day in the rose garden Eliot, guilt-torn and
exhausted from years of unhappiness and a painful separation from
his wife, experienced a temptation to deny the present by returning
to the road not taken in 1914, a temptation exactly analogous to
that of Thomas à Becket which generated the lines which now
open 'Burnt Norton'. The temptation to try to go back and take
a different road, to cancel history and create an alternative present,
constitutes an intersection where the lives of Becket, Christ and
Eliot come together. This intersection and the might-have-been
life that it brought to Eliot's attention are part of the abstraction he
uses in writing 'Burnt Norton'.

Eliot's meditation is resumed and completed in the other three
Quartets, begun some five years after 'Burnt Norton'. The experi-
ence memorialized by the moment in the rose garden becomes
the first of many examples of a point of intersection between time
and timelessness, of a fragment of time which takes its meaning
from and gives its meaning to a pattern – a pattern at once in
time, continuously changing until the supreme moment of death
completes it, and also out of time. Since individuals live and have
their being only in fragments, they can never quite know the whole
pattern, but in certain moments they can experience the pattern in
miniature. These timeless moments in time – 'the moment in the
rose-garden, / The moment in the arbour where the rain beat, /
The moment in the draughty church at smokefall' ('Burnt Norton'

II; CPP, 173) – provide for Eliot the means of conquering time. This moment of sudden illumination, in and out of time, Eliot associates with the Word-made-flesh, the Incarnation, and also with the word-made-art, poetry. The configuration of part and pattern, especially in these three dimensions (personal experience, religious illumination, art), emerges through repetition; the pattern is both the main subject and a major principle of form in *Four Quartets*.

In *Four Quartets*, Eliot solved the case of the missing abstraction both for himself and his reader by allowing the poem itself to generate the pattern which undergirds it and gives it meaning. On the simplest level, the abstraction is born of the fact that there are *four* meditations, all different, and yet obviously all of a kind. Just as Frazer abstracted one myth from many; just as the listener abstracts a Mozartian symphony, heard only in the mind's ear, from the actual symphonies, or the spectator abstracts a Shakespearean tragedy, performed only in the theatre of the mind, from the various tragedies; so the reader of *Four Quartets* inevitably if unconsciously abstracts an Eliotian quartet. This poem in the mind is private to each reader, but because it is generated by the text all readers share, it agrees to a remarkable extent with the abstractions constructed by other readers. The poem in the mind is at once spatial (it exists all at once in mental space) and temporal (it is always changing). 'The knowledge imposes a pattern, and falsifies, / For the pattern is new in every moment' ('East Coker' II; CPP, 179). In order to perceive the pattern, one must temporarily spatialize it. Such spatialization inevitably falsifies, but it is necessary because it is the only way of glimpsing the still point at the centre of all movement.

The quartet in the mind emerges automatically from the fact that each of the *Four Quartets* explores the same general subject; each is named for a place; and each has approximately the same form. The general subject of the sequence is time and human existence in and out of time. Valerie Eliot says that her husband considered affixing as an epigraph to the entire sequence the line from *Pickwick Papers*, "'What a rum thing time is, ain't it Neddy?'" (CFQ, 28). Thus a modern 'philosopher', Dickens' Mr Roker, would have balanced the ancient Heraclitus. The overall exploration of time and eternity includes an exploration of parallel antitheses such as movement and stillness, change and changelessness, part and pattern. Each poem in the sequence explores these intertwined mysteries. The meaningfulness of Eliot's treatment is immeasurably enriched by the fact that the form of the sequence is itself a perfect illustration of the twin mysteries.

The poems in Eliot's meditation are also parallel in being named for places. The first, of course, is named for the manor house in Gloucestershire visited by Eliot and Emily Hale. The title of the second, 'East Coker', refers to the village in Somerset from which, in the seventeenth century, Eliot's family had emigrated to America, and to which, after his death, Eliot's own ashes were to be returned. The mystery of beginnings and ends – 'In my beginning is my end', 'In my end is my beginning' – in and out of history is explored in this quartet. The third poem takes its title from a treacherous group of rocks, the Dry Salvages, located off the coast of Cape Ann, Massachusetts, where Eliot had passed his childhood summers. These rocks, the cold and seemingly limitless ocean in which they are anchored, and the great Mississippi River of his childhood are the major symbols in this meditation. The last quartet takes its title from a tiny village in Cambridgeshire, Little Gidding, which in the seventeenth century had been a community of dedicated Christians under the leadership of Nicholas Ferrar. Eliot, who visited Little Gidding in 1936, admired the example of this small group which had renounced position and wealth for a life of work and prayer. Each of these four places is associated with Eliot's part/whole pattern, with his stillness/movement theme. He insists on the importance of specific places as he does of specific moments. The timeless moment, in fact, can only occur in a specific place – a rose garden, a draughty church, a rain-washed arbour. The places permit glimpses of what is beyond place; they constitute, in a special sense, a way to transcendence. 'Only through time time is conquered' (CPP, 173); only through place place is conquered.

As all the *Quartets* explore the same theme, as all point to a specific place, so all have the same general form. The first part of each consists of a meditation on time and consciousness, arranged as statement/counterstatement/recapitulation. The second consists of a highly-structured poetical passage followed by a relatively prosaic passage, both on the general subject of being trapped in time. The third explores implications of the first two in terms of a journey metaphor, of some concept of movement of the self in and out of time. The fourth is a brief lyric or prayer. The fifth begins with a colloquial passage and then ends with a lyric which secures closure by returning to the beginning and collecting major images. The fifth section in each quartet incorporates a meditation on the problem of the artist who must still move in stillness, keep time in time (both continuously move in step, and continuously be still).

Repetition is not only evident in the overall skeleton or frame of *Four Quartets*. It is also present within the sequence, within each quartet, and within each section as Eliot organizes his system of echoes. 'East Coker' III provides a clear example of Eliot's focus on repetition as a way of beginning to understand and attempting to communicate what is ultimately beyond both understanding and communication. The poet offers three parallel similes for human existence, each containing a parallel realization of emptiness. The first is that human existence is like a play in which one becomes aware of the unreality of the scene only between the acts when the props are rolled away. The second compares life to a ride on a train which stops between stations, replacing movement and talk with stillness and silence and forcing the passengers to notice the empty faces of their fellow travellers. The third image adds the suggestion that in illness, under ether, one becomes aware of one's own emptiness.

Eliot continues with a series of parallel images regarding the insight available by waiting receptively in darkness. His images – running streams, winter lightning, garden laughter – are *about* echoes. In turn, they *are* echoes – echoes of 'Burnt Norton' and, more basically, echoes of something (becoming/being) which cannot be seen or heard or experienced except through echoes. At this point, the poet turns to the reader with a strikingly prosaic and arguably perverse confession. 'You say I am repeating / Something I have said before. I shall say it again. / Shall I say it again?' (CPP, 181). In a series of parallel and incantatory paradoxes, he resumes his echo of himself by echoing St John of the Cross, and then he repeats himself again with three paradoxes which, echoing Heraclitus, summarize the position that the way of self-denial and the way of self-fulfillment are one and the same. The experience of catching an echo of laughter, of ecstasy in a garden (the personal rose garden, the mythic hyacinth garden, the theological Eden), an echo which requires agony but points beyond it to a redemption of ecstasy, is repeated time and again in *Four Quartets*. The exercise of and the insistence on repetition in 'East Coker', then, are part of the poet's deliberate attempt to instruct his reader on the principle he used in constructing his poem and the principle by which it is to be appreciated.

The last poem, like the first one, presents special difficulties in a sequence largely dependent on the power of repetition. By the time he came to 'Little Gidding', Eliot had mastered his structural principle and his theme, but, as Helen Gardner's work on the composition of the poems makes clear, he had far more trouble with this poem than with the other three. A 'final' poem in a sequence which is about both movement and stillness could by its very perfection privilege stillness and thus blur the twin mysteries the poet was trying to hold in balance. 'Little Gidding' had at once to accommodate itself to the pattern generated by the existing poems and to crown that pattern by adding a work which would enable the quartet in the mind of both the poet and the reader to keep realizing itself. The fact that a new and, in one sense, a final abstraction was emerging from the creation of 'Little Gidding' risked subverting the basic premises explored in the work as a whole. The challenge was to complete what was in essence always in progress, to close what was always open. The poet accomplishes this in part by making his conclusion a repetition of his beginning, by returning to the images of 'Burnt Norton' I and deepening the significance of the laughter of the children in the garden. He points beyond the garden by pointing back to it; he takes us beyond our first world by enabling us to know it for the first time; he completes his line by taking us in a circle. The circle is at once a movement and a completion of movement, a return and a new start. The return does not, however, take us back to the exact place from which we started, nor does it take us to a resting place, but to a beginning which moves toward an end, which in turn is a beginning.

The importance of repetition as structure and theme in *Four Quartets* is inseparable from the musical analogy suggested by the title. The musical analogy is not the focus of this paper, but it must be noted that musical form reveals structure through repetition at the same time that it resists reduction to specific meaning. The theme, development and recapitulation of musical form are perfect for the interplay between pattern and movement which is at the heart of *Four Quartets*. Musical structure is at once diachronic (temporal, linear, related to melody) and synchronic (simultaneous, vertical, related to harmony) and thus contains within itself one of the primary mysteries Eliot is working with in *Four Quartets*. Eliot's use of repetition and his appropriation of musical form have much in common with Lévi-Strauss's analysis of myth and music. The function of repetition, Lévi-Strauss maintains in 'The Structural Study of Myth', is to reveal the structure of myth. In his studies of the myths of South American Indians in *The Raw and the Cooked*, Lévi-Strauss attends carefully to repeated elements in different versions of one myth and is able thereby to discern the underlying structure or pattern of the myth. In *Four Quartets*, Eliot repeats many versions of a single pattern, a pattern which emerges as a pattern simply by being repeated with variations. In *The Raw and the Cooked*, Lévi-Strauss claims that music 'is the only language with the contradictory attributes of being at once intelligible and untranslatable' (18). He thus organizes his text as a piece of music with an overture followed by a theme and variations, with inter-ludes and a coda. He includes in his text analogies to many other musical forms, including a short symphony, a toccata and fugue, and a rustic symphony. In the overture (introduction), he justifies his use of the musical analogy in language which, with very few changes, could be applied to *Four Quartets*. The correspondences between Eliot's work in *Four Quartets* and Lévi-Strauss' work on myth can be explained partially in terms of Eliot's mastery of the social scientists whose work Lévi-Strauss was using and also in terms of Eliot's comprehension of the problems of language and myth which Lévi-Strauss was to take up and extend in his own particular scientific discipline.

V

The way up and the way down are the same.

Heraclitus

The error of traditional anthropology, like that of traditional linguistics, was to consider terms, and not the relations between them.

Lévi-Strauss

From the first lines of 'Burnt Norton' – 'Time present and time past / Are both perhaps present in time future' – through the last line

of 'Little Gidding' – 'And the fire and the rose are one' – Eliot in
Four Quartets forces his reader to attend to opposites, to paradoxes,
puzzles and contradictions. Thus the way up and the way down
are one and the same, the end is the beginning and the beginning
the end, the darkness is the light, the stillness is the dance, and the
fire and the rose are one. Eliot's focus on contraries, everywhere
apparent, could be illustrated with any number of passages. In
'East Coker' III, for example, he uncompromisingly insists on his
oppositions.

> And what you do not know is the only thing you know
> And what you own is what you do not own
> And where you are is where you are not.   (CPP, 181)

He continually points to what is *not* there, to what is not said,
not heard, not known, not understood. This insistence on absence
is a part of the pattern of oppositions, for it is presented as
simultaneously an insistence on presence. The focus on opposites,
similarly, is itself a part of the pattern, for it is also a focus on
reconciliation.

Attention to Eliot's obsession with polarity in *Four Quartets*
reveals a major principle of form in this sequence. In simulta-
neously emphasizing disparate terms, Eliot is actually displacing
focus from the terms themselves to the relation between them.
For example, in the paradox which in a special sense summarizes
the entire sequence – 'the fire and the rose are one' – the
terms themselves (fire, rose) disappear as separate terms and are
replaced by the relation between them which enables the poet
to predicate identity. Eliot's habit of focusing on contraries as
a way to overcome them, as I have shown in a study of Eliot's
dissertation (1990), goes back at least to his graduate studies on
F.H. Bradley. Bradley's destruction of metaphysics in *Appearance
and Reality* is based in part on the view that although one can only
conceive of things or ideas in terms of what they are not (that is,
dualistically), one is inevitably nudged by this way of seeing into an
ongoing dialectical process which transcends oppositions.

Eliot's tendency in his later work to think in terms of opposites
rather than of fragments can be associated with his movement
beyond the linear Darwinian models which had been so useful in
his early work. In *The Waste Land*, he had adapted the comparative
method of Frazer and the social scientists to formulate a working

model for 'making the modern world possible for art'. The reference point in the poem is an ancient unified myth, an ancestor to which all contemporary myths can be related through descent. In *Four Quartets* Eliot moves beyond the evolutionary model and anticipates a spatial/temporal model somewhat similar to the one outlined in the late 1940s, the 1950s and the 1960s by Lévi-Strauss. In *The Raw and the Cooked*, the first of his four-volume *Mythologiques* (1964–71), Lévi-Strauss argues that the mythic mind sees in terms of binary oppositions, with a primary opposition being nature (the raw) and culture (the cooked). In analysing myth, Lévi-Strauss breaks the story down into various elements. He then generalizes the concrete elements into binary opposites, and ends by claiming that the purpose of myth is the production of a model capable of overcoming opposition. Thus he sees mythmaking as a primitive form of dialectic. But Lévi-Strauss's ambitions go beyond the primitive mind. He begins with ethnographic experience, but he universalizes his findings. His stated purpose is to draw up an inventory of all mental patterns, to discover the hidden structure of the human mind, and to describe how it works (10).

Four Quartets came before *The Raw and the Cooked*, and thus there is no question here of influence. But certainly Eliot in his great meditation sees reality in ways which overlap with those later outlined by Lévi-Strauss. The poet and the anthropologist had a number of important theoretical models in common, including Hegelian dialectic and Darwinian evolution. Eliot's doctoral studies included systematic work in the social sciences, and his journalistic activity contains evidence of continuous and highly-informed interest in comparative religion, sociology, psychology and anthropology. Eliot based his 'mythical method' primarily on Frazer, and Lévi-Strauss begins 'The Structural Study of Myth' (1955) with an 1898 quotation from Franz Boas, a contemporary of Frazer who used roughly the same method. Lévi-Strauss's epigraph, taken from Boas's introduction to James Teit's 'Traditions of the Thompson River Indians', refers to the precise method Eliot adapted for *The Waste Land*. 'It would seem that mythological worlds have been built up only to be shattered again, and that new worlds were built from the fragments.' Like Lévi-Strauss, Eliot begins with consideration of models drawn from linear evolution and ends with a synchronic model.

Eliot's focus on binary opposites in *Four Quartets* tends, then, to direct his reader away from terms *qua* terms to the relation which both unites and separates them. From a slightly different point of view, Eliot may be seen as alerting his reader to the point at which opposites almost or momentarily touch, to intersections or gaps between such polarities as time and eternity, and to the possibilities which are opened by these intersections. The first part of 'Burnt Norton' I, for example, introduces age-old puzzles about the meaning of time and eternity, about linear and cyclical patterns in time. The second part describes an experience, the first of many in *Four Quartets*, in which the opposition between time and time-lessness is resolved, not through synthesis, nor through dialectic, but through intersection. In this moment of intersection between time and eternity in a rose garden (a gift, not an achievement), this moment of echoed joy, time and eternity meet and overlap in such a way that both their sameness and their difference are apparent. Laughter echoes from 'our first world' (childhood, first love, Eden and more), a world which in being 'first' was in time, and in time was lost. But in being a world 'round the corner' just beyond 'the first gate', a world into which the reader is invited by the thrush, that world is present and eternal. Even after the bird says 'Go, go, go . . . human kind / Cannot bear very much reality' (CPP, 172), the children's laughter and the bird's song and the unheard music continue to echo in the garden of the poem ('Burnt Norton' V, 'Little Gidding' V). And in one of many lines in which the poet addresses his reader directly, 'My words [containing the hidden laughter] echo / Thus, in your mind' (CPP, 171). The 'leaves', then, continue, both in time and out of time, to 'contain' the laughter of the might-have-been children. And the figured leaves, the dancing leaves, refer in a repeated pun to the leaves of the book of this poem.

A recurrent example of the intersection between time and eternity can be seen in part III of 'Burnt Norton', 'East Coker' and 'The Dry Salvages'. In the central part of each poem, a horizontal, temporal journey through the darkness unexpectedly intersects with a vertical journey into the darkness which leads, in a paradoxical way, into the light. A train ride on metalled rails suddenly reveals an alternative journey which is not progression but descent, descent which is also ascent. Part V of each quartet points to another intersection, that between words as words (in time) and words as art (both in and out of time). Eliot is again pointing not to terms or words, but to the cracks between words as the placeless 'place' where meaning might be found, as the place to go to get beyond time and place.

Another way of approaching Eliot's emphasis on relation is by noticing his fascination with intermediate states. The voices of the hidden waterfall and of the children in the apple tree in the last part of 'Little Gidding' are 'half-heard' in the 'stillness / Between two waves of the sea' (CPP, 198). 'Betweenness' or relation-in-itself is also important in the earlier poems, and in 'The Hollow Men' 'betweenness' is at the heart of the poem.

> Between the idea
> And the reality
> Between the motion
> And the act
> Falls the Shadow . . .   (CPP, 85)

The poet continues with several other parallel statements, all emphasizing the relation between opposites, the gap opened by noticing polarities. The shadow also falls between the conception and the creation, the emotion and the response, the desire and the spasm, the potency and the existence, and the essence and the descent. The effect here and throughout *Four Quartets* is the displacement of focus from term to relation. Eliot's *modus operandi* in the *Quartets*, then, leads readers to an absence or a gap or a puzzle and then leaves them there for reflection on what can only be guessed, glimpsed, imagined, half-heard. This method is reminiscent of that of Socrates, who systematically nonplussed his auditors or led them to an aporia or a fertile impasse.

VI

> Though there is but one Centre, most people live in centres of their own.
>
> Heraclitus

> The hint half guessed, the gift half understood, is Incarnation.
>
> 'The Dry Salvages' V

An essential part of Eliot's approach to form in *The Waste Land* is the appropriation of a specific myth as a reference point. The myth of choice, Frazer's Urmyth, is privileged in that it is presented as the original myth from which all others descended and of which they are evolved fragments; it is privileged by being prior in time and by being totally comprehensive. Frazer constructed his monomyth by tracing myths and mythic fragments back through time to a reconstructed hypothetical abstract parent myth. An essential part of Eliot's approach to form in *Four Quartets* is the problematization of all imaginable reference points. 'Where is the summer, the unimaginable / Zero summer?' he asks in 'Little Gidding' (CPP, 191). The overall sequence can be seen as a radical critique of linear models such as Frazer's monomyth and, at the same time, a critique of cyclical models such as the one outlined in Yeats' *A Vision*. In the very first lines of 'Burnt Norton', the poet calls into question both linear and cyclical notions of time and complicates any concept of poetic structure based on traditional models.

Eliot's re-evaluation of the relation of past and future includes a critique of the theory of evolution. This critique, implicit throughout the sequence, is explicit in 'The Dry Salvages' II.

> It seems, as one becomes older,
> That the past has another pattern, and ceases to be a
>   mere sequence –
> Or even development: the latter a partial fallacy
> Encouraged by superficial notions of evolution,
> Which becomes, in the popular mind, a means of
>   disowning the past.   (CPP, 186)

The use of 'seems', 'mere', 'partial' and 'superficial' cancels any suggestion of an outright rejection of linear movement. But Eliot does reject the popular notion of evolution which sees the past as primarily a prelude to the present or as a stage in the development of the race, and he clearly rejects the idea that the present is the highest stage in evolution. He subverts, in brief, the very notions that Frazer, an unabashed positivist, had used in constructing his monomyth, because such concepts oversimplify the present and undercut the reality that the past and future are part of a pattern which is always present.

Eliot's abandonment of the strenuous metaphysics of high modernism was accompanied by the move towards a position rooted in Christian humility. The 'centre' in his new system is not a key myth, but a key pattern. Importantly, the pattern is one shared with his reader – not because, as with the Frazerian model, the myth is a universal common ancestor to all beliefs, but because the model exemplifies a universal and an individual pattern which is new in every moment. He introduces the pattern in 'Burnt Norton' and reiterates it throughout that poem and its successors. In 'Burnt Norton' II, he describes his newfound centre (or wisdom or meaning, depending on how one translates Heraclitus) in terms of a dance between stillness and movement.

> At the still point of the turning world. Neither flesh nor
> fleshless;
> Neither from nor towards; at the still point, there the dance is
> . . .
>
> Except for the point, the still point,
> There would be no dance, and there is only the dance.
>   (CPP, 173)

The key principle or pattern is both diachronic and synchronic, linear and cyclical at once. It is an idea of presence in which past and future, time and timelessness, intersect and are reconciled – not once and for all, but again and again. In the passage from 'The Dry Salvages' II quoted above, the poet describes the intersection as 'moments of happiness', of 'sudden illumination' in which lost experience is restored 'In a different form, beyond any meaning / We can assign to happiness' (CPP, 186). Past experience, including the prehistoric history of the race, does not cease to exist, but continues, like a buried stream, to move beneath and as part of the present; moreover, the past is sometimes vividly revived in moments which are in and out of time. Beginning with the experience in the rose garden of 'Burnt Norton', many versions of the moment of illumination are presented in the *Quartets*. None of these moments is in itself complete or perfect; each is suggestive, full of hinting – a pledge rather than a full realization of transcendence.

The intersections of time and eternity in *Four Quartets* operate on many levels, including the personal, the aesthetic, the religious, the racial and the cultural. All of the intersections are religious in the radical sense; that is, they function quite literally as re-binders, re-unifiers (*re-ligare*). They are not specifically or necessarily Christian, but as Eliot says in 'The Dry Salvages' V, the supreme example of the key pattern is the meeting of time and eternity, becoming and being, in the Incarnation of Christ.

> The hint half guessed, the gift half understood, is Incarnation.
> Here the impossible union
> Of spheres of existence is actual,
> Here the past and future
> Are conquered, and reconciled.   (CPP, 189–90)

This passage describes the incarnational principle which Eliot adopts as his reference pattern in *Four Quartets*. It is dynamic and open-ended; it contains both past and future, although, unlike the monomyth, it faces forward and stimulates the reader to do the same. The reader, compounded of spirit and flesh, mind and matter, provides another example of the incarnational principle. The poem, in which words move in and out of time, in which words intersect with pattern, is in many ways the most immediate instance of the incarnational principle for the sensitive reader.

Again, the principles behind *Four Quartets* can be elucidated by comparing and contrasting Frazer's monomyth in *The Golden Bough* with Lévi-Strauss's 'key myth' in *The Raw and the Cooked*. The model changes from biology to geology, from a temporally focused model to a model allowing for a far more complex interplay of temporal and spatial levels. Lévi-Strauss chooses a myth of the Bororo Indians of central Brazil as his 'key myth' not because he considers it ancient or superior or central, but because he intuits that it is a rich example of a pattern which he believes is present in many times and places. In *Four Quartets*, Eliot begins with a moment in a rose garden, a moment of happiness or illumination. He did not choose it for its antiquity or its universality, but for its richness in a specific present situation. That it is one version of a pattern present in the Edenic and many other myths corroborates the choice as a fine one. The experience in the rose garden is in time, and yet it suggests the intersection between time and the timeless. It is present, and yet it points to 'our first world' and by implication to paradise; it is on several levels both an end and a beginning. It is privileged structurally by appearing first and last in the poem and by being repeated; and because it is associated with such motifs as Eden, first love, salvation and transcendence, it is thematically charged. The experience in the rose garden, finally, hints at incarnation; it acts as a pledge of a principle which in

'The Dry Salvages' he half guesses and half understands to be the Incarnation.

In *Four Quartets*, to summarize, Eliot remains interested in the problem of form he had struggled with in his early work. The poetry he writes in response to that challenge changes, however, for as he indicates in 'East Coker' V, 'one has only learnt to get the better of words / For the thing one no longer has to say, or the way in which / One is no longer disposed to say it' (CPP, 182). In mastering the mythical method, he outgrew the emotions and ideas which that method enabled him to express, and he was forced in the *Quartets* to make a new start 'with shabby equipment always deteriorating'. His attitude towards reference points changes, a change that makes all the difference in his art. Traditionally, the reference point was a given in art. In the early twentieth century, the reference point was made up or brought or constructed. In *Four Quartets*, the reference point is both there and not there. 'Where is the summer, the unimaginable / Zero summer?' (CPP, 191). In the face of the aporias opened by human experience, he cultivates and masters a poetic involving an acceptance of absence (gaps) as openings to transcendence in life and in art.

References

Brooker, Jewel Spears, 'The Case of the Missing Abstraction: Eliot, Frazer and Modernism', *Massachusetts Review* 25 (1984), 539–552.
———, 'T.S. Eliot and the Revolt Against Dualism: His Dissertation on F.H. Bradley in Its Intellectual Context', in Laura Cowan, ed., *T.S. Eliot: Man and Poet*, Orono, Maine, National Poetry Foundation, 1990, 303–19.
Derrida, Jacques, *Writing and Difference*, trans. Alan Bass, Chicago, University of Chicago Press, 1978.
Lévi-Strauss, Claude, 'The Structural Study of Myth', (1955) trans. Claire Jacobson and Brooke Grundfest Schoepf, in David H. Richter, *The Critical Tradition*, 1989.
———, *The Raw and the Cooked*, trans. John and Doreen Weightman, New York, Harper & Row, 1969.

6

Risking Enchantment: The Middle Way between Mysticism and Pragmatism in Four Quartets

Donald J. Childs

During an interview with Françoise de Castro in 1948, several years after the publication of *Four Quartets*, T.S. Eliot was prompted by the interviewer's observations about the inhibition of mysticism by intellect in Valéry's creative process to talk about mysticism in general:

> Eliot then said what seemed to me the centre and luminous point of the entire interview: 'But intelligence pushed to its depths leads to mysticism.'
>
> 'Do you not believe,' I asked him . . ., 'that intellect and mysticism are two faculties which are opposed in human nature?' A sign of denial was his only response, and this affirmation: 'All human faculties pushed to their depths end in mysticism.'
>
> (my translation from the French, 3)

What Eliot means is not further explained in the interview, but in certain respects this comment is not surprising. That mysticism had been an interest of Eliot's from a very early time is clear from Lyndall Gordon's *Eliot's Early Years* (1977). That he understood intellect to be an important part of mysticism is a point made in his Clark Lectures of 1926, in which he celebrates 'the development and subsumption of emotion and feeling through intellect into the vision of God' (Lecture 3, 10). That mysticism continued to interest Eliot in the 1940s is clear from the example of *Four Quartets*, his most mystical poem. But to appreciate fully what Eliot means by his claim that all human faculties are ultimately grounded in mysticism, and to appreciate the function of the 'mysticism' of *Four Quartets*, we must review the philosophical version of this claim articulated in the dissertation of 1916, for Eliot's interest in mysticism at the time of *Four Quartets* is continuous in an important respect with his philosophical interests of thirty years before.

The mysticism of *Four Quartets* was evident to readers from the moment of publication. In the 1940s, Helen Gardner pointed to passages from *The Cloud of Unknowing*, Dame Julian of Norwich, Walter Hilton and St John of the Cross (168, 181, 184). Critics like Gardner, celebrating *Four Quartets* as 'Eliot's masterpiece' and finding themselves largely in sympathy with his Christian turn of 1927, accept the allusions to Christian mystics as clues to Eliot's spiritual state during the process of composition (2). Sister Corona Sharp represents the culmination of this trend, documenting the references to Christian mystics (especially St John of the Cross) and thereby explaining the integrity and coherence of Eliot's spiritual quest. In 'Little Gidding' 'the mystical journey ends . . . in "complete simplicity" or total self-giving. Having passed through the fires of purgation, the soul is ready to go forth from this life' (275).

Others, equally intrigued by the mystical dimensions of *Four Quartets*, have preferred to explore the influence of Eastern mysticism upon the poem. P.S. Sri, finding that 'the Indian face of Eliot has not been quite captured', suggests that Eliot is 'a *kavi*, a poet who attempts to see deep into the design of the universe' (4, 124). Cleo Kearns regards the references to Eastern mysticism in *Four Quartets* as serving a more secular epistemology. Arguing that Eliot defines the reading process as involving ceaseless surrender to a new point of view and then renunciation of it, she finds that in *Four Quartets* the 'Indic tradition, among many other points of view, is essential to this renunciation, for only through its counterpoint can Eliot enact the destabilization of an old perspective and the movement to a new one, which is all we know, at least in this life, of transcendence' (245).

Agreement that *Four Quartets* is a mystical poem, however, obscures the fact that 'mysticism' is a rather difficult word to define. In its derogatory sense, it is equivalent to 'occultism'. In its more usual religious sense, it signifies the experience of contact between the human and the divine. There is also a more general philosophical application of the word to denote an experience of insight into the ultimate nature of reality. For still others, mysticism is a manifestation of psychological illness. Recent debate among philosophers has concerned the question of whether the experience denoted by the word is the same in whatever system of belief it occurs, or whether the experience is culture-bound (see Katz, 1–9). A precise definition of the general phenomenon is not necessary for my purposes. I am interested instead in understanding as mystical the experience of ultimate reality that Eliot treats both in his dissertation and *Four Quartets*. Depending upon our perspective, the moments traditionally marked 'mystical' in *Four Quartets* – the moment in the garden when the lotus rises, the moment 'Quick now, here, now, always', the moment of 'Midwinter spring' when 'The soul's sap quivers' (CPP, 176, 191) – will seem to be Eliot's location of the point of contact between the human and the divine, between *samsara* and *nirvana*, between Bradley's appearance and reality, or between Bergson's clock time and *durée*. From my point of view, these moments mark the point of tension between what Eliot calls in his dissertation the subject side and the object side of human experience.

Eliot uses the distinction between subject and object to explain the divide between the traditional philosophical positions of idealism, on the one hand, and realism or materialism on the other. Our metaphysics will vary with our point of view. The objective or material world can be understood as the projection of a subject's consciousness, or the subjective or ideal world can be understood as a phenomenon caused by the interaction of objects:

> We have no right, except in the most provisional way, to speak of *my* experience, since the I is a construction out of experience, an abstraction from it; and the *thats*, the browns and hards and flats, are equally ideal constructions from experience. . . . Everything, from one point of view, is subjective; and everything, from another point of view, is objective; and there is no *absolute* point of view from which a decision may be pronounced. . . . For feeling, in which the two are one, has no history; it is, as such, outside of time altogether, inasmuch as there is no further point of view from which it can be inspected. (KE, 19, 21–2)

Given that the union of the two points of view remains always hypothetical, the subject-object dichotomy is a condition of human knowledge and experience, a consequence, in part, of language that depends on the distinction between subjects and predicates.

The point of the dissertation is to argue that the assumption

that the two points of view are united in feeling or immediate
experience is metaphysically false, or at least irrelevant: 'In the
growth and construction of the world we live in, there is no one
stage, and no one aspect, which you can take as the foundation'
(KE, 151). Being in general and human being in particular cannot
be reduced to subject or object. Rather, being (from the point of
view of human being, a point of view we cannot escape) is the
reference between them, the suspension between these extremes.
Eliot's argument about language, knowledge and experience is
the same: there is no language without a speaker, no knowledge
without a knower, no being without a human being. In each
case, subject and object penetrate each other, their interpenetration
producing language, knowledge and being.

As in Yeats' phases one and fifteen in the cycle of the moon,
so in the dissertation – human being does not reside at either the
subjective or objective extreme and human beings cannot experi-
ence either extreme: 'if anyone assert that immediate experience
["an all-inclusive experience outside of which nothing shall fall"],
at either the beginning or the end of our journey, is annihilation
and utter night, I cordially agree' (KE, 31). 'East Coker' and 'Little
Gidding' speak of this 'beginning' and 'end' of human experience;
'The Dry Salvages' speaks of our journey 'Here between the hither
and the farther shore'; and 'Burnt Norton' warns of the threat to
human being beyond the beginning and end that bracket human
experience:

> the enchainment of past and future
> Woven in the weakness of the changing body,
> Protects mankind from heaven and damnation
> Which flesh cannot endure.   (CPP, 173)

As human beings, we are 'Caught in the form of limitation /
Between un-being and being' (CPP, 175). There is no point of
view other than human being from which being can be inspected.

It is the dissertation's discussion of the attempt to transcend the
subject–object dichotomy that is relevant to the comment in the
Castro interview about the importance of mysticism. Eliot inherits
from Bradley and the philosophers of the idealist tradition the
assumption that there must be a moment – called 'immediate
experience' or 'feeling' – in which 'as yet neither any subject
nor object exists' (Bradley, 406–7). From this point of view, Eliot

observes,

> Experience . . . both begins and ends in something which is
> not conscious. . . . At the beginning then consciousness and
> its object are one. . . . As we develop subject and object side,
> they seem to approximate independence. . . . That objects are
> dependent upon consciousness, or consciousness upon objects,
> we most resolutely deny. . . . But if we attempt to put the world
> together again, after having divided it into consciousness and
> objects, we are condemned to failure. . . . Yet the original unity
> – the 'neutral entity' – though transcended, remains, and is never
> analysed away.   (KE, 28–30)

Eliot concludes that this faith in the ultimate oneness of reality is
the essence of metaphysics: 'in a metaphysical theory there is an
attempt to bind together all points of view in one' (KE, 163). But
despite our recognition that our metaphysics is a matter of faith,
we cannot escape our faith. As Michaels observes, for Eliot, 'To
acknowledge the conventionality of our own account of the real is
to acknowledge its contingency without undermining its validity,
its power over us' (196).

Metaphysics is always an extrapolation from local epistemologi-
cal practice, practice located in a particular place at a particular time.
Our world, our reality, comes from a dialectic of local points of
view: 'What makes a real world is difference of opinion' (KE,
165). The practical dialectic moves in the direction of unity, moves
towards an absolute:

> the life of a soul does not consist in the contemplation of
> one consistent world but in the painful task of unifying (to
> a greater or less extent) jarring and incompatible ones, and
> passing, when possible, from two or more discordant viewpoints
> to a higher which shall somehow include and transmute them.
> (KE, 147–8)

Eliot concludes that by the nature of human being – a being
he regards as inevitably social, constructing its reality through
agreement (through a coming to *one* mind about what constitutes
reality) – 'We are forced to the assumption that truth is one, and
to the assumption that reality is one' (KE, 168).

Human being is thus born into a world already constructed in
the direction of a certain oneness or *logos*, a world still engaged

in the constructive effort. The conclusion offered during the Castro interview follows. Pursue to its depths the subject-side or object-side formulas that try to 'put the world together' and you are bound to arrive at the original unity that all epistemological practice locates at the beginning and end of the distinction between consciousness and objects. In the terms of the interview: 'All human faculties pushed to their depths end in mysticism'.

With regard to *Four Quartets*, the important point to note about the dissertation's discussion of the basic mysticism involved in human knowledge and experience is the fact that it has its roots in Eliot's pre-dissertation analysis of the philosophies of Henri Bergson and William James. The reappearance of these two philosophies in *Four Quartets* marks the reappearance there of Eliot's interest in the basic mysticism of human being and the reappearance as well of the dissertation's determination to resist the urge to resolve the subject–object dichotomy into oneness.

On the one hand is Bergson, high priest of the Life Force. On the other is James, judging the worth of ideas by their practical consequences or 'cash value'. As Eliot knew them, they both offered themselves as honest brokers between the ideal and the real, hoping (in Bergson's terms) to solve a good number of metaphysical disputes 'by merely getting rid of the clumsy symbols round which we are fighting' (1889, xix). Eliot allowed neither claim, however, treating James as representative of the subject side of philosophy and treating Bergson as representative of the object side. His response to their limitations was to embark on his own search for the middle way between the ideal and the real. In articulating the difference between Bergson and James several years before writing the dissertation, I suggest, Eliot made the first move in articulating the different impulses *within* himself that he would figure in *Four Quartets*.

Living in a world overwhelmed by science and materialism, Eliot was attracted by Bergsonism, it would seem, by the promise of union with the Life Force – what he later dismissed as a 'promise of immortality' with a 'somewhat meretricious captivation' (1924, 29). In *Creative Evolution*, Bergson argues that life is a vital impulse that has divided itself into instinct and intelligence in order to wend its way through matter: the intellect has developed into such an efficient instrument for enabling life to overcome matter that it has subordinated intuition completely – relegating it to the land of daydream and sleep, where the practical restraints of the intellect relax. We can regain awareness of the ceaseless flux, the perpetual movement that is reality only by rediscovering the 'potentialities of intuition' that slumber within us: 'Let us try to see, no longer with the eyes of the intellect alone, which grasps only [what the intellect has] . . . already made and which looks from the outside, but with the spirit. . . . To movement, then, everything will be restored, and into movement everything will be resolved' (1907, 192, 264). It is this desire to achieve union with the movement of the vital impulse that earned Bergsonism the label 'mystical' from both its admirers and detractors and prompted Bertrand Russell to attack it 'with all imaginable ferocity' (343).

This is the mysticism Paul Douglass finds in *Four Quartets*. He argues that, largely through the influence of Bergson's mystical philosophy, the poem finally sorts out the relationship between Being and Becoming – 'the crucial issue of Eliot's career as a poet'. The point of the first quartet, Douglass claims, is to make the mystic way more fully real to its readers: '"Burnt Norton" enacts, insofar as it can, a process of awakening to the meaning of an intuitive experience'. The syllogistic reasoning at the beginning of 'Burnt Norton' is therefore abandoned: according to Bergson and Eliot, reality cannot be thought; it must be intuited (105–6, 95, 93).

Although Bergsonism is hardly mentioned in the dissertation, it is the subject (in whole and in part) of two papers Eliot wrote in the 1911–14 period at Harvard before leaving for Europe, where he wrote the dissertation. As early as 1911 Eliot speaks of Bergsonism as 'a rather weakling mysticism' and marks Bergson as one who has failed to occupy a middle ground between the ideal and the real, between subject and object (1911, 22). Quoting Bergson as contradictorily locating reality first in consciousness and then in matter, Eliot asks: 'Where . . . is the reality – in the consciousness, or in that which is perceived? Where is the one reality to subsume both of these, and can we or can we not know it?' (1911, 18–19). These are the general questions that animate the dissertation. Their connection to *Four Quartets* is suggested by an interesting echo: Eliot finds in the Bergson of *Creative Evolution* that 'Reality, though apparently *one* at bottom . . ., divides itself into a Cartesian dichotomy – the way up, consciousness, and the way down, matter' (1911, 13–14). Bergsonian flux is thereby aligned with Heraclitean flux ('The way up is the way down'), and the early interest in

Bergson and the subject–object dichotomy is thereby insinuated into 'Burnt Norton'.

The impact of Bergson upon *Four Quartets* has long been acknowledged (see Smidt, Smith and Bergsten). Evidence of the Bergsonian mystical impulse surviving alongside and within the references to classical representatives of Western and Eastern mysticism in *Four Quartets* is not hard to come by. The opening lines of 'Burnt Norton' are highly charged with Bergsonian echoes. Although inflected by Eliot's Anglo-Catholic perspective, and informed by his biography, the lines about time inevitably also recall Bergson's 'time' philosophy:

> Time present and time past
> Are both perhaps present in time future
> And time future contained in time past.
> If all time is eternally present
> All time is unredeemable.
> What might have been is an abstraction
> Remaining a perpetual possibility
> Only in a world of speculation.   (CPP, 171)

On the one hand, talk of redeeming time reveals the Anglo-Catholic's concern about Original Sin, and talk of the apparent impossibility that things 'might have been' otherwise reveals the regret of the husband separated from Vivienne Eliot at having impulsively forsaken Emily Hale twenty years before. On the other hand, however, the lines acknowledge a philosophical concern about determinism (the hypothesis seems to be that the unfolding of time was determined in the beginning and contains the evidence of its determination in every moment) and so implies a concern about the relationship between time and free will – the very question raised in these very terms in Bergson's first work, known in English as *Time and Free Will* (1889). Similarly, Eliot's observation that 'To be conscious is not to be in time' echoes Bergson's claim that 'We do not *think* real time. But we *live* it' (CPP, 173; 1907, 46).

Douglass documents many such Bergsonian elements in the poem. He concludes that because of Bergson the 'world we see at "Little Gidding"'s conclusion is a transfigured one in which history may be defined not as a nightmare, a chaos, but rather as an unending process of self-discovery, full of suffering, certainly, but also full of growth and divine love' (99). Bergson's emphasis on life as creation helps to make sense of the familiar compound voice (known as one's own and yet belonging to another) in 'Little Gidding': the point is to emphasize the '*dédoublement* . . . at the heart of the intuition, the revelation. The words themselves have engendered the world in which they are heard. . . . There is a sense in which the moment *creates itself* ' (102). Unconsciously, here, and consciously, in talk of the interpenetration of beginnings and endings, the poet is reconciling himself 'to a world in which the only finality is a continuous Becoming' (103). Douglass finds, in the end, that 'the poet takes his place with those who accept, not deny life, knowing that every vital action is a leap to a fall but nevertheless part of the creative impulse of the universe' (104).

I agree with much in Douglass's reading of *Four Quartets*, but I do not agree that the aspect of the poem 'in which the moment *creates itself* ' ought to be traced in the first instance to Bergson's influence. Eliot was from the beginning unhappy with Bergson's notion of the vital impulse. Although Eliot initially regarded Bergson as an idealist (he was interested in his early paper 'to show certain inconsistencies – idealism vs. realism – in B[ergson]'s position . . . based on the conviction that the idealistic is . . . the more fundamental' [1911, 11]), he came to regard him as representing the object side of experience. It is Bergson's '*élan vital* or "flux"' that he judges in his dissertation to be just as much an object-side abstraction from immediate experience as any object (KE, 19). And so Bergson represents for Eliot one half of the metaphysical impulse.

The philosophy that comes to represent, in both the dissertation and *Four Quartets*, the other half of this impulse – the subject-side explanation of experience – is a version of James' pragmatism. It prevents the dissertation's arrival at Bradley's Absolute, and it complicates the poem's drive towards a mystical 'still point' – towards the moment when 'the fire and the rose are one' – for there is a part of Eliot that accepts James' claim that truth is always in process, ever a function of human need. Bergson certainly impressed Eliot initially with his talk of creative evolution, but James' claim that the human being is the truly creative agent in the world was one that Eliot struggled with much longer.

According to James, 'the truth of an idea is not a stagnant property inherent in it. Truth *happens* to an idea. It *becomes* true, is *made* true by events' (1907, 97). He offered pragmatism, then, not as a *philosophy* about truth or reality but as a *method* – a method for getting beyond squabbles about truth or reality. As James explains:

> The pragmatic method is primarily a method of settling meta-physical disputes that otherwise might be interminable. Is the world one or many? – fated or free? – material or spiritual? – here are notions either of which may or may not hold good of the world; and disputes over such notions are unending. The pragmatic method in such cases is to try to interpret each notion by tracing its respective practical consequences. What difference would it practically make to anyone if this notion rather than that notion were true? If no practical difference whatever can be traced, then the alternatives mean practically the same thing, and all dispute is idle. (1907, 28)

In the end, James describes absolute truth as merely the 'ideal vanishing-point towards which we imagine that all our temporary truths will some day converge', and so he advises that we 'live to-day by what truth we can get to-day, and be ready to-morrow to call it falsehood' (106–7).

   Since Peirce and James first articulated their versions of the philosophy, pragmatism has come to rival deconstruction as the champion of anti-Platonism. The pragmatist, Richard Rorty observes, is one who 'sees the Platonic tradition as having outlived its usefulness' (xiv). In the Platonic tradition, to know the Good is to do the good, to know the Truth is to speak the truth. According to the pragmatist, however, thinking about Truth will not help us to say something true; thinking about Goodness will not help us to act well (Rorty, xv). Truth and Goodness have no essence. They are concepts relative to time and place. In short, there is no ultimate Platonic text behind the world; the world is an infinite series of texts. The pragmatist finds that 'there is nothing deep down inside us except what we have put there ourselves, no criterion that we have not created in the course of creating a practice. . . .' (Rorty, xlii). The result of a rigorous pragmatism is a 'post-philosophical culture' – 'one in which men and women [feel] themselves alone, merely finite, with no links to something Beyond' (Rorty, xlii–xliii).

   Eliot is no pragmatist in Rorty's sense of the term; the Eliot of *Four Quartets*, after all, believes in God. He is what Rorty would call an intuitive realist, one who thinks that 'deep down beneath all the texts, there is something which is not just one more text but that to which various texts are trying to be "adequate"' (xxxvii). Eliot speaks in these very terms at the time of his conversion:

> I should say that it was at any rate essential for Religion that we should have the conception of an immutable object or Reality the knowledge of which shall be the final object of that will; and there can be no permanent reality if there is no permanent truth. I am of course quite ready to admit that human apprehension of truth varies, changes and perhaps develops, but that is a property of human imperfection rather than of truth. (Dobrée, 75)

But Eliot was in 1914 something of a pragmatist, was in 1916 a very sophisticated pragmatist (as Michaels has shown), and was at the time of *Four Quartets*, I argue, still in many ways a pragmatist.

'Pragmatism', Eliot writes in 1914, 'has perhaps seized the right view of the relation of philosophy [to] human life; philosophy *is* to fit a need' (1914, 21). Along these lines, he argues in the dissertation that the world is a practical construct. Recognizing this fact will put an end to metaphysical disputes:

> The process of development of a real world . . . works in two directions; we have not first a real world to which we add our imaginings, nor have we a real world out of which we select *our* 'real' world, but the real and the unreal develop side by side. If we think of the world not as ready made . . . but as constructed, or constructing itself, . . . at every moment, and never more than an approximate construction, a construction essentially practical in its nature: then the difficulties of real and unreal disappear.
>
> (KE, 136)

Talk of satisfying needs, of construction and of practicality and the desire to get beyond metaphysical squabbles echoes James. Indeed, the dissertation's concluding chapter accepts the pragmatic criterion for truth: a theory must be 'capable of making an actual practical difference'; 'all that we care about is how [a truth] works' (KE, 161, 169).

That Eliot retained this 1916 pragmatic cast of mind alongside his Anglo-Catholicism is confirmed by his post-conversion poetry. In *Ash-Wednesday*, for instance, the language of the dissertation endures:

> Because I know that time is always time
> And place is always and only place
> And what is actual is actual only for one time
> And only for one place
> I rejoice that things are as they are and
> I renounce the blessèd face
> And renounce the voice
> Because I cannot hope to turn again
> Consequently I rejoice, having to construct something
> Upon which to rejoice   (CPP, 89)

The poet's recognition of his situation in a certain time and place is generally pragmatic. To accept that 'what is actual is actual only for one time / And only for one place' is also generally pragmatic. But to accept the loss of what seems to have been present once (a sustaining vision of a blessed face and voice), and to begin from this post-vision time and place to 'construct' the object of belief – that is, 'something / Upon which to rejoice' – is to use the very terms of the dissertation. Renouncing the blessed face and voice, and rejoicing that things are as they are, is like the renunciation of 'immediate experience' and the cordial acceptance of the consequences of this renunciation that we see in his dissertation: 'if anyone assert that immediate experience, at either the beginning or end of our journey, is annihilation and utter night, I cordially agree' (KE, 31). In *Ash-Wednesday*, part of Eliot's religious struggle is to allow within his poem not just the dogmatic Truth of Christianity, but also the small-t truth of pragmatism. Within these lines one can hear the murmur of the dissertation: 'the line between the experienced, or the given, and the constructed can nowhere be clearly drawn' (KE, 18).

The same determination to accept his time and place – to accept not only his own philosophical situation in particular, but also the situation of human beings in general between the extremes of 'un-being and being' within a world of constant becoming – is evident in 'East Coker' (1940):

So here I am, in the middle way, having had twenty years –
Twenty years largely wasted, the years of *l'entre deux guerres* –
Trying to learn to use words, and every attempt
Is a wholly new start, and a different kind of failure. . . .

         And so each venture
Is a new beginning, a raid on the inarticulate
With shabby equipment always deteriorating
In the general mess of imprecision of feeling,
Undisciplined squads of emotion. . . .

There is only the fight to recover what has been lost
And found and lost again and again: and now, under conditions
That seem unpropitious. But perhaps neither gain nor loss.
For us, there is only the trying. The rest is not our business.

                               (CPP, 182)

This discovery that language is unable to express a presence or
essence – that every attempt to use words 'Is a wholly new
start, and a different kind of failure', a 'raid on the inarticulate
/ With shabby equipment always deteriorating' – aligns this
moment in *Four Quartets* with the dissertation's insistence on
the remoteness of the Absolute from any verbal formula that
tries to embody it. The emphasis upon the present moment (the
'now'), even though it seem 'Unpropitious', and the emphasis
on 'only the trying', are all pragmatic, recalling *Ash-Wednesday*'s
celebration of the need to construct something upon which
to rejoice.

But most pragmatic of all is the conclusion that 'The rest is not
our business'. This is the properly pragmatic conviction of the
dissertation that metaphysics as the science of ultimate questions
is none of our business:

The Absolute . . . is neither real nor unreal nor imaginary. But
. . . a metaphysic may be accepted or rejected without our
assuming that from the practical point of view it is either true
or false. The point is that the world of practical verification has
no definite frontiers, and that it is the business of philosophy to
keep the frontiers open. (KE, 169)

There is trying and testing, but the rest is not our business. In the
end, then, we find in both the dissertation and *Four Quartets* the

pragmatic insistence that truths be tested and verified instead of referred to an inaccessible ideal standard.

In addition to the dissertation's analysis of the human being's metaphysical impulse toward the oneness of this ideal standard, the aspect of Eliot's early work in philosophy most important for an understanding of this work's bearing on *Four Quartets* is his discussion of the point at which Bergsonism and pragmatism meet. Eliot argued in 1914 that Bergsonians and pragmatists agree insofar as both regard history as a 'process in which human purposes are illusory'. The problem with Bergson and James is 'their confusion . . . of human and cosmic activity'. Bergson makes everything cosmic, makes everything part of the Life Force. 'Bergson denies human values', Eliot complains; for him, 'history is a vitalistic process in which human purposes do not exist' (1914, 21, 20, 20–1).

'The error of pragmatism', he writes, 'is, I believe, exactly the reverse':

> for pragmatism man is the measure of all things. [It] is a 'practical' philosophy. You choose a point of view because you like it. You form certain plans because they express your character. Certain things are true because they are what you need; others, because they are what you want. (1914, 20–1)

Eliot's description of pragmatism is a caricature: he implies that we approach reality with a shopping list of things we need, whereas the pragmatic claim that reality is convention means only that reality is contingent, and not that it is the result of a decision (see Michaels, 194). As Eliot notes in his dissertation, 'we have not . . . a real world out of which we select *our* "real" world' (KE, 136). But the fact that Eliot resorts to caricature reveals the design of the rhetoric: there must be straw figures of the subject and object sides of experience for the mediating rhetoric of Eliot's philosophical prose to function. Pragmatism measures human experience from the subject side, postulating the object; the Bergsonism of *Creative Evolution* measures experience from the object side, postulating the subject. It is the contemplation of this dichotomy with which the dissertation begins and it is the inevitable failure of philosophers to get beyond it that Eliot explains in his conclusion.

As far as Eliot is concerned, neither of these philosophies will do. On the one hand, he complains, Bergson emphasizes the reality of a fluid psychological world of aspect and nuances, where purposes and intentions are replaced by pure feeling. By the seduction of his style we come to believe that the Bergsonian world is the only world, and that we have been living among shadows. It is not so. Bergson is the sweet siren of adventurous philosophers and our world of social values is at least as real as his. (1914, 20)

On the other hand, the pragmatist's insight that philosophy is a human instrument designed to fit a need, he writes, 'does not strike me as a great emancipation; it strikes me as a tedious truism'. Pragmatism, he says, does not release us from our need to pretend that our philosophical theories are final: 'What pretension to finality does Plato make for his theory . . . that any man who uses his mind to theorise must not make?' (1914, 7) 'It may be true', he concedes, 'that man does not live by bread alone, but by making fictions and swallowing them alive & whole. This seems to reduce the high cost of living by eliminating living' (1914, 15).

Here is part of the argument and imagery of *Four Quartets*. First there is the argument by Bergsonian, Christian and Indian mystics alike that the moment of illumination reveals (as in Plato's metaphor of the cave) the distinction between reality and its mere shadow. The sunlight fills the empty pool; presence is overcome by absence; meaning seems to be revealed. Then there is Eliot's reservation about the Platonic language of light and shadow, for, given the values of light and shadow defined in the early essay, one finds a significant ambiguity in this mystical moment of illumination in 'Burnt Norton'. It is not clear what has been revealed, what truth it is that humankind cannot bear. Is the light (presumably the light of the Gospel of John that becomes the Word by the end of this poem) real, marking all else as merely shadow? Or is shadow real (the darkness that comes with the cloud), marking the momentary light as merely an illusion? It is not clear which of these phenomena the bird is calling 'reality'. The ambiguity is no accident; it comes from Eliot's disenchantment with the 'meretricious captivation' of this sort of 'promise of immortality' that he had encountered in Bergsonism. His fear was that the inner light was no more trustworthy than the inner voice, 'which breathes the eternal message of vanity, fear, and lust' (SE, 27). As always, the test is pragmatic; these moments 'can be judged only by their fruits' (SE, 405).

And yet pragmatism is no simple alternative to this mystical moment, Bergsonian or otherwise. One therefore also finds in 'Burnt Norton' the twenty-year fear of pragmatism's replacement of the spiritual part of our diet by fiction. The mysterious, lyrical fourth section of the poem focuses upon this fruitless option. The puzzling rhetorical questions serve to mock the pragmatic proposition that reality is a function of human need. The passing away of the sun (as in the first section of the poem, symbolically the reality outside the human being) exposes the ludicrousness of the suggestion that we could replace the sun: 'Will the sunflower turn to us, will the clematis / Stray down, bend to us: tendril and spray / Clutch and cling?' (CPP, 174). How can the world's being depend on human being? This section of the poem ironically reverses the bird's claim that humankind cannot bear very much reality: it is no longer to bear reality in the sense of 'to endure' reality; it is to bear reality in the sense of 'to sustain, support, create' reality. According to Eliot, 'the great weakness of Pragmatism is that it ends by being of no *use* to anybody' (SE, 454).

The problem Eliot identifies in 1914 as shared by Bergson and James is the problem he himself faces in *Four Quartets*. The problem, Eliot writes, is that, 'so far as I can see', neither 'has formed a clear conception of what the word *human* implies' (1914, 19). It is this definition of human being that Eliot continues to pursue in *Four Quartets*. He seems to assume that we all know intuitively what human being is: 'The question can always be asked of the closest-woven theory: is this the reality of *my* world of appearance? and if I do not recognize the identity, then it is not' (KE, 168). Bergson and James, he suggests, contradict this intuitive knowledge: 'they give us two forms of escape from reality as we know it in ordinary experience, a reality in which we find a constant friction between the mechanical and the volitional. One exalts mechanism, the other impulse. It amounts to the same thing' (1914, 22).

Bergson claims that we do not live fully until we become one with the Life Force; Eliot therefore dismisses his conversion to Bergsonism as a 'meretricious captivation'. He criticizes pragmatism for a similar sleight of hand: 'if *all* meaning is human meaning, then there is no meaning. If you assume only human standards, what standards have you?' 'Complete freedom', he writes, 'or complete determination', which he believes

Bergsonism offers, 'for a human being, is unthinkable' – and he means *literally* unthinkable (1914, 19). If, as the Bergsonian claims, human being is determined by an ultimate force (is bounded by a greater being), then we confront the 'unthinkable' spectre of complete determination. If, as the pragmatist claims, human being is constructed freely (it is bounded by un-being), then we confront the equally 'unthinkable' spectre of complete freedom.

To think that we are either completely free or completely determined is to contradict human being. The metaphysical extremes of subject-side and object-side points of view are literally unthinkable, Eliot argues in the dissertation (for the most part accepting Bradley's deconstruction of relational logic), because they inevitably imply one another. And so the syllogistic reasoning at the beginning of 'Burnt Norton' wrestles with the spectre of complete determination and the fourth section of the poem wrestles with the idea of complete freedom, knowing each of these conceptions of human being inadequate. Eliot's position is that we are determined by the world and we determine the world (as in 'Tradition and the Individual Talent' [see Davidson, 75–96]). The process is a dialectic of transcendence: 'the life of a soul does not consist in the contemplation of one consistent world but in the painful task of unifying (to a greater or less extent) jarring and incompatible ones, and passing, when possible, from two or more discordant viewpoints to a higher which shall somehow include and transmute them' (KE, 147–8). He makes a similar point in 'Little Gidding':

> what you thought you came for
> Is only a shell, a husk of meaning
> From which the purpose breaks only when it is fulfilled
> If at all. Either you had no purpose
> Or the purpose is beyond the end you figured
> And is altered in fulfilment.   (CPP, 192)

Our purposes react with our time and place to produce our world, just as the individual talent reacts with tradition to produce the literary world.

The poet of *Four Quartets* is suspended between the object-side and subject-side points of view, between suggestions that human being is a function of outer determination by object and a projection of desire from within the subject. The poet apparently longs for release from this suspension between contradictory metaphysics, longs for 'The inner freedom from the practical desire, / The release from action and suffering, release from the inner / And the outer compulsion' (CPP, 173). Reference to the inner and outer compulsion recalls the respectively pragmatic and Bergsonian explanations of reality as determined from within by the subject and from without by the object. But Eliot recognizes immediately that there is nothing but annihilation and utter night beyond the extremes that bracket human being:

> the enchainment of past and future
> Woven in the weakness of the changing body,
> Protects mankind from heaven and damnation
> Which flesh cannot endure.   (CPP, 173)

Such, according to Eliot, is *human* being, a balance between the 'annihilation and utter night' he cordially acknowledges in his dissertation and the 'heart of light' of which both *The Waste Land* and 'Burnt Norton' speak. We live in the 'partial ecstasy' and the 'partial horror' of a complication of object-side and subject-side points of view. As human beings, we are 'Caught in the form of limitation / Between un-being and being' – that is, we are caught between the Bergsonian hypothesis of an absolute vital being as responsible for human being and the pragmatic hypothesis of a lack of being beyond human being.

The journey of *Four Quartets* is towards recovery of the dissertation's 'cordial' acceptance of the vision of human being, and therefore reality (they are the same thing for Eliot in the dissertation) as this very suspension between the absolute and the relative. In both works, the main energy derives from the question of the relationship between belief and reality. Although a metaphysics always pretends to be true for all people and for all time, Eliot argues, 'A metaphysic may be accepted or rejected without our assuming that from the practical point of view it is either true or false' (KE, 169). The 'shaky ground and vanishing goal' of Eliot's philosophy, Michaels concludes, is 'the suspension of what . . . we might call belief':

To acknowledge the conventionality of our own account of the real is to acknowledge its contingency without undermining its validity, its power over us. Another way of putting this would be to say that what Eliot means when he calls reality conventional is that the real is what we *believe*, and that we cannot anchor our beliefs in something more real than they are. And yet, while there is nothing more real than our beliefs, it is clearly impossible to regard them as just one set of conventions among others since, if they really are our beliefs, we must believe them. (199, 196)

The achievement of the dissertation is to redefine reality not as subject or object, but as belief. From this point of view, the achievement of *Four Quartets* is similar: the poet is determined to acknowledge both his experience of belief as absolutely powerful and valid ('The hint half guessed, the gift half understood, is Incarnation') and his experience of belief as local and practical (located in East Coker and Little Gidding, for instance, 'Where prayer has been valid') (CPP, 190, 192).

The poem is therefore a dynamic tension between the rather mystical experience of belief as absolutely powerful and valid and the experience of belief as a series of propositions that (from the pragmatic point of view) do not work. In the mystical moments of *Four Quartets*, the poet offers for inspection the moment when absolute reality seems to be apprehended, the moment when not to believe is impossible. The part of Eliot that converted to Bergsonism in 1910 and to Anglo-Catholicism in 1927 wants to accept the mystical moment as illumination, as revelation of ultimate reality. It seems that the presumption of the poet describing the mystical moment is that description of that moment is equivalent to description of reality. But there is a part of Eliot that remains a pragmatist, that continues to be disturbed by his own pragmatic questions about what we identify as 'objective' truth: 'So long as our descriptions and explanations can vary so greatly and yet make so little practical difference, how can we say that our theories have that intended identical reference which is the objective criterion for truth and error?' (KE, 168–9).

Thus the fear of committing himself to a particular formula of words that would then be subject to pragmatic inspection: 'do not call' the moment fixity; we can only say '*there* we have been' and 'cannot say' where or for 'how long' (CPP,

173). On the one hand, the poet cannot specify time and place because the experience is ostensibly outside time and place; but, on the other hand, he cannot specify time and place for fear of the sceptical reaction of the pragmatic dimension of his sensibility that regards all experience – indeed, regards reality itself – as a function of time and place. There is a part of Eliot in *Four Quartets* that still understands the mystical moment as he did in the dissertation – as the experience of the power of one's beliefs, as the experience of the epistemological and metaphysical practice of one's age, as an experience of belief not as contingently but as absolutely valid. The attempt as poet to express this experience in propositional or descriptive form inevitably exposes the contingency of the belief, for the belief is always a formula expressed in words – words that 'Crack and sometimes break, under the burden', words that 'will not stay in place, / Will not stay still', words that are 'shabby equipment always deteriorating' (CPP, 175, 183).

In the dissertation Eliot argues 'Without words, no objects' (KE, 132). A similar suspicion may be responsible in part for *Four Quartets'* fussing about words, for if there are no words that will suffice in defining an object, 'how can we say that our theories have that intended identical reference which is the objective criterion for truth and error' (KE, 168)? Disrupting the Christian Eliot's conviction that variation in the 'human apprehension of truth' is 'a property of human imperfection rather than of truth', I suggest, is the nagging suspicion of the pragmatic Eliot that variation in the apprehension of truth is indeed a property of truth – the suspicion, that is, that 'Truth *happens* to an idea. It *becomes* true, is *made* true by events' (James, 97).

The very language of the affirmation that 'The hint half guessed, the gift half understood, is Incarnation' reminds us that there is another half of the hint and gift to be guessed and understood – reminds us that the line between the gift and the construction placed upon it can nowhere be clearly drawn (CPP, 190). And so, at times in *Four Quartets*, opposing the conviction that life is or should be a progress vertically towards the Absolute, is the suspicion that life is merely a lateral process, a drift from one contingent belief to another:

> There is no end, but addition: the trailing
> Consequence of further days and hours,
> While emotion takes to itself the emotionless
> Years of living among the breakage
> Of what was believed in as the most reliable –
> And therefore the fittest for renunciation.
>
> (CPP, 185)

This section of 'The Dry Salvages', having asked 'Where is there an end of' this process of 'addition', and having decided that 'There is no end', concludes as the dissertation does that we must accept the vision of life as a practice with no ultimate purpose: 'We cannot think . . . / . . . of a future that is not liable / Like the past, to have no destination' (CPP, 186). A similar point is made in 'Little Gidding': 'Either you had no purpose / Or the purpose is beyond the end you figured / And is altered in fulfilment' (CPP, 192). In both the dissertation and 'The Dry Salvages', Eliot observes that we create a practical fiction simply to cope with what the dissertation marks as 'annihilation and utter night' and what the poem marks as 'the final addition', the threat of 'Death': 'We have to think' of the fishermen 'as forever bailing, / Setting and hauling' – 'Not as making a trip that will be unpayable / For a haul that will not bear examination' (CPP, 186). This sense of there being no end to the process of belief, and the sense also that the fiction of an end as a valid and valuable purpose is necessary, ironically preface the introduction of 'the one Annunciation' – a version of the 'one' in which we are forced to think truth and reality culminate.

Four Quartets, like the dissertation, thus marks human being as suspension between the absolute and the relative, between the object to which our knowledge strives to become adequate and the subject that tries to make the world adequate to its desire. The poet is suspended between the hope that his belief is founded upon ultimate reality and the fear that his belief is a fiction. In the grip of belief – in the rose garden, sudden in a shaft of sunlight, in the 'distraction fit' – the absolute is undeniable: '*there* we have been', in its presence (CPP, 190, 173). The poem in part documents the experience of the mysticism of metaphysics, the experience the dissertation describes as being 'forced to the assumption that truth is one, and to the assumption that reality is one' (KE, 168). The poem actually concludes on this note, seeking the 'complete simplicity' in which 'the fire and the rose are one' (CPP, 198). But the poem's assertion in its last section that 'We shall not cease from exploration' echoes the dissertation's conclusion 'that the world of practical verification has no definite frontiers, and that it is the business of philosophy to keep the frontiers open' (CPP, 197; KE, 169). As always, the irresistible impulse towards the absolute is resisted by the suspicion that there is no such absolute for the exploration to discover.

In the interference of the poem's mystical and pragmatic moments with each other, Eliot approaches once more – this time in a different medium – the awareness of 1916 that 'the line between the experienced, or the given, and the constructed can nowhere be clearly drawn' (KE, 18). In the words of the poet in 'East Coker',

> There is, it seems to us,
> At best, only a limited value
> In the knowledge derived from experience.
> The knowledge imposes a pattern, and falsifies,
> For the pattern is new in every moment
> And every moment is a new and shocking
> Valuation of all we have been.   (CPP, 179)

The key words in the dissertation's title – knowledge and experience – reappear here as though to recall the advice of 1916: 'think of the world not as ready made . . . but as constructed, or constructing itself . . . at every moment, and never more than an approximate construction, a construction essentially practical in its nature' (KE, 136).

In the end, by tracing the 1948 observation that 'All human faculties when pushed to their depths end in mysticism' back to the dissertation's reservations about the mystical presupposition of all metaphysical speculation, and by following Eliot's opposition of Bergson and James through the dissertation's opposition of subject-side and object-side points of view and through *Four Quartets'* opposition of mystical and pragmatic moments, we can see that *Four Quartets* does not locate reality exclusively in what are traditionally identified as its mystical moments. The poem also demonstrates the dissertation's pragmatic awareness that ultimate reality is in fact a practical construction. But despite the disagreement between the Christian Eliot and the pragmatic

Eliot – the former convinced that there is an objective truth and reality, the latter convinced that there is only subjective truth and reality – the agreement of Eliot the word-bound mystic and Eliot the world-bound pragmatist that the expression of an objective truth and reality is not possible in language ironically leads to the same conclusion: we must construct something upon which to rejoice.

References

Bergson, Henri, *Time and Free Will: An Essay on the Immediate Data of Consciousness*, trans. F.L. Pogson, 1889; rpt London, Allen & Unwin, 1921.

———, *Creative Evolution*, trans. Arthur Mitchell, 1907; rpt London, Macmillan, 1911.

Bergsten, Staffan, *Time and Eternity: A Study in the Structure and Symbolism of* Four Quartets, Stockholm, Svenska Bokförlaget, 1960.

Bradley, F.H., *Appearance and Reality: A Metaphysical Essay.* 2nd. edn 1893; rpt Oxford, Oxford University Press, 1930.

Castro, Françoise de, 'Interview with T.S. Eliot' (1948), Hayward Bequest, King's College Library, Cambridge.

Davidson, Harriet, *T.S. Eliot and Hermeneutics*, Baton Rouge, Louisiana State University Press, 1985.

Dobrée, Bonamy, 'T.S. Eliot: A Personal Reminiscence', in Allen Tate, ed., *T.S. Eliot: The Man and His Work*, London, Chatto & Windus, 1966, 65–88.

Douglass, Paul, *Bergson, Eliot and American Literature*, Lexington, University Press of Kentucky, 1986.

Eliot, T.S., 'A Paper on Bergson' (1911[?]), Eliot Collection, Houghton Library, Harvard University.

———, 'The Relation Between Politics and Metaphysics' (1914), Eliot Collection, Houghton Library, Harvard University.

———, 'A Prediction in Regard to Three English Authors', *Vanity Fair* 21.6 (February 1924), 29, 98.

———, *The Clark Lectures: Lectures on the Metaphysical Poetry of the Seventeenth Century*, Eliot Collection, Houghton Library, Harvard University.

Gardner, Helen, *The Art of T.S. Eliot*, 2nd edn 1959; rpt London, Faber & Faber, 1968.

James, William, *Pragmatism*, 1907; rpt Cambridge, Mass., Harvard University Press, 1975.

Katz, Stephen, ed., *Mysticism and Philosophical Analysis*, London, Sheldon Press, 1978.

Kearns, Cleo McNelly, *T.S. Eliot and Indic Traditions: A Study in Poetry and Belief*, Cambridge, Cambridge Univeristy Press, 1987.

Michaels, Walter Benn, 'Philosophy in Kinkanja: Eliot's Pragmatism', *Glyph* 8 (1981), 170–202.

Rorty, Richard, *The Consequences of Pragmatism*, Minneapolis, University of Minnesota Press, 1982.

Russell, Bertrand, *The Autobiography of Bertrand Russell*, London, Allen & Unwin, 1967.

Sharp, Sister Corona, '"The Unheard Music": T.S. Eliot's *Four Quartets* and St. John of the Cross', *University of Toronto Quarterly*, 51.3 (1982), 264–78.

Smidt, Kristian, *Poetry and Belief in the Work of T.S. Eliot*, 1949; rpt London, Routledge & Kegan Paul, 1961.

Smith, Grover, *T.S. Eliot's Poetry and Plays: A Study in Sources and Meaning*, Chicago, University of Chicago Press, 1956.

Sri, P.S., *T.S. Eliot, Vedanta and Buddhism*, Vancouver, University of British Columbia Press, 1985.

(For support during the writing of this essay, I am indebted to the Webster Fellowship Programme of Queen's University at Kingston and to the Postdoctoral Fellowship Programme of the Social Sciences and Humanities Research Council of Canada.)

7

Negative Theology and Literary Discourse in Four Quartets: A Derridean Reading
Cleo McNelly Kearns

INTRODUCTION

Eliot's poetry, it is commonly said, is deeply influenced by what is known in theology as the apophatic tradition and in mystagogia or spiritual training as the 'negative way'. Negative theology, as usually defined, assumes that any attempt to specify the characteristics or mode of being of the divine is not simply inadequate, which would be a truism, but essentially misleading and even false, because divinity is so far beyond the categories of human understanding and ontology as to make them a hindrance rather than a help to its apprehension. 'If anyone thinks that he has known God,' Meister Eckhart teaches his disciples, 'even if he did know something, he did not know God.' Eliot puts the case with greater urbanity, but he makes a similar point:

> In order to arrive at what you do not know
>   You must go by a way which is the way of ignorance.
> In order to possess what you do not possess
>   You must go by the way of dispossession.
>
> ('East Coker' III; CPP, 181)

For Eliot, however, who was a rigorous and lifelong sceptic in the sense that Jeffrey Perl has eloquently articulated in his *Skepticism and Modern Enmity* (1989), every direct statement requires an immediate counterstatement, lest it be reified into an absolute and lose its purchase on reality. Hence Eliot is quick to juxtapose his invitations to the negative way with equally pressing invitations to a positive alternative. Over and against the heart of darkness, we have then the 'heart of light'; over and against the way back, the way forward ('East Coker' III). Indeed, it would be quite possible to imagine *Four Quartets* as claiming, in direct opposition to the apophatic passage first cited, that 'to know what you already know

/ You must go by a way which is the way of knowledge', and that
'to possess what you already possess / You must go by a way of
repossession'. Some such stance is implied, surely, in the famous
peroration of 'Little Gidding':

> We shall not cease from exploration
> And the end of all our exploring
> Will be to arrive where we started
> And know the place for the first time.   (CPP, 197)

This juxtaposition of negative and positive modes is in fact
quite characteristic of much that goes by the name of apophatic
theology or the negative way in the Judaeo-Christian tradition,
and of much of Eliot's poetry as well. Sometimes this collocation
even takes the form of a direct statement of identity. Heraclitus
said it long ago: 'the way down *is* the way up'. Eliot takes this
aphorism as the epigraph to 'Burnt Norton', and it stands over all
four of the quartets as both a mandate and a description, pointing
to their curious attempt at a double and very nearly simultaneous
exploration of these apparently opposed directions. 'This is the one
way', 'Burnt Norton' says of the negative path, 'and the other /
Is the same'. (III; CPP, 174)

Turning to the poetic as well as the philosophical implications
of these two ways, we can see at once some of the problems their
collocation raises. Among other things, both in the several religious
traditions on which Eliot draws, and in his poetic tradition as well,
the way down is the way of asceticism and abstraction, while the
way up is the way of erotic experience, metaphor and imagination.
The negative way seeks, through a process of progressive elimi-
nation of the partial, to attain a posture of complete humility and
self-erasure before the void; the positive way calls for escalating
degrees of recognition and self-affirmation, proceeding from like
to like to a place commensurate with contemplation of the whole.
Likewise, the negative way, or way down, seeks to move the
consciousness beyond the body and its images; while the affirmative
way, or way up, seeks to move it more deeply *into* them, and with
more and more degrees of conscious spiritual awareness. The
problem of their combination within a single discourse has haunted
gospel narrative, Biblical theology, and, in a more extended sense,
Western poetic discourse for many centuries.

The consequences for poetry of this combination of the way up and the way down are especially difficult to work out. For negative theology, at least as commonly understood, is not only apophatic, but apophantic; it involves a purgation not only of desires, but of phantasms, images and sounds, and of overinvestment in human emotions, actions and relationships as well. 'I no longer strive to strive towards such things,' says the penitential voice of *Ash-Wednesday*, thinking of 'art' and 'scope' and the haunting sensory impressions and emotional tonalities the poem seeks in vain to move beyond (CPP, 89). Positive theology, on the other hand, not only affirms but cultivates these phantasms, actions and relationships as an integral part of the approach to the divine. Each implies an entirely different rhetoric, as well as a different spiritual, mental and emotional stance, and each is equally subject to imitation, travesty and reduction to the merely literary in transmission.

In what way, then, are these paths 'the same'? How can there be a poetics that reconciles them or, better yet, actually demonstrates what the critical Buddhist and later Zen traditions tried to indicate: their secret alliance with each other? The difficulties involved here are not simply those of facile self-contradiction. They also lie more deeply in the danger of what Yeats called *vacillation*, a distracting wavering between radically different points of view, modes of activity, attitudes toward the world and poetic values which, though their goal is the same, cannot be combined short of that goal, lest one be misappropriated as an avoidance or denial of the other.

This vacillation is dramatized in *Ash-Wednesday*, which explores its uneasy implications for the fate of poetry as well as for the fate of the soul. The poem begins in renunciation of the quest for the 'blessed face', and with a corresponding evocation of the negative way and a commitment to follow it. Then it deviates wildly from this commitment into a positive garden of images. Aware of the ambivalence that threatens the integrity of the initial project, the narrator fears he will end up among those who 'affirm before the world and deny between the rocks' (V; CPP, 97). His fear here is not the usual fear of the committed, that one will deny in public what one believes in private, but its reverse, the fear that one will affirm before the microphone what one questions in the study, and that in either case one's negations will be as shallow as one's affirmations.

This vacillation or ambivalence seems to shift as the poem moves on to a direct formulation and apparent endorsement of the positive way, especially as opposed to the simulacrum of the negative experienced in psychological depression or anxiety. 'Where shall the word be found, where will the word / Resound?' *Ash-Wednesday* V asks, seeking the conditions for a genuine positive *or* negative way. Certainly not in the travesties of negation created by mere worldly disillusion:

> For those who walk in darkness
> Both in the day time and in the night time
> The right time and the right place are not here
> No place of grace for those who avoid the face
> No time to rejoice for those who walk among noise and deny
>   the voice   (CPP, 96)

There is a double negative in these lines, for they define not what is, but what is *not* the true negative way, and prefer to it, if only as a *pis aller*, a positive affirmation which has at least the merit of avoiding triviality. The images, the affirmations, the 'face' and 'voice' which then move in to accompany this reversal of ways, the 'blessed sister' who incarnates the fountain and the garden and the forward movement toward light are certainly better than the anomic disillusion of the fashionable cynic. And yet, as we later read, it is only the '*weak* spirit' that 'quickens to rebel' by affirming 'the bent golden-rod and the lost sea smell', and only the '*blind* eye' that creates 'the empty forms between the ivory gates' (VI; CPP, 98: *emphasis added*). We are left in a state of uneasy suspension between the negative way to which the poem first commits itself and the positive one it ambivalently affirms in order to attain its resolution.

To overcome that vacillation, and to write a stronger poem in its stead, without sacrificing the energy to be gained from a move beyond the easier reductions of negativity, is the project of *Four Quartets*. This project requires the collocation of opposing negative and affirmative ways not in a mode of ambivalence and vacillation but in a mode of wisdom, a wisdom based on consistency and rigour, rather than indecision, and one which will not allow itself to be seduced into a one-sided commitment to affirmation even to achieve poetic power or dramatic resolution. But the practical and theoretical questions for poetry and for mystagogia alike raised by this project are acute. It is all very well to call negative and positive paths 'the same', but it remains an open question whether one person can pursue both at the same time and whether one poem can incorporate both effectively.

PRAYER AND RHETORIC IN DERRIDA'S NEGATIVE WAY

The question behind *Four Quartets*, then, is first to what extent collocations between negative and positive ways, between apophatic and analogic discourse, enact avoidance, vacillation, self-contradiction and bad faith, and to what extent they are genuine mediations; and second, their effect on the poetics of the text. Eliot's resources for addressing these questions came not only from traditions other than classical within Western discourse, but also from his understanding of Hindu and Buddhist points of view. In the work of Nagarjuna in particular, Buddhism offered a sophisticated attempt to develop a position which would call into question both every affirmation with respect to the divine and every negation as well. Nagarjuna evolved a system of logic which has been compared not only to that of F.H. Bradley, subject of Eliot's dissertation, but to Derridean deconstruction as well (see Magliola, Kearns and Jackson). Charged with the task of inculcating or creating the conditions for a very subtle awareness of *sunyata*, or the positively charged void in his teaching, Nagarjuna developed a fourfold logic which may be codified in the form 'not this, not that; not *not* this, not *not* that'. The influence of this kind of logic on Eliot as he glimpsed it in his philosophical studies was profound (see Kearns and Perl).

Easy to caricature – a problem to which we shall return – this logic of double negation has in fact a classic apophatic and mystagogic function; it exists not as pure speculation, but within a context of meditative practice and spiritual teaching. Eliot was well aware of that context, and understood perfectly the difference between honing the mind on this logic and learning to live by it in its original cultural and discursive context. The first he attempted; the second he forewent. He became neither a Buddhist nor a religious philosopher, but chose instead to be a Christian and a poet, and this choice has important consequences for understanding the exact resonance of the negative way in his work, as well as for the important distinctions between philosophical, theological and literary discourse it entails. Nevertheless, without some mention

of Buddhist and Hindu apophatic thought, often so much more
rigorous than its cousins in the West, we cannot begin to trace
the Eliotic 'way down', much less understand how it may be,
simultaneously, a 'way up'.

In order to establish even more extended parameters for
discussing this question and its bearing on the poem, we need,
however, a far more refined sense of the way apophatic discourse
works than any adduced so far, even in Eliot's Indic sources.
We will find them, I suggest, in a semi-autobiographical or at
least auto-exegetical piece by Jacques Derrida, 'How to Avoid
Speaking: Denials'. In this article, Derrida replies to the question
of whether his work lies within the mode of negative theology
with a highly qualified *no*. The qualifications, however, are *so* high,
and involve such fine distinctions as to be (mis)interpretable, as
Derrida himself is the first to admit, as a kind of *yes*. How, after
all, as Derrida points out, given his own presuppositions about
textuality, could he stop his texts from being read in this light?
In the name of what external authority? The resulting dilemma is
Kafkaesque, and Derrida's wry tone and aphoristic style testify to
his sense of a position not dissimilar to Kafka's. As Derrida points
out, again rather wryly, of his own case, 'Those who would like to
consider "deconstruction" a symptom of postmodern nihilism could
indeed, if they wished, recognize in it the last testimony – not to
say martyrdom – of faith in the present *fin de siècle*. This reading
will always be possible. Who could prohibit it? In the name of
what?' (1986, 7; all further page references are to this essay unless
otherwise noted)

The first thing to note about negative theology, Derrida points
out, and indeed about any form of apophatic discourse, even
philosophical discourse that tries to avoid theological presup-
positions altogether, is that, while extremely various, its many
manifestations share a common distrust of language in general
and of propositional language in particular (4). There are good
reasons for this distrust, for any decision to express the 'way down'
in propositional or conceptual language, the language of definition,
naming and semantic attribution, has, almost inescapably, already
a positive or affirmative dimension, an implicit 'way up' which
threatens to undercut it. As Kafka remarked, 'doing the negative
thing is imposed on us, an addition; the positive thing is given
to us from the start' (36–7). It is extremely hard to defeat or

circumvent this affirmative dimension of speaking long enough to explore even the possibility of a deeper wisdom or a darker point of view.

Apophatic discourse has this positive dimension in part simply because it is already a decision to speak, and the act of speaking, especially when it takes on the particular intensity of so many apophatic texts, presumes both a promise, an injunction for which the text wishes to be responsible, and a destination, an interlocutor whom it wishes to address. Speech always works, to put it in Eliot's rather different terms, from within the parameters of an earlier 'Annunciation' or at least 'annunciation' ('The Dry Salvages' II). It is generated by 'the drawing of this Love and the voice of this Calling', a force which, whether theologically or textually construed, whether put in capitals or lower case, always precedes and occasions it (CPP, 197). To speak, then, implies in its very way of working a certain degree of affirmation, the call of an other and the responsibility to an other, whether that call emanates from the divine origin, 'the Word', or simply a prior text, 'the word'. Furthermore, speech always carries within itself some trace or mark of that call and responsibility. As Derrida insists, 'The most negative discourse, even beyond all nihilisms and negative dialectics, preserves a trace of the other. A trace of an event older than it or of a "taking place" to come' (28).

As Patricia Miller Cox has pointed out, the term 'trace', when used in this way, is closely paralleled to Plotinus' use of the term *ichnos* in a theological context (cited in Jackson, 460), and indeed Derrida himself translates *ichnos* as 'trace' when it occurs in the *Divine Names*. This trace of the promise of Edenic language is both indicated and distanced in all the little words and phrases that seek to protect negation from simple-minded or logocentric affirmation in apophatic discourse, words like 'as if' (*quasi*) or 'without' (*sans*) or phrases like 'let me put it this way'. These words and phrases help to postpone affirmation and to destabilize the propositional nature of language, while at the same time they point ahead or behind to the possibility of these fulfilments. Just so the little 'say that' in the lines from 'Burnt Norton' ('say that the end precedes the beginning') protects the quasi-quality of the discourse, so that we are less prone to take its paradoxes at a literal level, where they will be

easily reducible to nonsense, as if the spirit or meaning had
to work in the same way as the grammar of the sentence. At
the same time it permits a certain kind of liaison between spirit
and word, a transference which is attenuated but not entirely
broken.

The 'trace of the other', this point of transference between
opposite or at least incommensurate discourses, may be viewed
as theological, ontological, material or even what Derrida would
call *grammatological*. Whether it is permanent or momentary, a
matter of truth or textuality, is secondary, for Derrida, to the
recognition that it is *already always in place*. 'Language has started
without us, in us and before us', Derrida insists; 'this is what
theology calls God' (29). Overlaying the marks of the trace,
however, and often obscuring them, is precisely the question
of text or Text, word or Word. To put this differently, the
term 'God' even in the apophatic sentence 'God is not *x*' may
always be read in two ways. It may point either to 'God' as a
perhaps misleading word for the trace or *différance* that is both
the limit, the particular occasion and the contradictory *aporia*
which conditions the possibility of speaking at all, or to God
as the certainly misleading self-presence of what we might call
logos-talk. We tend, as a culture, to lean heavily on the second,
metaphysical, theologizing and universalizing reading, even in texts
which seek to subvert that tendency.

Recognition of the trace, Derrida insists, leads us in the con-
trary direction, not to the God of the philosopher-theologians,
or even to that direct and congruent reversal of the usual
understanding of his image so often implied in apophatic theo-
logy, but on the contrary to what he calls a *différance* which,
although it may be said, for purposes of argument, to generate
language and meaning in some way, is what we might call
infinitely finite, a singular or particular, and cannot be thought
of in terms of ultimate or absolute cause or origin in any sense
(29; cf. also Derrida 1973). *Différance* and its traces are not,
then, at least as far as Derrida is concerned, to be baptized
or classicized, much less to be regarded as revelation in any
form. The term 'God', if speakable at all, is speakable only in
this differential, deconstructive sense. As Derrida says, thinking
of such negative theologians as pseudo-Dionysus and Meister
Eckhart:

> The power of speaking and of speaking well of God already
> proceeds from God. . . . This is what God's name always names,
> before or beyond other names; the trace of the singular event
> that will have rendered speech possible even before it turns
> itself back toward – in order to respond to – this first or last
> reference.
>
> (28)

Negative theology shares with deconstruction the desire to break
or destabilize the logocentric, theologizing usage and return to that
other usage of the signifier 'God' which is more closely associated
with trace, call, promise and recognition of otherness. Though
deconstruction, unlike negative theology, focuses primarily on the
exposure of this trace, it may find in negative theology a discourse
more open to such exposure, a discourse in which, so to speak, half
its work, the work of destabilizing the connection to metaphysics,
has been done, though the other half, the work of revealing the
trace and its particularity and singularity, remains as yet untouched.
The term 'God' may have, then, in deconstruction, even though
veering inevitably into undue proximity with the term *logos* or
rational significance, a certain rough linguistic, mystagogic and
even pedagogic function, if only in drawing attention to the
problem of the trace.

Faced, however, with the task of defeating or circumventing
cultural and conceptual links between affirmative *logos* and the
divine, both the negative theologian, who wishes to avoid the
name of God lest he or she limit that divine, and the apophatic
philosopher, who wishes to bracket, suspend, or question that
name for other or different reasons, are alike in a difficult position.
The strong logocentric tendency of the culture works against the
task, but so does the problem of defining the 'other' that is the
source of promise, call or responsibility. For as soon as that 'other'
is posited, even in negative terms, even as *trace*, or *différance*, or the
some three dozen substitutions for those terms Vincent Leitch has
counted in Derrida's work (43), it begins to take on a substantive
and universalistic character. Not only is metaphysics a sovereign
ghost hard to expel from the republic of letters, but the trace or
différance always tends to present itself as a classic universal, rather
than as that particularity or singularity that both Derrida and the
Judaeo-Christian tradition have always asserted – Jerusalem against

Athens – that it must be.

Furthermore, to deny this universalizing or logocentric signifi-
cance may always be read as no more than a psychological defence
or an unduly baroque and pretentious way of speaking. Nothing,
it might seem, can be done in either the apophatic mode or
the deconstructive mode, given the presence of an ineluctable
metaphysical tendency which will always pre-empt the empty
space of negation with the fulness of its logos-bearing word, or turn
negation itself into a universal sign with an automatic reference or
mechanical and predictable discursive function. Hence the very
structure of the act of speaking of divine things itself dictates that
almost any such speaker will end up writing, or appearing to write,
a positive theology at base.

Given this difficulty, apophatic discourse must always tend to
seem a rather literary and supplemental turn, an 'addition', as
Kafka calls it, a rhetorical stunt or troping on more straightforward
ways of speaking. It seems to call less for deconstruction than
for debunking, so that we can all proceed more expeditiously,
if only in the direction of what William James liked to call, with
appropriate banality, 'the religion of healthy-mindedness'. And this
debunking, Derrida points out, will not be hard to do, for nothing
is such an easy mark for caricature, for travesty, for imitation as a
fully-developed apophatic position. It is indeed extremely difficult
to keep epigones and parodists alike from reducing it to a mere
mechanics of reiteration. 'For those who have nothing to say or
don't want to know anything, it is always easy to mimic the
technique of negative theology', Derrida writes acerbically (5),
thinking, no doubt, of examples close to home. As 'Burnt Norton'
says, it is the 'Word in the desert' which is most attacked by the
temptations of parody and reduction, the 'crying shadow in the
funeral dance' and the 'loud lament of the disconsolate chimera'
(V; CPP, 175).

Over this uncomfortable rhetorical position of negative theo-
logy, moreover, hangs a certain darker cloud, the charge of
deliberate mystification and double-dealing. After all, to make the
point in a slightly different way, the root meaning of *apophasis* is a
rhetorical device 'whereby', the OED tells us, citing a particularly
nicely turned definition, 'we deny that we say or do that which
we especially say or do'. Eliot comes close to this point in 'Burnt
Norton' II when he enjoins us, with regard to the 'still point', *not*

to call it 'fixity', for he uses the very word he seeks to forbid, a word which is, furthermore, abstract and vaguely unpleasant enough to induce, at least at the poetic level, precisely the momentary sense of stasis he wishes to avoid (CPP, 173).

Negative theology may seem to take comfort with respect to this critique in the equal and opposite discomfitures of its cousin and rival, positive theology or metaphysics. These are great, and they come from other inherent tendencies of language which we have yet to canvass here, but of which Derrida has written often under the rubric of deconstruction. These include not only the 'becoming theological' of discourse, its uneasy and often unfounded claim to include terms which are identical with their referents, but its countervailing heterodoxy and materiality as well. For, as it has been Derrida's specific calling to show, speech and language indicate not only a certain faith in the divine promise which underwrites words, but the recognition that this faith is never quite fully realized as well. 'One has only learnt to get the better of words', as Eliot puts it, 'For the thing one no longer has to say, or the way in which / One is no longer disposed to say it', and 'last year's words belong to last year's language / And next year's words await another voice' (CPP, 182, 194). There can be no full unmediated presence of word and thing on the same page, no moment of complete logocentric redemption – at least within time – but only a pointing forward or backward to an elsewhere in which they might possibly intersect. It is perhaps for this reason that Eliot almost never uses either the name of God or even that of Christ in either his poetry or his prose.

Still, negative theology cannot entirely rejoice in this discountenancing of a rival, for, abstracted from praxis, it is subjected to the same linguistic deflation as the positive way. After all, it too relies on language which is not only material and historically situated, but often heterodox to its intentions, and it is, as already pointed out, especially susceptible to that travesty and appropriation by the other which language necessitates to communicate at all. It is not simply, as *Four Quartets* puts it, that 'Words strain, / Crack and sometimes break' under their burdens, or that every effort to use them is a 'raid on the inarticulate / With shabby equipment always deteriorating' (CPP, 175, 182), but that this breakdown is *essential to their ability to function as language at all*. There is no way for either positive or negative ways to claim immunity from this rhetorical danger, for the danger is imbricated in the very medium of expression of them both. As Derrida puts its succinctly, 'the risk is inscribed in the structure of the mark' (5).

In traditional negative theology, Derrida goes on to show – theology that, with Dionysus or Eckhart, takes place within an explicit context of faith and praxis and therefore wishes to work toward a certain hyper- rather than anti-essentiality, a God-beyond-God – there are ways of mitigating this risk, though it can never be completely eliminated. There is first the establishment of what Derrida calls a kind of 'esoteric sociality', a place apart, a restricted zone, a cultic space which is structured around a secret or supposed secret which must be defended against reduction, misrepresentation and blasphemy. (For a further exploration of the political, literary and philosophical implications of this construct, see Kenneth Burke). Secondly, there is the insistence on some kind of context of praxis, which is often indicated within the text by the inclusion of prayers, invocations and apostrophes or direct addresses to students, disciples or readers. These make at least an implicit connection between negative and affirmative modes. As Derrida says, speaking of prayer in particular:

> Between the theological movement that speaks and is inspired by the Good beyond Being or by light and the apophatic path that exceeds the Good, there is necessarily a passage, a transfer, a translation. An experience must yet guide the apophasis toward excellence, not allow it to say just anything, and prevent it from manipulating its negations like empty and purely mechanical phrases. This experience is that of prayer. (41)

Sometimes the prayer, the invocation and the apostrophe to the disciple or reader are woven into the text so closely as to blend curiously with one another. 'O Trinity beyond being,' Dionysus begins in the example Derrida analyses most closely, 'direct us to the mystical summits more than unknown and beyond light . . . This is my prayer. And you, dear Timothy, be earnest in the exercise of mystical contemplation.' (47). As Derrida points out, Dionysus here prays in a way we take first as direct discourse, made on his own behalf and recorded at what, for us, is some past moment in time. But he then makes of this prayer a quotation, and part of an apostrophe to his student, Timothy. By writing both his prayer and his apostrophe down, furthermore, he includes us, his potential readers, in the address, even further situating the text in a concrete situation, the here and now in which we read.

The prayer which seeks to protect negative theology against nihilistic or rhetorical reduction, then, becomes not or not just a pure, private, unique, spontaneous and unrepeatable petition or doxology to an unknowable God, but a form of speaking and writing designed to be heard, read and reiterated by an interlocutor, and beyond even that interlocutor by a wider audience, a multiplicity of addressees, whom it wishes to solicit. As Derrida concludes his analysis of Dionysus' text:

> It is addressed to the best reader, to the reader who ought to allow himself to be led to become better, to us who presently believe we are reading this text. Not to us as we are, at present, but as we would have to be, in our souls, if we read this text as it ought to be read, aright, in the proper direction, correctly: according to its prayer and its promise. He also prays – that we read correctly, in accordance with his prayer. None of this would be possible without the possibility of quotation (more generally of repetition) and of an apostrophe that allows one to speak to several people at once. (48)

This 'multiplicity of addressees' is a necessary condition of the injunction or call to propagation of the faith, the vocation of the promise, that founds negative discourse in a practical context. The apostrophe to Timothy and to us, his future readers, signals for Derrida in Dionysus' text a 'pedagogy which is also a mystagogy and a psychagogy', one in which 'the gesture of leading or directing the psyche of the other passes through apostrophe' (48).

Here, however, we come full circle, for the reiterability of speech and writing, their capacity for self-citation and quotation, for indirect as well as direct discourse, are problematic as well as protective. They 'bend' – the term is Derrida's – the pure spontaneous interior utterance or prayer toward exteriority, and hence toward the possibility of reduction, travesty and even blasphemy. Hence the double bind of the esoteric sociality of negative discourse, that it must open itself to repetition and mimicry in contexts inappropriate or heterodox to its original intentions in order to fulfil those intentions at all.

For those, moreover, who receive negative theology in those heterodox contexts, and who wish to bracket, question or suspend the divine promise and vocation that founds it, these strategies of prayer and apostrophe or address are not only to be avoided on principle, but are self-defeating in essence. Without such protections, however, their work is especially susceptible to reduction to a form of mere denial, nihilism or self-indulgent literariness. Such has often been the fate, for example, of both Nietzsche and Heidegger, not to mention that of Derrida himself. As Derrida puts it:

> Without the divine promise which is also an injunction, the power of these *synthemata* would be merely conventional rhetoric, poetry, fine arts, perhaps literature. It would suffice to doubt this promise or transgress this injunction in order to see an opening – and also a closing upon itself – of the field of rhetoricity or even of literariness, the lawless law of fiction. (23)

Here we touch bottom and begin moving up, however, for the risk of the reduction of the negative way to nihilism or rhetoricity also creates, Derrida insists, not simply a problem but also an opportunity. When the operations of the 'lawless law' of literature inherent in apophatic discourse begin to become clear, they also serve to draw attention to the material, heterodox, unfinished quality of texts, to their contexts, their historical situation, and their matrix in the here and now, as well as to their reiterability, their propensity for mechanization and for travesty. Hence, the suspension of the divine promise and the release of the 'lawless law' of literature close a speculative, heavenly, other-worldly place for apophasis, but open up a practical, finite and this-worldly one which can and must, provisionally at least, be maintained. For after all, as Bradley put it long ago, only in this finite this-worldly place can Goodness and Beauty *in any place* be realized. The sheer rhetoric of apophasis, then, for all its faults and problems, does help to work against a relentless 'becoming theological' of language to inaugurate what we might call a 'becoming material', or, to reinstate theology with a difference, a *becoming incarnational* of language. In this sense, the 'risk . . . inscribed in the structure of the mark', which we may call the risk of sheer literary linguisticality, is in fact, as Derrida puts it – also, perhaps even for theology proper – a 'piece of luck' (5).

Even this 'piece of luck', however, can't fully or automatically isolate the negative way from the trace of the affirmative one and vice versa. Language, after all, is and remains *both* inherently theological and inherently material and it bears the trace or mark or cross of both. This double dimension of linguisticality, to affirm or negate either aspect of which generates the twin illusions of logocentrism on the one hand or logophobia on the other, creates the space, the place, the occasion, the intersection at which negative and positive ways may meet and cross. It also provides the medium for understanding the identity in difference of both. The resulting tension, so easily called duplicity, leads again to a Kafkaesque situation, which we may read as tragedy or comedy depending on our bent.

PRAYER AND RHETORIC IN THE NEGATIVE WAY OF 'FOUR QUARTETS'

To link Eliot's exploration of the negative way in *Four Quartets* with Derrida's 'How to Avoid Speaking' may seem an indulgence in one of those metaphysical conceits by which, as Samuel Johnson put it with some distaste, 'the most heterogeneous ideas are yoked by violence together'. The Derrida/Eliot parallel has, however, been suggested, though not fully explored, by several critics (notably Davidson, Perl and Brooker and Bentley), and it certainly takes on plausibility when we consider both the common lineage of these figures in late idealist and pragmatist philosophy and the remarkable parallels, and in some cases profound interactions, between their philosophical positions and those of certain Buddhist schools. If nothing else, moreover, Derrida and Eliot share a common literary fate, for each has attained a certain fame or notoriety on the basis of views which often vary from simple misunderstanding to outright travesty of their work, and yet each must on principle refrain as much as possible from explicit dissociation from those misreadings, for each believes that a certain vulnerability to them is intrinsic in the decision to speak or write in a certain manner in the first place.

The real question, however, is not whether Derrida and Eliot thought alike or experienced the same problems, though a case can be made that in many ways they did. (Indeed a great deal of Derrida's *oeuvre* might be read as an attempt to specify 'what was believed in as the most reliable − / And therefore the fittest for renunciation' [CPP, 185].) Rather, it is to what extent the texts of one can illuminate those of the other. In the case of *Four Quartets* and 'How to Avoid Speaking' the potential for this illumination is

great, for with the Derridean analysis of negative theology in mind
we can understand better not only the curious, oblique discourse
of *Four Quartets* – part prayer, part meditation, part exercise in the
romantic sublime – but also that rhetoricity or literariness which
threatens both to fulfil and to defeat its purposes and with which it
seeks an accommodation that will violate neither the status of the
text as poetry nor its function as spiritual training. The juxtaposition
of Derrida's essay on negative theology and Eliot's poem of the
negative way may then clarify the way of working and the potential
wisdom of both.

Before turning to the poem, however, let me say that the
question as to whether Eliot's general point of view belongs to
what Derrida calls the hyper-essential and theological tradition of
the negative way or, with Heidegger, to the more radical and
philosophical anti-essentialist camp is one I wish, in this context
at least, assiduously to avoid. If forced to adjudicate this issue, I
would probably argue along lines already laid down by Harriet
Davidson and Jeffrey Perl that, in philosophy at least, he was
more radically negative and anti-essentialist than hyper-essential in
tendency. This question, however, is not so easily broached, much
less settled, for it entails, among other things, a reconsideration of
the whole distinction between theology and philosophy implicit in
its terms, not to mention the vexed issue, still under sharp debate,
of whether or not a genuine Judaeo-Christian faith – which Eliot
obviously endorsed – can be collocated with a radically apophatic
position in any way at all.

(A rough canvass of positions on this issue will indicate its com-
plexity: Heidegger, it is clear, thought no such collocation possible;
the philosophers and theologians John Caputo, Robert Magliola
and Joseph O'Leary, *inter alia*, disagree. The contributors to Henry
Ruf's useful anthology *Religion, Ontotheology and Deconstruction* fall
out on several sides of the debate and help clarify what is at stake.
Derrida, as we have seen, does not know what would prevent a
form of theologically affirmative deconstruction, though he himself
would not be comfortable with that reading of his work. He
also admits, however, that Heidegger's critique of ontotheology,
which he in general follows and even attempts to exceed, does
not meet all the relevant cases of Christian, not to mention Islamic
and Judaic, theological discourse [1982, x]. More work on these
matters clearly lies ahead.)

Wherever Eliot would have fallen out or did fall out in this debate, however, there is no doubt about his full exploitation of both the 'risk' and the 'piece of luck' inherent in apophatic discourse in the 'structure of the mark'. Indeed, *Four Quartets* is one of the most sustained meditations in our tradition on the problems of language and rhetoricity as they bear on practical and poetic expressions of the negative and positive ways alike. The poem makes, in the course of that meditation, full and careful use of the tropes and strategies of place, prayer and apostrophe that seek to protect the 'way down' against reduction, and full use, as well, of that destabilization of propositional syntax, whether negative or affirmative, which, as Derrida puts it, 'deconstructs grammatical anthropomorphism'. At the same time, it moves into the space created by the 'lawless law' of literature, a space in which any verbal or textual construct may participate at once both in committed praxis and in sheer rhetorical play.

This 'lawless law' of literature in *Four Quartets* entails not only the problem of the relationship of writing and iterability to the immediacy and efficacy of prayer and praxis, but the ease with which the negative way may be reduced to a protocol and a travesty as well. It is, after all, as we have seen, precisely the problem of the word in the desert, that negative word so easily attacked and mimicked by the 'loud lament' of every passing 'disconsolate chimera'. Eliot is well aware of the rhetorical irritations attendant on expressions of the negative way. Part of his way of dealing with them is simply to insist. 'You say I am repeating / Something I have said before', he says, and answers, with self-reflexive irony:

> I shall say it again.
> Shall I say it again? In order to arrive there,
> To arrive where you are, to get from where you are not,
> You must go by a way wherein there is no ecstasy.
>
> (CPP, 181)

Such insistences are one way of dealing with the problem. Another way is to attempt to develop, within the parameters of the poem itself, the discernment that will allow a reader to tell the difference between approximations of genuine discourse and its mimetic or mechanical travesties and simulacra. Eliot tries for this purpose the extremely risky strategy of allowing his poem to parody its own most obvious moments of lyric intensity. The sublime style with which, in *Four Quartets*, opposites like 'garlic and sapphires in the mud' are 'reconciled among the stars', or 'comets' and 'Leonids' bring the world to destruction (CPP, 172, 178) makes for a strong effect, but these passages are very close, in fact, to parodies of themselves and their symbolist precursors alike. This proximity precipitates a certain deflation, an effect of which the poem goes on, immediately, to make us bitingly aware. 'That was a way of putting it . . .', we learn, 'a periphrastic study in a worn-out poetical fashion' (CPP, 179).

This strategy, however, as Eliot well knows, may backfire, because, just as bad money drives out good, just as contaminated water pollutes the whole well, so in the presence of parody the supposed 'original' it parodies – itself only an approximation and thus not beyond reproof – may be sullied as well. There is no discourse in *Four Quartets*, however elevated, or indeed however self-protectingly flat, prosaic, precise and cautious, that can be guaranteed against reduction to a mocking literary imitation. This potential literary-linguistic inflation and deflation, this theatricality and adulteration inherent in apophatic discourse, is perhaps best displayed and at the same time defeated by 'East Coker''s supremely effective self-debunking similes for the negative way: the moment when the tube train stops too long at a station, and the moment when the scenery is changed between acts on a stage. These similes, which approach the level of metaphysical conceits, call attention to the rhetoricity of negations while at the same time they undercut the potential self-dramatization involved in that rhetoricity. They thus draw the teeth from the critique by holding up for scrutiny that element of self-dramatization which most vitiates the usefulness of apophatic discourse as a mystagogia or spiritual practice.

Take, for instance:

> I said to my soul, be still, and let the dark come upon you
> Which shall be the darkness of God. As, in a theatre,
> The lights are extinguished, for the scene to be changed
> With a hollow rumble of wings, with a movement of darkness
>   on darkness,
> And we know that the hills and the trees, the distant panorama
> And the bold imposing facade are all being rolled away –
>   ('East Coker' III; CPP, 180)

Here the double entendres and mockeries of inflation involved in those rumbling 'wings' and that 'imposing facade' brilliantly display both the duplicity of language, with its lurking and uncontainable potential for theologization and materialization alike, and the sheer rhetoricity to which the negative way is so often prone. Here Eliot deals with the risk 'inherent in the structure of the mark' by displaying and exploiting it to a point that is at once extremely accomplished in terms of poetics and extremely accurate in terms of spiritual practice as well.

Much of *Four Quartets*, as the individual titles of its parts indicate, is concerned with naming or delineating the 'place apart' in which this and other explorations of the negative way can go on without the impositions of propositional language, and hence without the censoring implications either of orthodoxy or of heresy, the need to say *yes* or *no* to the easy affirmations and negations it attempts to move beyond. Is that place to be 'Burnt Norton', with its implications of fire, emptiness, dryness and desert, these co-existing, however, with the hovering reality of that first Eden, site of our strongest visions or memories of presence? Perhaps – or perhaps this 'place' is merely one first-level approximation in a discourse that, like all negative protocols, must proceed by approximations and eliminations, including the relinquishment or renunciation of this first Edenic possibility.

On first reading, we seem to have found the 'place', as the lotos of affirmation rises, with its unbearable reality, out of the 'heart of light' in the dry pool (I). The three later quartets, however, added by way of supplement after Eliot thought he had finished the poem, encourage us, if we have not already done so, to take the invitation to 'descend lower' even more deeply to heart. The 'places' delineated by the following quartets take up this challenge in turn, each pitching its tent further and further from home, further and further on the downward way. Hence we move through the open fields of 'East Coker', across the empty seas of 'The Dry Salvages' and ultimately to 'the world's end', to 'Little Gidding'. This last place apart is a strange place indeed, an underworld meeting point with the spirits of the dead located behind a pigsty, a dull facade and a tombstone.

This meeting point, with its echoes of Aeneas at the gates of Hades and Pound's libation of blood in the *Cantos*, is a place of esoteric sociality *par excellence*, an opening at once literal and figurative – or perhaps neither quite literal nor quite figurative –

into an underworld of which the dark, occluded and even cultic nature has been insufficiently appreciated. It is not, however, a place which requires of its initiates a propositional assent to a series of dogmatic statements or beliefs. Such a test would entail precisely the logocentrism, the secure propositionality, the investment in predicative language, that each quartet in its own way has sought to call into question. No creed is necessary or even possible in this space because 'what you thought you came for' would be 'only a shell, a husk of meaning' in any case. Furthermore, you are not here 'to verify, / Instruct yourself, or inform curiosity', but simply to 'kneel / Where prayer has been valid' (CPP, 192).

The address to 'you' here and the association of the 'place apart' with prayer are the classic marks which seek to protect the negative way from misappropriation, and they are found throughout the quartets in different forms. Their presence, however, as we have already established, does not guarantee what we might call a successful apophasis. First of all, to be thoroughly rigorous, the way down must call even those ghostly indications of affirmation into question. It must open up, at least potentially, to the dark abyss in which neither promise nor destination, neither calling nor prayer, is automatically assumed. If we move back to 'East Coker', we can see Eliot exploring this abyss, moving gingerly further and further out and down 'On the edge of a grimpen, where is no secure foothold' (CPP, 179). 'The Dry Salvages' too speaks of a 'calamitous' situation, an 'unprayable' prayer, the prayer of the 'bone on the beach', prompted by the merely verbal annunciation that parodies, but does not achieve, genuine promise or calling. Here there is no achievement, no end, no telos, but only 'addition', and even the injunction to move downward is sheer noise, a 'clamour' which announces only death (CPP, 185).

That death, however, is at least a limit, and in this limitless wasteland, this infinite entropy of disseminations, a limit is an advance. At least it allows for some sort of ultimatum, for 'the bone's prayer' is a prayer to 'Death its God'. Once fully admitted into the poem, this ultimate negation, properly confronted at last at its most darkly potent, with the capital punishment implied in its capital D, precipitates a reversal that involves less a change of direction than a change of address. There is no answer to the drifting movement of pain except Death, and yet that Death is a kind of answer-without-answer, and as such it offers the first whisper of a new orientation.

Immediately after confronting it, we hear of 'the hardly, barely prayable / Prayer of the one Annunciation' (CPP, 186). These shifts in typography from lower to upper case change the state of play in the poem, for this Annunciation, unlike the one mentioned before, is unique, not subjected to reiteration, not reducible to a series of repetitions. The previous word *annunciation* is a common noun belonging to the discourse of predication and infinitely applicable as signifier to a number of signifieds and situations; the current word *Annunciation* signals a theological event, as much invocation and address as reference, and calling to mind unmistakably a sacred context.

As invocation and address, this Annunciation implies a reinstate-ment of that promise, that calling, that fulfilment of the word as Word which founds discourse. This calling recurs, however, not as a result of avoiding or denying the negative way, but as a result of following it rigorously as far as it will go. (The process is exactly similar to Dante's descent into Hell, which proves, *without change of direction*, to have been the whole time an ascent toward Purgatory at the other pole of the world as well.) The capital D signals that extremity, and the capital A answers to it by beginning its reinscription in the context of promise, calling, prayer, apostrophe and practice. The difference between them, however – between death and Death, annunciation and Annunciation – is only a matter of the tiniest shift, the barest trace, the slightest mark. This trace does not take place at the semantic or conceptual levels; indeed, like the *a* in *différance*, it even remains silent when the poem is read aloud. It remains nonetheless a potent force which changes the values of every statement with which it is brought into proximity.

The promise implied in the 'one Annunciation' is partially redeemed in part IV of 'The Dry Salvages', but only partially, for this section takes the form of a prayer *for* a prayer, a kind of double deferral by which the perhaps not quite fully Marian 'Lady, whose shrine stands on the promontory', is asked to pray, and pray again, and again to 'repeat a prayer' on behalf of others (CPP, 189). She is asked to engage in this repetition in fact on behalf of those who have gone down the negative way to a point where the spoken sound, the clamour and clang of the angelus, the church's perpetual affirmation, cannot reach them.

At this point, perhaps indeed only writing, the silent capital of the word on the page, can make any difference at all. Like the prayers which frame Dionysus' explorations of the negative way, this quasi–Marian prayer can hold only for a moment, if ever, its promise of purity and immediacy as a spontaneous utterance of a believing speaker; seconds later it appears a literary set piece. But perhaps it is no less efficacious for that; perhaps a literary set piece is exactly the *pharmakon*, the medicine or poison for which the sickness onto death of the situation calls.

Prayers and apostrophes throughout *Four Quartets* participate in this movement back and forth from revelation to rhetoricity, from interiority to writing, from secure association with a believing speaker to detached suspension in an indeterminate linguistic space, and they do so sometimes with disconcerting speed. These prayers and apostrophes are often couched, for instance, in a discourse that begins by seeming direct, but that turns out moments later to be quotation or self-citation with the rhetorical needs of a particular audience in view. This is true not only of the Marian prayer just cited, which seems at first a pure lyric break and then a literary *tour de force*, but of other prayers and apostrophes as well. In 'The Dry Salvages' III, for instance, a voice descants:

> O voyagers, O seamen,
> You who come to port, and you whose bodies
> Will suffer the trial and judgement of the sea,
> Or whatever event, this is your real destination.

(CPP, 188)

This anonymous apostrophe seems to greet us from the eternal narrative present, its 'this' a shifter which points to an immediate, universal and fairly ultimate context, 'the time of death', just outside the text. It turns out, however, at least according to the next two lines, to be the discourse, or to be *like* the discourse, of a particular speaker at a past time with an individual disciple's situation in mind: 'So Krishna, as when he admonished Arjuna / On the field of battle.' Likewise with Dame Julian's 'Sin is behovely, but / All shall be well, and / All manner of thing shall be well'. This occurs twice in 'Little Gidding', once with enough disjuncture in diction to indicate its source in another somewhat distant text, then secondly with enough editorial excision to lose a little its air of antique citation and become one with the narrative voice, a voice we internalize and make our own in a kind of immediate presence as we read (CPP, 195, 198).

This shifting back and forth from revelation to rhetoricity in *Four Quartets* is also generated by syntactical devices which help to destabilize secure propositions, either affirmative or negative, and protect the discourse from inflation and reduction alike. We have already spoken of the little words, the '*quasi*'s and 'without's, the 'say that's and 'so's and 'as if's, which remind us both of the promised fulfilments of language and its faltering approximations of those promises. Perhaps the most telling of these is the deceptively nonchalant phrase that introduces, apparently from left field, the wisdom of *The Bhagavad Gita* in 'The Dry Salvages' III: 'I sometimes wonder if that is what Krishna meant – / Among other things – or one way of putting the same thing' (CPP, 187).

This little quasi-speculative phrase, 'I sometimes wonder', opens the section, and the colon at the end of these lines points forward to what follows. But its shifter, 'that', may also be taken as referring to the discourse immediately preceding, a discourse about the dark power of time with indeed strong overtones of the *Gita*. The phrase thus has the retroactive function of drawing attention to the sheer textuality, the bravura 'writeness' of both the previous and the following passages. The 'time the destroyer' and 'fare forward traveller' lines, so powerful in their own context, then become, by this sudden disjunctive framing, texts for citation or reference rather than transparent media for the immediate apprehension of a certain truth, a truth which they seem to convey with such overwhelming presence when we are actually reading them.

Eliot's handling of syntax works at its best, however, when he contrives to allow it to inscribe a redeeming trace of the negative way at the very centre of the affirmative passage which ends the *Quartets*, but in such a manner as to defeat, at least at the propositional level, the binary split between these apparent oppositions and to indicate how they can be 'the same'. The point of intersection or crossing of these two paths cannot, of course, be fully specified, predicated or named, for no specification, predication or name could refer to it without privileging one or another of its opposing aspects. Indeed, as Derrida says of similar instances of intersection in his own thought, this moment when affirmations and negations coincide is *not* a concept or a name, even though it may lend itself to conceptualization and naming at a preliminary or approximate level. Rather, it is more like a field of force, which we can only trace in the alignments it produces. (Derrida's multiplying terms, such as *trace, différance, pharmakon, supplement,* etc., indicate his own traversal of these approximations.) To come closer to it in language, however, takes, in the end, something besides conceptualization in definitive or even quasi-definitive terms. It takes 'another syntax, one that exceeds even the order and the structure of predicative discourse'. Such approximations must be written, Derrida concludes, 'completely otherwise' (4).

What that 'completely otherwise' way of writing might look like we may perhaps discern in the curious sentences which are not quite sentences which conclude 'Little Gidding'. These sentences begin, ordinarily enough, with the direct discourse and predicative statements inaugurated by 'We shall not cease from exploration'. But are these statements so direct? If we look just above them on the page, we find the line 'With the drawing of this Love and the voice of this Calling' followed by no particular punctuation, merely the white space, the pause for breath, of a blank line on the page (CPP, 197). There are at least two possible ways to read the relationship of this single, haunting line with what follows: first as an ordinary adverbial phrase modifying the final stanzas without any particular change of discourse, and secondly as if it introduced them as some indirect discourse or citation spoken by that voice, which citation itself provides or explicates their substance. We could, that is, read the line as continuous with what follows, or as if there were a break, a colon, or the words 'which says that' introduced what follows.

True, no colon is specified, for its presence would anchor the ensuing lines squarely in the mode of citation when their status is perhaps better left ambiguous. The absence of the colon or of some explicit 'which says that' reserves their potential of functioning *both* as pure prayer and as quotation, as logos and rhetoricity. But so many passages in the quartets have worked this way before (including, as we have seen, the introduction of Krishna's wisdom) that we can't fully suppress the shadow of this aspect of citation, which falls, lightly enough, across the rest of the verse, reminding us that great poetry it may be, but fully achieved logocentric revelation it is not. It is, partly at least, merely the echo of a perhaps purely textual preceding vibration.

As for the following and final statements or (non-) sentences themselves, their nouns sometimes seem, on closer examination, to lack any predicates at all. What verb, for instance, answers to 'The voice of the hidden waterfall'? Or consider the final instance:

> Quick now, here, now, always –
> A condition of complete simplicity
> (Costing not less than everything)
> And all shall be well and
> All manner of thing shall be well
> When the tongues of flame are in-folded
> Into the crowned knot of fire
> And the fire and the rose are one.   (CPP, 198)

Not only does the 'condition of complete simplicity' never find a verb – an absence we hardly feel except, perhaps, as a momentary skipped heartbeat – but the final statements, 'all shall be well' and 'the fire and the rose are one' are both in future, not in present time. The verse spacing allows us to overlook this deferral, for it is easy – and not entirely wrong – to take the clause, 'And the fire and the rose are one' out of context and read it as a single ringing affirmation. Not entirely wrong, but not entirely right, either, for we would hardly be surprised, at the conceptual, if not the poetic level, to find this line reframed as a quotation. It might, that is, be supplemented in turn, so that it would read something like: '". . . And the fire and the rose are one." / So Julian to her disciples on the field of pain.'

Should this implication or re-writing offend against the purity of the verse, the offence is a risk inherent, as I have been arguing throughout, in the structure of the mark. Before deciding to mitigate or reduce it, moreover, we should, perhaps, consider carefully Derrida's final question, a question which is not, or not merely, rhetorical:

> Perhaps there would be no prayer, no pure possibility of prayer, without what we glimpse as a menace or as a contamination: writing, the code, repetition, analogy or the – at least apparent – multiplicity of addresses, initiation. If there were a purely pure experience of prayer, would one need religion and affirmative or negative theologies? Would one need a supplement of prayer? But if there were no supplement, if quotation did

not bend prayer, if prayer did not bend, if it did not submit
to writing, would a theiology be possible? Would a theology be
possible? (62)

Perhaps it would, perhaps not. But the menace or contamination
of writing, the code, repetition, the multiplicity of addresses and
indeed of origins are all, for good or ill, built into poetry in a
far more obvious way than they are to theology proper, whether
negative or positive. In this respect poetry participates doubly both
in the risk, but also in the luck of the mark. It testifies and must
testify to a multiplicity of origins and ends, some textual, some
hors-texte, some arising from the word, some from the Word.
Only by virtue of this multiplicity can *Four Quartets* trace both
the way up and the way down at the same time. The result,
at least in *Four Quartets*, may be as valuable for mystagogia and
spiritual practice and even for its more secular version, *paideuma*,
as it is for philosophical and theological debate.

References

Brooker, Jewel Spears, and Joseph Bentley, *Reading the Waste Land:
Modernism and the Limits of Interpretation*, Amherst, University of
Massachusetts Press, 1990.
Burke, Kenneth, *The Rhetoric of Religion*, Boston, Beacon, 1961.
Caputo, John, *Radical Hermeneutics: Repetition, Deconstruction, and the
Hermeneutic Project*, Bloomington, University of Indiana Press, 1987.
Davidson, Harriet, *T.S. Eliot and Hermeneutics: Absence and Presence
in 'The Waste Land'*, Baton Rouge, Louisiana State University
Press, 1985.
Derrida, Jacques, *Speech and Phenomenon and Other Essays on Husserl's
Theory of Signs*, Evanston, Northwestern University Press, 1973.
———, *Limited Inc., a, b, c*, Paris, Galilee, 1977.
———, 'Letter to John P. Leavey, Jr.' in *Semeia* 23, ed. Robert
Detweiler, Atlanta, Scholars' Press, 1982.
———, 'How to Avoid Speaking: Denials', in Sandford Budick and
Wolfgang Iser, eds, *Languages of the Unsayable: The Play of Negativity
in Literature and Literary Theory*, New York, Columbia University
Press, 1986).
Jackson, Roger R., 'Matching Concepts: Deconstructive and Foun-
dationalist Tendencies in Buddhist Thought', *Journal of the American
Academy of Religion* 52 (1989).
Kafka, Franz, *Dearest Father: Stories and Other Writings*, New York,
Schocken, 1954.

Kearns, Cleo McNelly, *T.S. Eliot and Indic Traditions: A Study in Poetry and Belief*, Cambridge, Cambridge University Press, 1987.

Leitch, Vincent, *Deconstructive Criticism: An Advanced Introduction*, New York, Columbia University Press, 1983.

Magliola, Robert, *Derrida on the Mend*, West Lafayette, Indiana, Purdue University Press, 1984.

Perl, Jeffrey, *Skepticism and Modern Enmity*, Baltimore. Johns Hopkins University Press, 1989.

(I acknowledge with gratitude the helpful comments of Derek Attridge, who read an early draft of this article with scrupulous care.)

8

The End of Tradition and the Beginning of History
Michael Levenson

I

'I can never re-read any of my prose writings without acute embarrassment,' Eliot wrote in 1942. 'I shirk the task, and consequently may not take account of all the assertions to which I have at one time or another committed myself; I may often repeat what I have said before, and I may often contradict myself.' (OPP, 26) The remark is from 'The Music of Poetry'. Two years later, in 1944, in the address 'What is a Classic?' he cheerfully acknowledged that he was construing the term 'classic' in only one of its possible senses, insisting that 'I do not bind myself, for the future, not to use the term in any of the other ways in which it has been used. If, for instance, I am discovered on some future occasion, in writing, in public speech, or in conversation, to be using the word 'classic' merely to mean a standard author in any language', then – intones Eliot – 'no one should expect one to apologize.' (OPP, 53) But can one be so sure?

There is no mannerism more recurrent in Eliot's later criticism than the offhand allusion to his earlier critical positions and the disarming confession that he no longer holds some of the most celebrated opinions of the brash young fellow who wore the same name. I say 'mannerism', but it is more than that. The problem of Eliot's relation to his own past writings, as he himself well realizes, raises the question of the consistency, coherence and integrity of the self – specifically the integrity of the self as it is obliged to live through time.

In another public address of the wartime period, 'The Social Function of Poetry', Eliot offers something like a first principle of his self-historiography. He has been discussing the differences in sensibility between different nations, and between those who speak different languages, and then he goes on to say:

But people do not only experience the world differently in different places, they experience it differently at different times. In fact, our sensibility is constantly changing, as the world about us changes: ours is not the same as that of the Chinese or Hindu, but also it is not the same as that of our ancestors several hundred years ago. It is not the same as that of our fathers; and finally, we ourselves are not quite the same persons that we were a year ago. (OPP, 20)

Together these instances, only a few among the many, allow me to formulate the problem of the temporality of the self or, to put it another way, the historicity of identity. It is the ambition of this essay to unfold these difficulties as they arise both in *Four Quartets* and the body of discursive writing surrounding them. The boundaries around the individual poems are largely ignored here, because the issue is one that most often eludes Eliot's conscious control and that burrows through the walls of form.

The writing of *Four Quartets* involved Eliot in a deep persistent worry, not that he would be leaving old beliefs behind and that he would be exposing himself to charges of self-contradiction, but that as the poem extended itself, it would show no development at all, contradictory or otherwise. The fear is the fear of poetic stasis, of torpid self-repetition. John Hayward reported Eliot's anxiety during the completion of the sequence, the concern that 'he was simply repeating himself and so running into the risk of producing an elegant parody of the earlier poems in the group.' While writing 'East Coker' Eliot had expressed the same worry. 'It may be quite worthless,' quotes Hayward, 'because most of it looks to me like an imitation of myself' (CFQ, 25, 16–17). In 'East Coker' the concern penetrates the poetry: 'You say I am repeating / Something I have said before. I shall say it again. / Shall I say it again?' (CPP, 181). One might have expected the question ('Shall I?') to precede the answer ('I shall'), but Eliot is plainly not feeling so resolute. 'Shall I say it again?' records a deep confusion, not merely a question posed to the will – Shall I choose, after all, to say it again? – but a genuine uncertainty: Shall I, in spite of all my choosings, find that I have said it again?

The presiding spiritual *topos* of *Four Quartets* is timelessness, but this *topos* stands in ambivalent relation to what one might think

of as the poetic *praxis* of the poem which binds Eliot tightly
to the movement of time. How to die into grace? – that is
one question. How to stay alive as a poet? – that is another.
For the life of the soul, the burden is to escape 'the waste
sad time / Stretching before and after' (CPP, 176). But for
the life of the lyricist the burden is precisely to live *after* the
before, to take up a position in time that will validate the poetic
utterance as a living utterance. This is what occurs in response
to the opening lyric ('What is the late November doing') of the
second movement of 'East Coker': 'That was a way of putting
it – not very satisfactory: / A periphrastic study in a worn-out
poetical fashion . . .' (CPP, 179). Even perfect familiarity with
the poem cannot remove the shock of moving from the lyric
to the critique. The opening lines bear no sign of diminished
conviction, and if they can be understood as 'a worn-out poetical
fashion', this is only because one firm conviction has yielded
to another. The poetry enacts the principle found also in the
criticism, that 'we ourselves are not quite the same persons that
we were a year ago' or indeed the same poets that we were a few
lines ago.

Here is how the *Quartets* resist the danger of repetition: they
thematize the necessity of change. They insist upon discontinuity
in both the poetry and the poet's life; they devalue 'the knowledge
derived from experience':

> The knowledge imposes a pattern, and falsifies,
> For the pattern is new in every moment
> And every moment is a new and shocking
> Valuation of all we have been.   (CPP, 179)

One way of putting the question of this essay is to ask what these
'new and shocking' moments have to do with those 'timeless
moments' apprehended by the saint and only glimpsed by us
ordinary spiritual seekers. Or put another way, what does the
shock of poetry have to do with the poise of saintliness? Whatever
answers might ultimately be given to these questions, it is possible
to begin by simply discounting the moment of insincerity in 'East
Coker' when we are told that 'The poetry does not matter', and
to insist that a consuming unacknowledged struggle within the
Quartets is to accommodate the claims of poetry and the claims
of saintliness.

II

One of the most notable aspects of Eliot as a literary historian during the first phase of his career is the way that his celebrated emphasis on tradition masks the dominance of the present tense in his historical view. The stated principle in 'Tradition and the Individual Talent' is that the poet 'must inevitably be judged by the standards of the past', and that the significance of the poet lies in 'the appreciation of his relation to the dead poets and artists' (SE, 15). Certainly the rhetoric of the essay is the rhetoric of authority, an authority demanding self-surrender, the poet yielding to something grander, more ancient, more valuable. And certainly it is this dominant rhetoric which Eliot elsewhere wants to emphasize – for instance, in 'The Function of Criticism' where he cites the earlier essay and interprets it as positing 'something outside of the artist to which he owes allegiance, a devotion to which he must surrender and sacrifice himself in order to earn and to obtain his unique position.' (SE, 24)

But even within 'Tradition and the Individual Talent' there is a rival strain of emphasis, an emphasis on the constitutive and generative powers of the present tense. In its most radical guise – a radicalism too rarely acknowledged – this appears in the much-noted claim that the past may be 'altered by the present as much as the present is directed by the past' (SE, 15). The power of the present to alter the past, indeed the demand that the present can only live by altering the past, is by no means concealed in Eliot's argument, but to take the point as seriously as it deserves is to recognize its uneasy relation to the ideology of authority and self-surrender.

The dominant rhetoric of the earlier criticism is the rhetoric of sacrifice to the past, but the critical practice is the practice of *appropriation* by the present. We get an important clue to this in Eliot's characterization of the 'historical sense' in 'Tradition and the Individual Talent'. The historical sense, he writes, 'involves a perception, not only of the pastness of the past, but of its presence' (SE, 14). This is a telling moment, because it signals a transition which will occur repeatedly in Eliot's early literary history and which is precisely a transition from the pastness of the past to the presence of the past – that is, to what the last sentence of 'Tradition and the Individual Talent' describes as '*the present moment of the past*' (SE, 22; my emphasis).

The reopening of the literary past is the first polemical act in Eliot's criticism, but the decisive second act is the reappropriation of past to present – the making present of historical time. Early in *The Sacred Wood* is found the contention that 'The important critic is the person who is absorbed in the present problems of art, and who wishes to bring the forces of the past to bear upon the solution of these problems' (SW, 37–8). The past appears now as an instrument in the service of the present, and if we consider the sententious defence of literary theft – 'Immature poets imitate; mature poets steal' (SE, 206) – then it becomes clear how thoroughly the sacrifice of the contemporary poetic self can turn into its aggressive appropriations.

The larger question here is nothing less than that of the historicity of the literary tradition, and the difficult issue is what relation the making present of the past holds to that historicity. One recalls Eliot's assertion that 'the historical sense compels a man to write not merely with his own generation in his bones, but with a feeling that the whole of the literature of Europe from Homer and within it the whole of the literature of his own country has a simultaneous existence and composes a simultaneous order.' But if the historical sense is a recognition of *simultaneity*, then where is the movement of time? Eliot speaks of the development of the European mind, but immediately contends that it is a development which 'abandons nothing', 'which does not superannuate either Shakespeare, or Homer, or the rock drawing of the Magdalenian draughtsmen' (SE, 14, 16). Nothing abandoned, nothing lost, nothing superannuated – everything present in simultaneous order – where is the movement of history?

In the essay on Ben Jonson Eliot explains what it means to go to the centre of Jonson's work and temperament, asserting that 'we must see him unbiased by time, as a contemporary' (SE, 148). Unbiased by time, seen as a contemporary – this is the condition sought throughout those early historical studies – and what is that condition but an *overcoming* of history, an erasure of the *pastness* of the past, a devouring of the past in the hungry maw of the present?

To give the point its due generality, it can be said that Eliot is engaged in nothing less than the task of spatializing time.[1]

This is the real force in the image of a simultaneous order: temporal movement, evolution, development, these notions are transmuted into the image of an ideal order of monuments – a kind of trailer park of literary greatness – where all the dead poets congregate and arrange themselves into a systematic whole. There is no suggestion in this image that the lapse of time brings with it a fading, or a withering, or even an aging. All the past is present, and in place of the ravages of passing time, there are the consolations of space. Here, what Eliot calls a 'metaphorical fancy' in *The Use of Poetry and the Use of Criticism* is worth recording in full:

> From time to time, every hundred years or so, it is desirable that some critic shall appear to review the past of our literature, and set the poets and the poems in a new order. This task is not one of revolution but of readjustment. What we observe is partly the same scene, but in a different and more distant perspective; there are new and strange objects in the foreground, to be drawn accurately in proportion to the more familiar ones which now approach the horizon, where all but the most eminent become invisible to the naked eye. The exhaustive critic, armed with a powerful glass, will be able to sweep the distance and gain an acquaintance with minute objects in the landscape with which to compare minute objects close at hand; he will be able to gauge nicely the position and proportion of the objects surrounding us, in the whole vast panorama.
>
> (UPUC, 108)

Within this metaphorical fancy the spatializing of time is frank, vivid, sustained and consequential, and Eliot, it is tempting to say, reveals himself here as no historian of the literary tradition, but as its geographer – geographer of the whole vast panorama. Indeed it is well to consider how this conversion of time into space, of elapsed time into spatial simultaneity – how this leads to the unnerving paradox that Eliot, the most eloquent voice in defence of tradition, is also the most cunning enemy of historical time. To use the past to solve the problems of the present, to see the dead poets unbiased by time, as contemporaries, to see all history as a panorama displayed before the scanning eye of the critic – this is to take a view of tradition which avoids the challenges of temporality and jeopardizes the notion of literary change.

III

> Only a flicker
> Over the strained time-ridden faces
> > ('Burnt Norton' III; CPP, 174)

> The serenity only a deliberate hebetude,
> The wisdom only the knowledge of dead secrets
> > ('East Coker' II; CPP, 179)

> These are only hints and guesses,
> Hints followed by guesses;
> > ('The Dry Salvages' V; CPP, 190)

At this point something might be gained by a slow glance at a little word. The word is 'only', around which so much of Eliot's subtlety clusters – a word which incites devious movements whenever it appears. It has a curious career within the *oeuvre*, playing a key part in *The Waste Land*, occupying a minor but strategic position in *Ash-Wednesday*, then becoming a major protagonist in the verbal drama of the *Quartets*, while remaining almost entirely absent from the rest of the poetry. In what is almost always its first signification in Eliot, it enforces the sense of contraction and diminishment: *only* as 'merely'. From *all* to *only*, from imaginary plenitude to real limitation – this is a prominent vector, but it by no means exhausts the wanderings of the word. Consider a celebrated sequence from *The Waste Land*.

> Son of Man,
> You cannot say, or guess, for you know only
> A heap of broken images, where the sun beats,
> And the dead tree gives no shelter, the cricket no relief,
> And the dry stone no sound of water. Only
> There is shadow under this red rock . . .
> > (CPP, 61)

After the blank unrelieved scene of depletion ('Only / A heap') comes a slim opening toward recovery ('Only / There is shadow'). The sequence plainly utters what is so often quietly implied in Eliot's play with the word, namely that near the condition of loss is *another way*. The sense of *only* as 'merely', as 'nothing more than' or 'nothing but', stands close by *only* as 'except that', 'on the other hand', 'on the contrary'. In the midst of limitation, there you find exception. *The Waste Land* condenses the ambiguity in these lines from part V: 'Only at nightfall, aethereal rumours / Revive for a moment a broken Coriolanus' (CPP, 74).

In *The Waste Land* the ambiguity remains stunted, because the second significance, the hint of exception/escape, remains so faint and indeterminate. It is in the *Quartets* that the semantic machinery is set whirring. So, for instance, when we learn in 'Burnt Norton' that it is 'Only in time' that visionary experience can be reclaimed, we assume that we are in the familiar grip of limitation (CPP, 173). Sighing, we resign ourselves to hard necessity. But when the phrase reappears, climactically, a few lines later: 'Only through time time is conquered – ' it must register strangely on the attentive ear. Natural word sequence and rhythmic habit would lead one to expect an inversion: 'Only through time is time conquered.' This is the syntax, moreover, that most naturally yields the reading of *only* as 'exclusively', the reading that the previous lines have encouraged. By refusing the inversion, Eliot gently adjusts the semantic pressure, urging the sense of *only* from 'exclusively' to 'except for the fact that'. Make this substitution, and the line becomes a strongly self-contained restatement of the philosophic puzzle that the poem has teasingly built. Yes, our weak flesh binds us to time, involves us in the fallen realm of past and future; and yes, it is only in time, exclusively in its modality, that we can possess the moments of vision. All this would be cause for resignation – *except for the fact that* 'through time time is conquered.'

In the second section of 'The Dry Salvages' the sense of 'exception' becomes more marked even as the crisis of nihilism becomes more urgent.

> There is no end of it, the voiceless wailing,
> No end to the withering of withered flowers,
> To the movement of pain that is painless and motionless,
> To the drift of the sea and the drifting wreckage,
> The bone's prayer to Death its God. Only the hardly, barely
>   prayable
> Prayer of the one Annunciation.   (CPP, 186)

Here the semantic knot is tightened. It is not simply that limitation and exception, constraint and escape, are brought near to one another; it is that the former can bring about, can create, the latter. *Only* as depletion sets the conditions for *only* as liberation: 'And what you do not know is the only thing you know' ('East Coker' III; CPP, 181). Loss is gain, limitation is purification – this Eliotic motif plays itself out within the life of the small particle *only*.

But there remains a further, still more elusive, suggestion in this play of significance, one that can be drawn from the cry in *Ash-Wednesday*: 'but speak the word only' (CPP, 93). Under the heading of 'idiomatic uses', the OED lists a use of *only* in which the sense of 'no more than' passes into the sense of 'as much as'. Here in *Ash-Wednesday* the passage occurs, as indeed it occurs in *The Waste Land*: 'If there were the sound of water only' (CPP, 72). Both lines weld together the sense of a bare minimum – only the word, only the sound of water – with the sense of sublime sufficiency: The word! The sound of water!, as much as to ask, Who could want more?

It is this mix of deprivation and satisfaction that becomes so rhetorically potent, as for instance in the final twinned appearance of the word in 'Little Gidding': 'We only live, only suspire / Consumed by either fire or fire' (CPP, 196). Here *only* performs its routine labour in registering the dwindling of possibilities to 'no more than' fire or fire. But it also works its subterranean mysteries: How can one speak of dwindling when the possibility is 'as much as' life, as much indeed as eternal life. Eliot ends the first chapter of *The Idea of a Christian Society* with a sentence that serves as the best gloss on these lines. 'That prospect [of a Christian society],' he writes, 'involves, at least, discipline, inconvenience and discomfort: but here as hereafter the alternative to hell is purgatory' (ICS, 21). With just a thought, expressed in just such a tone, do the deprivations of *only* pass into a perfect sufficiency.

'Tradition' as it presided over Eliot's early understanding of time was first of all a plenitude. It was not a lineage but a totality – a totality varying in magnitude but never less than immense. It comprised 'the whole of the literature of [the poet's] own country' and 'the whole of the literature of Europe from Homer.' It comprised that large and ever-growing population called 'the dead'. What happens with the appearance of a new work 'is something that happens simultaneously to *all the works of art* which preceded it' (SE, 15; my emphasis). The language of plenitude – all, whole, and every – is the constant attendant of Eliot's reflection on tradition.

The way of *only*, as it has been traced here, contests the way of *all*. The history of its connotations begins with deprivation, restriction, limitation and exclusion, and the further refinements always derive from that head meaning. When *The Waste Land* contemplates 'only / A heap of broken images' (CPP, 61), it signals the disintegration of the well-composed totality of tradition. To recognize this is to acknowledge rival understandings of history: a spatial understanding which sees all historical time as extended before the discerning eye, and a temporal understanding which surrenders the hope of possessing an ever-receding past.

The first view, the view of tradition, begins as a secular perspective on the history of literature, and transforms into a theological perspective that one finds, for instance, in 'Little Gidding': 'history is a pattern / Of timeless moments' (CPP, 197). That, we find ourselves wanting to say, is what we once thought *literary* history was. Indeed, there is a powerful counterpart relationship between the structure constituted by the deposits of literary tradition, as this was formulated in 'Tradition and the Individual Talent', and the structure of moments as it is presented in the *Quartets*. Between 'literary monuments' and 'timeless moments' there is an underground continuity.

It is the official position of the *Quartets* that timeless moments populate the spiritual universe and that:

> Here the impossible union
> Of spheres of existence is actual,
> Here the past and future
> Are conquered and reconciled . . .   (CPP, 190)

And yet, with all those high modernist instances of instantaneous vision – the impression, the image, the vortex, the epiphany – the difficulty is to determine what happens after the 'timeless moment', what happens in the poetry, what happens in the life. How does one live, how does one write, when the visionary gleam has passed? Just slightly earlier, 'The Dry Salvages' had taught that:

>   to apprehend
> The point of intersection of the timeless
> With time, is an occupation for the saint —
> No occupation either, but something given
> And taken, in a lifetime's death in love . . .
>
>   (CPP, 189–90)

The category of the 'lifetime' thrusts itself into the meditations of the *Quartets*, as it had not in the earlier poetry. It quietly unsettles the stability of the official position, the official mystical position, the strenuous affirmation of an 'impossible union'. What is unsettling, first of all, is that while timeless moments never age, human beings do, and

>   As we grow older
> The world becomes stranger, the pattern more complicated
> Of dead and living. Not the intense moment
> Isolated, with no before and after,
> But a lifetime burning in every moment
> And not the lifetime of one man only
> But of old stones that cannot be deciphered.
>
>   (CPP, 182)

There is then a 'before and after' that is not, as 'Burnt Norton' would have it, 'ridiculous', the before and after unfolding in the thread of a life. A life-time given form, given grace, by a pattern of time-less moments — this is the tense, unsteady thought that interrupts the smooth lyric course of the poem. So in 'Little Gidding' the meeting with the 'familiar compound ghost' takes place at an 'intersection time' with 'no before and after'; and yet the burden of this messenger is to 'disclose the gifts reserved for age / To set a crown upon your lifetime's effort' (CPP, 194). It seems right to say that the major poems of the early career paid little heed to what Richard Wollheim calls 'the thread of life'. Readers have often noticed how the young Eliot so often affected the tones and postures of an aging poetic persona; Prufrock's premature fatigue epitomizes that gesture. But even old man Gerontion and endlessly aging Tiresias remain, like Prufrock, indifferent to a 'lifetime's effort'. This is simply not a category that attracts poetic notice. Not the aging of an imaginative apparatus that looks back on an unchanging, unchangeable past, but an overwrought imagination that sees past and future spread out equally before it, equally close at hand, contained, as it were, in time present – this was the condition of the early poetry. (Prufrock: 'I have known them all already, known them all'; 'And I Tiresias have foresuffered all' [CPP, 14, 69].)

The most banal explanation for the change is almost certainly the best: Eliot grew older. The poet who so early had made a trope of aging had grown as old as his trope. To that dull point, we can add another: that the rapid succession of modernist styles and aesthetic doctrines made the distance between present and past painfully evident. That a month after finishing *The Waste Land* Eliot would call it 'a thing of the past as far as I am concerned', and that he could disavow critical principles almost as soon as they had been embraced give clear signs of modernism's own temporality. It is common to remark on the quick ticks of modernist time, but no less pertinent is the complementary aspect of accelerated change: the growing mass of old material left behind as signs of self-obsolescence and as markers of a life-path that could be retraced only at the price of imaginative death.

This concern carries us back to the issue raised at the beginning of this essay – specifically, the issue of Eliot's bewilderment in the face of his own past work. As early as the preface to the second edition of *The Sacred Wood*, Eliot discovers that he can neither identify himself with his old essays, nor modify them to reflect his present views. He cannot identify with them because he has grown past them – and he cannot modify them because he would have to write another book to capture the 'expansion' of his interests. So much has happened, writes Eliot, 'that the chief value remaining to this volume, if any, is as a document of its time: and that is another reason for altering nothing' (SW, vii). This is the kind of remark he will frequently make in addressing his past criticism – he will leave the early essays unchanged because they belong to a distinct epoch in his life, an epoch whose integrity needs to be respected even if it can no longer define his present attitudes.

The suggestion here is that as Eliot becomes obliged to confront the fact of his own change – in the poetry, in the criticism, and indeed in his personal and public life – his understanding of historical time undergoes a deep transformation. The point can best be approached through some remarks in Eliot's late lecture on Goethe, 'Goethe as the Sage', delivered in 1955. In that address

Eliot begins with one of his most extended meditations on his own history as a critic. He refers to his earlier, distinctly dismissive remarks about Goethe – most notably the comment that Goethe 'dabbled in both philosophy and poetry and made no great success of either' – and he takes that early dismissal as an occasion for raising one of the two large questions of his essay:

> [W]hat is the process by which one becomes reconciled to those great authors to whom in one's youth one was indifferent or antipathetic – not only why it takes place, but why it ought to take place; not only the process but the moral necessity of the process.

> (OPP, 208)

At this point Eliot offers a sketch of the development of personal taste and private critical judgement, elaborating an account which he had been offering in more primitive terms for some time. He divides the growth of judgement into three distinct phases. In the first, which he associates with adolescence, the reader is swept with enthusiasm beyond the impulse of the moment and without exercising any real critical faculty. In the second phase, the critical faculty is roused; the circle of appreciation is widened; but characteristically there remains a limitation in literary enjoyment and critical insight which show themselves in a lingering antipathy to authors of acknowledged greatness – Goethe and Milton being prominent examples in Eliot's own career. Finally, in the third stage, the stage of critical maturity, one turns the critical eye back upon the self and asks why one has failed to enjoy imaginative achievement which has been found delightful by those 'as well qualified or better qualified for appreciation than ourselves.' Why does one loathe Milton? Why does one recoil from Goethe? In attempting to understand this kind of failure, 'one is seeking for light, not only about th[e] author, but about oneself' (OPP, 209). And what Eliot has learned, he lets us know, is that in his own case critical maturity has brought two great changes: first a narrowing of his literary predilections, a desire to read fewer and fewer poets; and second, an urge to settle accounts with certain grand figures he feels that he wronged in his callow years.

In itself this genealogy of the critical faculty is rather predictable and unexciting, but it has, I think, decisive importance for any effort to understand Eliot's emerging view of the spiritual life and the literary tradition. And this is because the image of an individual life history – which in Eliot's case is preeminently the life history of a poet or a critic – becomes the paradigm for temporality. Eliot's understanding of his own evolution as a critic serves as a key to his new understanding of historical evolution. The history of the self becomes a figure for history as such.

It will be possible to elaborate this point by considering Eliot's attempt to resolve one of the most vexing problems in his critical thought – the notorious problem of 'belief'. It will be recalled that in the 1929 essay on 'Dante' he had struggled with the question of how much of Dante's theology we ourselves need to believe in order to read the poem with full satisfaction, and he had come to the tentative conclusion that, while we cannot ignore the philosophic and theological commitments since they are the *matter* of the poem, we are not asked to make them our own: 'You are not called upon to believe what Dante believed' (SE, 258). What is necessary rather is a suspension of both belief and disbelief.

Thus Eliot in 1929. Four years later in the lecture on 'Shelley and Keats' which became part of *The Use of Poetry and the Use of Criticism*, the position alters. This presumably is because with Shelley, Eliot must admit that his revulsion from the Shelleyan philosophy does indeed hinder his enjoyment of the poetry – he may be able to suspend his disbelief in Dante's Catholicism, but he cannot do so when faced with the creed of a vegetarian anarchist. And yet Eliot is highly reluctant to conclude that we can only appreciate the work of a poet whose beliefs we share; he comes then to the following view:

> When the doctrine, theory, belief, or 'view of life' presented in a poem is one which the mind of the reader can accept as coherent, mature, and founded on the facts of experience, it interposes no obstacle to the reader's enjoyment, whether it be one that he accept or deny, approve or deprecate. When it is one which the reader rejects as childish or feeble, it may, for a reader of well-developed mind, set up an almost complete check. (UPUC, 96)

The problem of belief is thus recast in the terms of life history. Why are some beliefs an obstacle to poetry and others not? – because some beliefs are childish or adolescent, while others are adult. 'I was intoxicated by Shelley's poetry at the age of fifteen,' writes Eliot, and this, he explains, is because an adolescent reader is the only one capable of enjoying an adolescent poet (UPUC, 96–7). But this is plainly a fragile enjoyment; the reader who outgrows adolescence also outgrows all those poems written under the infatuation of adolescent belief. The only secure poetic appreciation can be that between consenting adults.

The central concept in this increasingly ascendant critical conceit is *maturity*. It had played a minor role in Eliot's essays from the start, but it becomes steadily more dominant as his career unfolds, and by the lectures of the forties it becomes perhaps the most fundamental notion in his critical thinking. In the 1944 paper 'What is a Classic?' Eliot writes that:

> If there is one word on which we can fix, which will suggest the maximum of what I mean by the term 'a classic', it is the word *maturity*. ... A classic can only occur when a civilization is mature; when a language and a literature are mature; and it must be the work of a mature mind. (OPP, 54–5)

To define maturity, as Eliot immediately concedes, may be impossible, but 'if we are properly mature, as well as educated persons, we can recognize maturity in a civilization and in a literature, as we do in the other human beings whom we encounter.' This last rhetorical move helps to illuminate what is meant by saying that Eliot comes to take individual life history – now defined as the progress of a life towards maturity – as the basis for historical perceptions.

> Time present and time past
> Are both perhaps present in time future,
> And time future contained in time past.
> If all time is eternally present
> All time is unredeemable.   (CPP, 171)

As against this view in 'Burnt Norton', it might be said that in 'Tradition and the Individual Talent' time was redeemable exactly to the extent that it was eternally present, perpetually *simultaneous*. The failure of the ideal of simultaneity, the loss of the synoptic, synchronic assimilation – this is what incites Eliot into revaluation of life in time. It is what confirms the need, pressing everywhere through the late poetry, to 'Redeem / The time' (CPP, 94).

The official view in the *Quartets* holds that to redeem time is to conquer time; is to defeat the tyranny of the before and after; is to achieve an 'intersection' with the timeless. But a second view, less coherent, less sustained, contemplates overcoming the 'unredeemable' 'eternally present' not by curling in the ecstasy of timelessness, but simply by aging. From the standpoint of the older poet who has changed his poetic style, his critical precepts, and his religious faith, it is no longer possible to enjoy the Tiresian perception that past and future are spread out in an endless, ageless present. It is now too painfully evident that the past is another country.

The 'moments of agony', teaches 'The Dry Salvages', are permanent 'With such permanence as time has.' 'People change, and smile: but the agony abides. / Time the destroyer is time the preserver . . .' And, as this section of the poem ends, it reminds us that the ragged rock may be concealed, may be turned to human purposes, 'but in the sombre season / Or the sudden fury, is what it always was' (CPP, 187). Being what it always was is precisely what 'Tradition and the Individual Talent' had denied in its insistence that the past is modified by the present, given new values, endowed with new form. Relics of this attitude persist in the *Quartets*. But the counter-attitude, increasingly prominent, is that the past defies revaluation; the agony abides, preserved without benefit of change. Harry's return will be painful, says Agatha in *The Family Reunion*,

> because everything is irrevocable,
> Because the past is irremediable,
> Because the future can only be built
> Upon the real past.   (CPP, 288)

It is a large part of the burden of this essay that the 'real past', the real, irrevocable, irremediable past, is what Eliot had denied or suppressed in his early work. So much of the early poetry and criticism had relied on tropes of assimilation that when Eliot surrenders those tropes and acknowledges the past as beyond our will to transform, a deep shudder runs through all his writing. In place of the trope of assimilation, there is now the trope of abandonment. This is the underside of the figure of maturity; in a self, in a style, in a culture, maturity has its casualties. As Eliot writes in 'What is a Classic?',

> It is to be observed, that a society, and a literature, like an individual human being, do not necessarily mature equally and concurrently in every respect. The precocious child is often, in some obvious ways, childish for his age in comparison with ordinary children. Is there any one period of English literature to which we can point as being fully mature, comprehensively and in equilibrium?   (OPP, 56)

The answer he gives is no. But at the moment, more important than the answer is just the fact of Eliot's abiding reliance on the paradigm of individual history. It is the strength of this paradigm that brings Eliot to the perception that the passage of time leaves an irrecoverable loss — that as in an individual life, the movement towards literary maturity brings, as he once put it, an enrichment that is at the same time an impoverishment:

> We do not take kindly to the thought that, in order to gain one thing, we may have to give up something else of value. With these lost values the path of history is strewn and always will be . . . indeed, part of our pleasure in early literature, as of the delight which we take in children, is in our consciousness of many potentialities not all of which can be realized.
>
>   (OPP, 165, 167–8)

Gone is the notion of tradition as a simultaneous order; gone is the contention that the mind of Europe abandons nothing, superannuates nothing; gone is the easy confidence that we can see the dead poets as our contemporaries, 'unbiased by time'. Eliot's late appreciation of the pastness of the past — its heavy, opaque alterity — brings him to the recognition of lost critical values, lost imaginative opportunities: 'In the perfection of any style it can be observed, as in the maturing of an individual, that some potentialities have been brought to fruition only by the surrender of others' (OPP, 167).

To the question, 'What is a classic?', Eliot answers bluntly that Virgil is a classic, and then still more bluntly that Virgil is *the* classic, our only incontestable classic. 'No modern language', he writes, 'can hope to produce a classic, in the sense in which

I have called Virgil a classic. Our classic, the classic of all Europe, is Virgil.' The universality of Latin, the maturity of Roman culture, permitted the creation of the classical standard, and, continues Eliot, 'It is sufficient that this standard should have been established once for all; the task does not have to be done again' (OPP, 70).

Not to be done again, indeed impossible to do again – here is the acknowledgment of the irretrievable past, the irrecoverable example. At least up to the time of *The Use of Poetry and the Use of Criticism*, Eliot had continued to visualize an ideal state of perfect amalgamation – all the poets finally singing together – all the regions of the English literary mind brought into harmonious integration – an ideal inspired by the thought that the great poet is one 'who in his poetry re-twines as many straying strands of tradition as possible' (UPUC, 85). This is another image for the spatial recovery of lost time, but it is an image that comes under increasing strain. Part of Eliot's understanding of Virgil as classic depends on recognizing the *Aeneid* not as a strand that might be twined with other strands, but as itself an entire web.

And just because it is complete, because it achieves that literary maturity towards which the imagination must always strive, it creates that impoverishment which exists alongside enrichment; it is at once a cultural triumph and an historical obstacle, a great red rock which casts a shadow over all subsequent Latin poetry. The literary historical difficulty, the new literary historical difficulty for Eliot, is that every supreme poet 'tends to exhaust the ground he cultivates, so that it must, after yielding a diminishing crop, finally be left in fallow for some generations.' In less metaphorical terms, he explains, 'Not only every great poet, but every genuine, though lesser poet, fulfils once for all some possibility of the language, and so leaves one possibility less for his successors' (OPP, 64–5). And elsewhere: 'When a great poet has lived, certain things have been done once for all, and cannot be achieved again . . .' (NDC, 114).

Virgil, the classic, exhausted the entire Latin language, and it is the good historical fortune of English poetry – this is a key step in Eliot's argument – that its 'greatest poets have exhausted only particular areas' (OPP, 64). Shakespeare removed the possibility of dramatic greatness from his successors in the English language; Milton eliminated English epic grandeur; but

because the language is vaster than these two genres, there is
hope for the English poet that the post-Virgilian Latin poet could
never share.

> Words move, music moves
> Only in time; but that which is only living
> Can only die. Words, after speech, reach
> Into the silence. Only by the form, the pattern
> Can words or music reach
> The stillness, as a Chinese jar still
> Moves perpetually in its stillness.
>
> ('Burnt Norton' V; CPP, 175)

I quote this passage in part because it so neatly epitomizes the nearly
frictionless movement of *only* along its semantic continuum. The
first use gives 'exclusively', the second and third 'merely', and the
fourth ('Only by the form') condenses the ideas of limitation,
exception and sufficiency that have been seen here as central to
Eliot's uses of the word. In greater part, though, I quote the passage
because of its use of a second companion word: *still* or *stillness*.
Throughout the *Quartets* both variants are kept more distinctly
in the foreground than *only*, with their purposes more visible,
their ambiguities more deliberate. In the lines just preceding the
passage above we read that 'the light is still / At the still point
of the turning world.' 'In process' and 'at rest' − these are the
intimations that Eliot wants to hold together in a single excited
glance, as at the end of the first of these lines. Still as finality, still
as ongoing continuity; the doubleness in the concept of inertia
− this is a recurrent and highly visible conflation in the poem.
Moreover, Eliot wants to let the separate senses interanimate,
until we understand rest as a kind of process and movement, at
least the right kind of movement, as a poise like that of a gliding
bird. The difficult balance toward which Eliot aims can be seen
in the contrast between 'still and moving' in 'Burnt Norton' and
the recast version in 'East Coker': 'still and still moving' (CPP,
173, 183).

On its face this last phrase belongs to the basic strutwork of
the poem's mystical equations, the series of paradoxical identities
that fall under the head of the 'impossible union / Of spheres of
existence' and that include such phrases as 'Never and always',
'Neither flesh nor fleshless', 'the moment in and out of time',

and climactically, 'the fire and the rose are one.' But in its context
– 'Old men ought to be explorers / Here and there does not
matter / We must be still and still moving' – it belongs not to
the mystic's time but to that life-time of which I have made
so much.

And it is in the context of life-time, the time of self-identity
and self-recognition, that 'Little Gidding' puts *still* to important
use. 'I was still the same, / Knowing myself yet being someone
other – / And he a face still forming' (CPP, 193). 'Still' and 'only'
appear with such frequency and with such constant adjustment that
in moments of stress it is almost as if they alone could carry the
burden of implication: Only/ Still. Even when they are absent,
their echoes can be heard:

> We shall not cease from exploration
> And the end of all our exploring
> Will be to arrive where we started
> And know the place for the first time.
> Through the unknown, remembered gate
> When the last of earth left to discover
> Is that which was the beginning . . .   (CPP, 197)

The 'last left' – this is what the 'real past' does in the course
of life-time: it leaves permanent traces and shrinks the scope of
discovery. It exhausts possibilities 'once for all', until the 'only'
thing remaining is the first thing, and 'still' we must seek it.

Is it too much to say that going in search of the timeless Eliot
discovered the past? I think not. Brooding on the ambiguities
of maturity, recognizing that we gain by losing, that once an
imaginative possibility is realized it is realized once for all, he
came to recognize as he had not before the unyielding pastness
of the past. I suggest that we regard this as a change as notable as
any in his writing. Tradition (in the early view) is less daunting
than consoling as it gathers round the poet, leaving nothing behind,
politely rearranging the order of its monuments at the behest of
the strong poet. But history (in the later view), strewn as it is with
values irretrievably lost, is unaccommodating in its priority; it lives
only by erasing possibilities for the future. Now the monuments
no longer move; now it is we who move among them, changing
our minds as we change our angle of vision, trying to find some
uncluttered place to pitch our own stone.

Notes

1 Harold Bloom has put this well, writing that 'Eliot's idealized fiction (in "Tradition and the Individual Talent") is that vision of a "simultaneous order" that releases literary time from the burden of anxiety that is always a constituent of every other version of temporality.' *The Breaking of the Vessels* (Chicago: University of Chicago Press, 1982), 18.

9

Repetition and Order in the Wartime Quartets
A. Walton Litz

> Perhaps,
> The man-hero is not the exceptional monster,
> But he that of repetition is most master.
> > Wallace Stevens, *Notes Toward a Supreme Fiction*

In his essay on 'The *Pensées* of Pascal' Eliot observes that 'some forms of illness are extremely favourable, not only to religious illumination, but to artistic and literary composition. A piece of writing meditated, apparently without progress, for months or years, may suddenly take shape and word; and in this state long passages may be produced which require little or no retouch' (SE, 405). When the facsimile of *The Waste Land* manuscripts was published in 1971 critics immediately recognized in this passage a covert reference to part V of *The Waste Land*, which appears to have been written quickly and in an almost trancelike state of inspiration, drawing together the leading themes and images of the poem. In a different way, 'Burnt Norton' was also a poem that wrote itself, but in this case it was not physical or mental stress that drove the poem but a profound sense of time lost and the past recaptured. Eliot's visit to Burnt Norton in the late summer of 1934, accompanied by his close friend Emily Hale, was the catalyst, and the poem is infused with the sense of landscape as a structure of feeling that was sharpened by Eliot's visit to his native land in 1932–3. It opens with a meditation on 'Time present and time past' that, in slightly different form, was originally intended for Act One of *Murder in the Cathedral*, and the entire poem seems to flow easily from that passage. In its proportions 'Burnt Norton' follows the five-part pattern of *The Waste Land*, with a brief lyric (part IV) as its turning-point. Obviously Eliot found this pattern (which had emerged in 1921–2 from his virtual collaboration with Ezra Pound) congenial to the musical development of his themes. 'Burnt Norton' was written with no sequel in mind, and it stands at the end of *Collected Poems 1909–1935*, mysterious and compelling, as if it were a last visitation by the lyric muse.

After writing 'Burnt Norton' Eliot returned to his longstanding preoccupation with the theatre, and *The Family Reunion* – which dramatizes many of the poem's themes – would almost certainly have been followed by further work for the stage if the war had not intervened. 'Even "Burnt Norton",' Eliot told an interviewer in 1953, 'might have remained by itself if it hadn't been for the war, because I had become very much absorbed in the problems of writing for the stage and might have gone straight on from *The Family Reunion* to another play. The war destroyed that interest for a time: you remember how the conditions of our lives changed, how much we were thrown in on ourselves in the early days? "East Coker" was the result – and it was only in writing "East Coker" that I began to see the Quartets as a set of four' (Knowles, 101). In a draft of his essay 'The Three Voices of Poetry', Eliot called the last three quartets 'patriotic poems'; and although he later cancelled this description, the phrase is an accurate one (Ackroyd, 264). Almost against his will, Eliot found himself in the position of unofficial laureate to two nations, Britain and the United States, united as never before or since by a common danger. Sebastian Knowles has shown how the last three quartets are shot through with allusions to wartime events, and how they spoke with moving urgency to contemporary readers (ch. IV). Eliot may have returned to poetry in part because the dislocations of the war (and the temporary closing of the theatres) made it impossible to maintain the regular schedule that he needed for writing drama; but he also had a sense of responsibility to time past, present and future.

'East Coker', like 'Burnt Norton', was written quickly in January–February 1940. This was the time of the 'phoney war', a time to assess the past before confronting an unknown future, and Eliot worked as if Dunkirk were in view (the military imagery of parts IV and V anticipates the events of May–June 1940). He chose to replicate the five-part structure of 'Burnt Norton', and in the course of writing 'East Coker' he evolved the notion of four quartets based on the symbolism of the four seasons and the four elements (CFQ, 18). This discovery of a symmetrical structure for a long poem must have been exhilarating, but at the same time Eliot was aware of the dangers of boredom and irrelevant repetition that lurked in a pattern thrice repeated. In the final draft of the conclusion to part III of 'East Coker', where he adapted (as in

'Burnt Norton') lines from St John of the Cross, he inserted this gloomy preamble: 'You say I am repeating / Something I have said before. I shall say it again. / Shall I say it again?' (CPP, 181). Here the problem of creating diversity and interest within a repeated pattern is voiced within the poem, and it was only at John Hayward's insistence that a similar caveat was excised from part II of 'The Dry Salvages': 'One has to repeat the same thing in various ways / And risk being tedious' (CFQ, 132).

Clearly Eliot was uneasy and even defensive at the thought of replicating the same pattern and reorchestrating the same themes: when 'East Coker' was a work in progress he remarked that 'most of it looks to me like an imitation of myself' (CFQ, 16–17), and as the sequence developed the burden became greater. John Hayward remarked in July 1942, when Eliot was struggling with the revisions of 'Little Gidding', that the poet's chief fear was of 'simply repeating himself and so running into the risk of producing an elegant parody of the earlier poems in the group' (CFQ, 24–5). But in spite of these reservations the fixed sequence gave Eliot support and direction, since it catered to his natural tendency to write individual sections which would, with time and luck, cohere into larger wholes. When asked by the interviewer for *The Paris Review*, Donald Hall, about his method of building a long poem out of separately-written sections, Eliot replied, 'That's one way in which my mind does seem to have worked throughout the years poetically – doing things separately and then seeing the possibility of fusing them together, altering them, and making a kind of whole of them' (CFQ, 14).

Eliot believed that individual sections would, in the course of time, coalesce into a unified structure, and the terminology he frequently used – 'fused' into a 'whole' – echoes the famous passage on the imagination at the end of chapter XIV of *Biographia Literaria* that he had quoted in part at the turning point of his 'Andrew Marvell' essay to define true Metaphysical 'wit'. Coleridge says that the poet 'diffuses a tone and spirit of unity, that blends, and (as it were) *fuses*, each into each, by that synthetic and magical power, to which we have exclusively appropriated the name of imagination . . . [imagination] forms all into one graceful and intelligent whole' (II, 16, 18). Throughout his career Eliot maintained a Romantic theory of creativity, believing that the images and emotions thrown up from the unconscious would gradually take shape in the search for 'the right words in the right order' (OPP, 97), and that the moment of coalescence was, if not magical, beyond the powers of rational explanation ('Those are pearls that were his eyes'). This belief was his solace and assurance as he pressed on, more and more fitfully, with the writing of 'The Dry Salvages' and 'Little Gidding'.

As the last three quartets took shape in 1940–2 Eliot was discovering more about the possibilities of a long poem, and as always these discoveries are discussed indirectly in his literary criticism. It has often been noted that his June 1940 memorial lecture on Yeats expresses ideas that lie behind part V of 'East Coker' and part II of 'Little Gidding'; less well known are the notions about language, form and structure that emerge from his lecture 'The Music of Poetry' and the uncollected radio address on Tennyson, 'The Voice of His Time', both of which were delivered in February 1942. At that time the composition of 'Little Gidding', first drafted in June–July 1941, had been deferred for some months, and it was not until July 1942 that the poem was put back 'into the melting pot' (CFQ, 25). During this year-long hiatus Eliot was clearly mulling over the lessons he had learned and would have to apply once again, and we can recover some of these from the two essays.

In both the emphasis is on the building up of a unified structure out of diverse materials and separate 'poems'. Here *In Memoriam* is a model, and in speaking of it Eliot might be speaking of the *Quartets*. As in the *Quartets*, the 'intensity of the personal experience gives the poem its emotive force; but a long poem . . . would not be readable if it expressed no more than personal grief at the loss of a friend. The poem expresses Tennyson's attitude toward life, and in expressing that, expresses also the attitude of his age . . .' (Eliot, 212). This is precisely the quality – a discourse on general issues reinforced by 'acute personal reminiscence (never to be explicated, of course, but to give power from well below the surface)' – that gives *Four Quartets* their extraordinary power (CFQ, 24). Eliot also admired the overall organization of *In Memoriam*, which follows a 'logic of the emotions to form a continuous meditation on life and death.' In Tennyson's seasonal cycle, as in *Four Quartets*, 'Every season and every place brings another aspect of grief' (212). Most of all, he would have felt an affinity with Tennyson indicated by his title: 'The Voice of His Time'. For as he worked on 'Little Gidding' Eliot must have realized that he too was writing a 'complex and comprehensive expression of an historic phase of thought and feeling' (212).

In the more familiar 'The Music of Poetry' Eliot addressed a question that he raised six months later in a letter to John Hayward: what is the value of a title that suggests a musical form?

> I am aware of general objections to these musical analogies. . . . But I should like to indicate that these poems are all in a particular set form which I have elaborated, and the word 'quartet' does seem to me to start people on the right tack for understanding them ('sonata' in any case is *too* musical). It suggests to me the notion of making a poem by weaving in together three or four superficially unrelated themes: the 'poem' being the degree of success in making a new whole out of them. (CFQ, 26)

In *The Waste Land* Eliot had (with Pound's assistance) achieved a wholeness of a different kind. The poem is almost unbearably intense from start to finish, and the structure might be described as a mosaic of Arnoldian touchstones, passages that are often juxtaposed without conventional transitions and that must cohere in the mind of the active reader who is attuned to the emotional logic of the writing. *Four Quartets*, however, was the product of an older poet with a different poetic, one who had learned to value qualities other than nervous intensity. We might remember that Ezra Pound called *The Waste Land*, as it ran from 'April' to 'shantih', the longest poem in the English language, and advised Eliot: 'Don't try to bust all records by prolonging it three pages further' (L1, 497). What Pound meant was that Eliot had reached the bearable limits of sustained lyricism, in a poem devoid of passages of lesser intensity. It may be no accident that Eliot's recording of *The Waste Land* runs just under thirty minutes, the limit that Edgar Allan Poe set for the Romantic lyric.

In 'The Music of Poetry' Eliot declares that:

in a poem of any length, there must be transitions between passages of greater and less intensity, to give a rhythm of fluctuating emotion essential to the musical structure of the whole; and the passages of less intensity will be, in relation to the level on which the total poem operates, prosaic – so that, in the sense implied by that context, it may be said that no poet can write a poem of amplitude unless he is a master of the prosaic. (OPP, 32)

And he adds in a footnote: 'This is the complementary doctrine to that of the "touchstone" line or passage of Matthew Arnold: this test of the greatness of a poet is the way he writes his less intense, but structurally vital, matter.'

Perhaps more than the necessary repetitions, this practice of alternating the 'poetic' with the 'prosaic' has troubled readers of *Four Quartets*. The problem does not exist in those sections where the 'less intense' passage has a strong cadence. At the beginning of 'The Dry Salvages', for example, the sonorous Tennysonian rumination on the long rhythms of the sea ('The sea has many voices, / Many gods and many voices') is suddenly interrupted by an intense two-line Imagist poem: 'The salt is on the briar rose, / The fog is in the fir trees' (CPP, 184–5). Here the counterpoint in voice and mood is totally effective. Nor, I think, does the practice trouble us when the prosaic seems to be reaching beyond poetry into the silence, as when, in part V of 'The Dry Salvages', a passage of almost unbearable lyric beauty:

> The distraction fit, lost in a shaft of sunlight,
> The wild thyme unseen, or the winter lightning
> Or the waterfall, or music heard so deeply
> That it is not heard at all, but you are the music
> While the music lasts –

falls sharply away into something near prose itself.

> These are only hints and guesses,
> Hints followed by guesses; and the rest
> Is prayer, observance, discipline, thought and action.
>
> (CPP, 190)

The long, almost unscannable last line seems to say that these are values that lie beyond poetry. Such a line cannot be used too frequently, but when it is embedded in the context of highly-charged verse it has a strong emotional impact.

The real difficulty lies in part II of the first three quartets, where a highly organized lyric is followed by a passage of loose meditation. The falling-off from one form to another is never quite satisfactory, and Eliot must have been conscious of this weakness, since in 'Little Gidding' he follows the lyric of the four elements with the brilliant imitation of Dante, arguably the finest and most tightly organized (also the longest) passage of sustained power that he ever wrote. We know from the drafts and his own comments that the passage gave him immense trouble, but the result justified all his labours. Eliot seems to have thought of part II as the most 'open' section of the *Quartets*. In replicating the pattern of 'Burnt Norton' Eliot stayed remarkably close to the original line-lengths in the other four parts, but part II gradually expanded to over double the length as Eliot moved from 'Burnt Norton' to 'Little Gidding'. This makes sense in terms of the musical analogy, and shows Eliot's flexibility within the set form.

The most profound benefit Eliot derived from repetition was the thematic similarities that evolved in parallel sections of the poem. Part IV, for instance, is always a short lyric that uncovers the mystery of the quartet. The opening of part III of 'Burnt Norton', which uses the setting of the London Underground to describe an infernal descent, is paralleled in 'East Coker' by the Miltonic descent into inner darkness, in 'The Dry Salvages' by Krishna's plea for disinterestedness and in 'Little Gidding' by a meditation on the 'three conditions' of attachment, detachment and indifference – and in the first three quartets the passages share the motif of voyaging. The first half of part V is always devoted to the struggle with language and form, the attempt to incarnate feeling in words; and this leads to the concluding second half, which in each case speaks of the spiritual communion or Incarnation of which the poem – 'The complete consort dancing together' – is a material reflection. Here again Coleridge is relevant, with his notion of the poetic imagination reflecting in a secondary world the eternal I AM. And when Eliot comes in part V of 'Little Gidding' to his description of the ideal poem, he borrows his language once again from the close of chapter XIV of the *Biographia*. Coleridge says that the imagination:

reveals itself in the balance or reconciliation of opposite or discordant qualities: of sameness, with difference; of the general, with the concrete; the idea, with the image; the individual, with the representative; the sense of novelty and freshness, with old and familiar objects; a more than usual state of emotion, with more than usual order.

(II, 16–17)

Just as Yeats in 'Among School Children' welded the Symbolist image of the dance onto the more traditional Romantic image of organic unity, the flourishing tree, so Eliot in a long parenthesis adapts Coleridge's balanced phrases and adds to them the Yeatsian figure of the dancer that brought part II of 'Little Gidding' to a climax ('unless restored by that refining fire / Where you must move in measure, like a dancer').

> And every phrase
> And sentence that is right (where every word is at home,
> Taking its place to support the others,
> The word neither diffident nor ostentatious,
> An easy commerce of the old and the new,
> The common word exact without vulgarity,
> The formal word precise but not pedantic,
> The complete consort dancing together)
> Every phrase and every sentence is an end and a begin-
>   ning,
> Every poem an epitaph.   (CPP, 197)

In this passage the syntax, reminiscent of 'Among School Children', acts out the theme of reconciliation.

Another aspect of the double structure to part V found in the three wartime quartets is that it provides a double closure. Each of the three poems comes comfortably to rest at the end of the first section of part V:

> For us, there is only the trying. The rest is not our busi-
>   ness.
>
> ('East Coker'; CPP, 182)

> The hint half guessed, the gift half understood, is Incarna-
>   tion.
>
> ('The Dry Salvages'; CPP, 190)

> With the drawing of this Love and the voice of this Call-
> ing.
>
> ('Little Gidding'; CPP, 197)

The three poems could end easily on these lines, which in
many ways are more satisfactory closures than the passages to
follow. But in the case of 'East Coker' and 'The Dry Salvages'
Eliot feels he must throw the momentum of the poem forward
to the next one, while with 'Little Gidding' the last verse-
paragraph is a somewhat mechanical attempt to draw together
the leading themes and images of the previous poems, and to
return the reader to where his cyclical journey began in 'Burnt
Norton'.

Here again a passage from Coleridge is the best description of
Eliot's aims in the use of repetition. Writing to Joseph Cottle
on 7 March 1815, Coleridge said that 'The common end of all
narrative, nay, of all Poems is to convert a *series* into a *Whole*:
to make those events, which in real or imagined History move
on in a *strait* Line, assume to our Understandings a *circular*
motion – the snake with its Tail in its Mouth' (956). The
Quartets can – and must – be read in sequence, since they
trace a temporal arc of thematic and imagistic development.
But once they have been read and assimilated, it is easy and
necessary to see them as superimposed structures through which,
as through a series of overlays, we can discern the parallels
that bind the *Quartets* together. This is not the early modern
notion of 'spatial form', in which the whole work is reformed
in retrospect as a single image, but a more conservative late
modern approach that combines a strong linear development with
an equally strong effect of simultaneity – 'the snake with its Tail in
its Mouth'. The temporal and spatial readings are complementary,
but they remain distinct parts of a total experience. A similar
structure may be found in Wallace Stevens' *Notes Toward a
Supreme Fiction*, written at the same time as 'Little Gidding',
where three variations on a set pattern are presented through
the technique of parallel cantos. The result is a symmetry and
balance that reflect the Coleridgean bias of both works. At the
very centre of *Notes* Stevens gives us, just before the invoca-
tion to the Muse, his version of the close to chapter XIV of
Biographia:

Two things of opposite natures seem to depend
On one another, as a man depends
On a woman, day on night, the imagined

On the real. This is the origin of change.
Winter and spring, cold copulars, embrace
And forth the particulars of rapture come.

(392)

In Stevens's poem, as in *Four Quartets*, the sacred text of the 'new poetry' and the New Criticism has been translated into a form of belief. The difference, of course, is that Stevens can rest on the ample satisfactions of the mind and the physical world, while Eliot must move through that world 'Into another intensity / For a further union, a deeper communion.'

References

Ackroyd, Peter, *T.S. Eliot: A Life*, New York, Simon & Schuster, 1984.
Coleridge, Samuel Taylor, *Biographia Literaria, or Biographical Sketches of my Literary Life and Opinions*, 2 vols, ed. James Engell and W. Jackson Bate, Princeton, Bollingen, 1983.
————, *Collected Letters*, vol. 4, ed. Earl Leslie Griggs, Oxford, Clarendon, 1959.
Eliot, T.S., 'The Voice of His Time,' *The Listener*, 27.683 (12 February 1942), 211–12.
Knowles, Sebastian, *A Purgatorial Flame: Seven British Writers in the Second World War*, Philadelphia, University of Pennsylvania Press, 1990.
Stevens, Wallace, *The Collected Poems of Wallace Stevens*, New York, Knopf, 1954.

10

Origins of Form in Four Quartets
Louis L. Martz

'Burnt Norton' may be read in two contexts: as the first of the *Four Quartets*, or as the last of the poems in Eliot's collected volume of 1936. My own tattered copy of that volume bears the date of purchase, 'Oct. 1936', and I well remember the astonishment and puzzlement that the final poem of that book aroused – a poem published there for the first time, without warning, without preparation. That autumn I met on the street Donald Gallup, whose great collection of Eliot was already well advanced (he had shown me his rare copy of the book mistitled *Ara Vus Prec*). I stopped him, crying 'Donald! – I've just been reading the new collected Eliot.' 'Yes,' he said, 'and what, *what*, do you make of "Burnt Norton"?' 'Nothing,' I said. 'My eyes failed, and I knew nothing.' 'It's the same with me,' he said. And then, with the blowing of a horn, he turned and walked away, shaking his head.

That anecdote may not be precisely accurate in detail, but it does, I think, represent the response of early readers to 'Burnt Norton'. And now, after so many years of explication and annotation, we are still shaking our heads at this, the most elusive of all Eliot's poems. What did it mean in 1936? Certainly not the beginning of a sequence, for Eliot had no thought then of any sequel to this poem. It seemed to stand in stark isolation at the end of the book, an isolation created by the contrast it offered with the long sequence immediately preceding it, Eliot's unsteady experiment in public, didactic verse, the choruses from *The Rock*, with their deliberately simplified, declarative style. Those choruses, indeed, seemed to have the effect of cutting off 'Burnt Norton' from Eliot's earlier writing.

And yet it was evident, even in 1936, that 'Burnt Norton' was adapting the five-part structure of *The Waste Land*, for that structure was signalled by the use of a short lyric as part IV of the sequence. But what did it mean, what does it mean, to feel the five-part structure of *The Waste Land* working within so different a poem? To answer this question it may help to review the process by which *The Waste Land* gained its peculiar structure, emerging from the hands of Ezra Pound, as Eliot says, reduced to half its manuscript length.

First of all, without Pound's editorial intervention, we would not have the short lyric, 'Phlebas the Phoenician', appearing by itself as part IV of *The Waste Land*, and thus, presumably, we would not have the short lyrics constituting the fourth sections of all the *Four Quartets* – the short movement that helps to create analogies with Beethoven's late quartets. Indeed we might not have the Phlebas lyric at all, without Pound's advice, for Eliot, upset by Pound's slashing away at the eighty-two lines preceding this lyric in the manuscript, wrote to Pound, 'Perhaps better omit Phlebas also???' Pound was horrified: Eliot seemed not to understand the central principle of the poem's operation. 'I DO advise keeping Phlebas,' Pound replied. 'In fact I more'n advise. Phlebas is an integral part of the poem; the card pack introduces him, the drowned phoen. sailor, and he is needed ABSoloootly where he is. Must stay in' (L1, 505).

What Pound describes in that vehement answer is the sort of organization that Eliot later called musical, in his lecture 'The Music of Poetry', delivered in 1942, just as he was completing *Four Quartets*: 'The use of recurrent themes is as natural to poetry as to music,' Eliot says:

> There are possibilities for verse which bear some analogy to the development of a theme by different groups of instruments ['different voices', we might say]; there are possibilities of transitions in a poem comparable to the different movements of a symphony or a quartet; there are possibilities of contrapuntal arrangement of subject–matter. (OPP, 38)

So, in *The Waste Land*, after the embers of lust have smouldered in 'The Fire Sermon' – 'Burning burning burning burning' – the death of Phlebas by water provides a moment of serenity, quiet, poise, as Phlebas enters the whirlpool in whispers to a death not to be feared, but foreseen and accepted. The lyric acts as the lines about the still point act in the two poems of 'Coriolan', where, first, amid the turmoil of the crowd at the parade, the people think they find their answer in the military leader: 'O hidden under the dove's wing, hidden in the turtle's breast, / Under the palmtree at noon, under the running water / At the still point of the turning world. O hidden' (CPP, 127–8). But then, ironically, it appears in the second poem that the difficulties of a statesman have led him also to seek the still point: 'O hidden under the . . Hidden under the . . . Where the dove's foot rested and locked for a moment, / A still moment, repose of noon' (CPP, 130). The lyric of Phlebas acts as such a moment of repose, a nodal moment, tying together the strands of the poem, as Pound explained. And the fourth part, the short lyric, in all the *Four Quartets*, performs a similar function of poise and knotting, as the poem finds a temporary rest where themes and images and voices merge for a moment.

One voice of great importance speaks at the close of the Phlebas lyric, which is not simply a translation from Eliot's poem in French, *Dans le Restaurant*, for the closing lines are quite different. The French poem ends in an offhand, conversational tone: 'Figurez-vous donc, c'était un sort pénible; / Cependant, ce fut jadis un bel homme, de haut taille.' (Imagine then, it was a distressing fate; / Nevertheless, he was once a handsome man, of tall stature) (CPP, 51). In *The Waste Land* Eliot has changed the tone from conversational to prophetic by evoking the voice of St Paul addressing 'both Jew and Gentile' in his epistle to the Romans (ch. 2, 3): 'Gentile or Jew / O you who turn the wheel and look to windward, / Consider Phlebas, who was once handsome and tall as you' (CPP, 71).

A similar effect is created by Pound's critical slashing away of all those weak and in part offensive Popeian couplets at the outset of part III of *The Waste Land* manuscript. 'Do something different,' Pound advised (WLF, 127). So Eliot did: he pencilled on the back of the manuscript page a draft of the new opening passage, 'The river's tent is broken . . .' – lines that stress the eternal presence of the river within the waste land, culminating in the line that echoes the voice of the psalmist in exile: 'By the waters of Leman I sat down and wept', with its attendant question, 'How shall we sing the Lord's song in a strange land?' (Psalm 137:4).

A similar concentration upon the emergence of the prophetic voice is created by the removal of the monologue that opens *The Waste Land* manuscript, the monologue of the rowdy Irishman telling of a night on the town in Boston. This was excised by Eliot himself, perhaps under Pound's influence, perhaps because Eliot himself saw that the rowdy vitality of those singing, drinking men who stage a footrace in the dawn's early light does not accord with the voice that follows, the voice of one who is so reluctant to live that April becomes the cruelest month. That excision brings us quickly to the voice of a modern Ezekiel, speaking the famous lines:

> What are the roots that clutch, what branches grow
> Out of this stony rubbish? Son of man,
> You cannot say, or guess, for you know only
> A heap of broken images.   (CPP, 61)

Then these lines of true prophecy play their contrapuntal music against the voice of the false prophet, Madame Sosostris.

But I need to explain what I mean by the prophetic voice. With William Blake, we should discard the notion that the prophet's main function is to foretell the future. If, like Blake, we think of the biblical prophets, we will recall at once that they spend a great deal of time in denouncing the evils of the present, evils that derive from the people's worship of false gods and the pursuit of wealth and worldly pleasures. Prophecies of the future appear, but these are often prophecies of the disasters that will fall upon the people if they do not mend their evil ways. Denunciation of present evil is the primary message of the Hebrew prophet: he is a reformer, his mind is upon the present. But then he also offers the consolation of future good, if the people return to worship of the truth. Thus the voice of the prophet tends to oscillate between denunciation and consolation: he relates visions of evil and good, mingling within the immense range of his voice the most virulent excoriation and the most exalted lyrics. This, I think, is exactly the sort of oscillation that we find in Pound's *Cantos* and *The Waste Land*.

At the same time the true prophet never speaks for himself. In the basic Greek meaning of the word, a prophet is one 'who speaks for another', for God, for the gods, or for other human beings. The last function, to speak for others, is the prophetic role adopted by that poetical father of both Pound and Eliot, Walt Whitman, who proclaimed:

Through me many long dumb voices,
Voices of the interminable generations of slaves,
Voices of prostitutes and of deformed persons,
Voices of the diseased and despairing, and of thieves and dwarfs.
Of the trivial and flat and foolish and despised.

A prophet is one who speaks for another. Whitman desires to speak
for all Americans, diverse as they are; he desires to bind them
all together by the power of his voice. Thus in his enormous
catalogues, based upon the vistas of the biblical prophets, he
includes every aspect of human existence, seeking always to record
'What living and buried speech is always vibrating here.'

We can see, then, why Eliot at first thought of giving his poem
the strange title 'He Do the Police in Different Voices', an echo of
Dickens perhaps prompted by the way in which *Our Mutual Friend*
is so deeply concerned with death by water in the Thames and with
the ordure, rubbish and corruption on land in London.

Voices, voices – 'what living and buried speech is always
vibrating here' – voices of past and present, of life and death,
oscillating together – this is the method invented by Pound in
his early *Cantos* and brought to perfection by Eliot. Pound could
see what Eliot was doing because *The Waste Land* represented the
fulfilment of his own prophetic impulse, gradually revealed in the
seven cantos that he had written by the end of 1919. Eliot had
read those cantos, including the unpublished Canto VII, which a
postcard in the new collected *Letters* shows Eliot reading just as he
was embarking upon the composition of his own 'long poem'.[1]
The point is important because, as Ronald Bush has said, 'In
Canto VII Pound anticipated Eliot by applying what we now
call modernistic techniques to the themes, motifs and images of
"Gerontion" and prepared the way for *The Waste Land*' (225).

In Canto VII Pound attempts a synthesis of many 'voices',
oscillating between the past and the present and developing the
theme of the search for 'buried beauty' and 'Eros drowned'. It
is a poem in which, through this medley of many voices, one
feels the pulsating search for redemption of a dead land where
one hears 'Words like the locust-shells, moved by no inner
being; / A dryness calling for death.' Thus, after reading the
revised version of *The Waste Land*, Pound wrote to Eliot with
envy and generous congratulation: 'Complimenti, you bitch. I

am wracked by the seven jealousies, and cogitating an excuse for always exuding my deformative secretions in my own stuff, and never getting an outline' (L1, 498). But the shape, the 'outline' of the revised poem is largely due to Pound's removal of Eliot's own 'deformative secretions' – excisions which allow the prophetic voice to emerge with concentrated power. So in the pub scene of part II that insistent voice five times cries out in clock-like cadence: 'HURRY UP PLEASE ITS TIME'. This is more than the voice of a bartender. In the context of the whole revised poem this becomes another prophetic voice crying, 'Repent, for the time is near.'

Then, at the exact centre of the revised poem, the great central voice emerges out of the sordid sexual scene, the voice of the prophet three times identified as 'I Tiresias', merging all the earlier voices identified by the capital letter 'I':

> (And I Tiresias have foresuffered all
> Enacted on this same divan or bed;
> I who have sat by Thebes below the wall
> And walked among the lowest of the dead.)

Eliot knows well what he is saying in his famous note: 'Tiresias, although a mere spectator and not indeed a "character", is yet the most important personage in the poem, uniting all the rest. . . . What Tiresias *sees*, in fact, is the substance of the poem' (CPP, 78). Tiresias, we might say, is the name of the prophetic voice that dominates this poem and emerges at the close in the most powerful voice of all, the voice of the Thunder, uttering its Sanskrit commands. Without the shaping of Pound's editorial hand we would still have had an interesting poem, but the voices brought together by 'I Tiresias' would have been overshadowed, blunted, obscured.

All this is not designed to detract from Eliot's achievement, but to define a contrast between this prophetic poem of many voices – including Pound's subtextual voice – and the quite different five-part poem that first appeared in 1936.

In 'Burnt Norton' Eliot's reprise of the five-part form of *The Waste Land* pays tribute to the outline discovered by Pound in that 'sprawling' manuscript, and he proceeds to use its musical form towards other ends. The form of 'Burnt Norton' recognizes the existence of an earlier self – that collaborative self of different voices – but proceeds to explore the creation of another self. Or, to adapt Eliot's own words about *The Golden Bough*, 'Burnt Norton' remembers that vanished mind of which the present mind is a continuation.[2] The result is that the poem's place at the end of Eliot's volume of 1936 serves to indicate another way of writing and another attitude toward life, an attitude earlier implied in the reluctant recovery of joy in sensory life at the close of *Ash-Wednesday*, where

> the lost heart stiffens and rejoices
> In the lost lilac and the lost sea voices
> And the weak spirit quickens to rebel
> For the bent golden-rod and the lost sea smell
> Quickens to recover
> The cry of quail and the whirling plover   (CPP, 98)

– or in 'Marina', where the renewed man prays, 'let me / Resign my life for this life, my speech for that unspoken, / The awakened, lips parted, the hope, the new ships' (CPP, 110). These poems serve as preludes to the rose garden of 'Burnt Norton'.

That garden, like *The Waste Land*, is inhabited by echoes, but they no longer function in the way of *The Waste Land*. The prophetic oscillation between degraded images from modern life and brighter images of past belief is no longer needed, for – 'Quick now, here, now, always' – all images of the past are eternally present. The many echoes in the rose garden have been carefully pointed out over the years: intimations of Augustine and Bergson on the problem of time; an echo of *Alice in Wonderland* – a favourite echo of Eliot, since he took such pleasure in pointing it out to readers who had not noticed it; echoes of Kipling's 'They'; echoes of Lawrence's poignant and to Eliot cruel story 'The Shadow in the Rose Garden'; above all, though briefest of all, an echo of Dante's *Paradiso* in the phrase 'heart of light', evoking the passage where Dante, encircled by 'the two garlands of those sempiternal roses', hears a voice speaking 'del cor de l'una de le luci nove' – 'from the heart of one of the new lights' (*Paradiso*, 12:28).

The last echo leads back to the ecstatic experience of the speaker after his return, late, from the hyacinth garden of *The Waste Land*:

Your arms full, and your hair wet, I could not
Speak, and my eyes failed, I was neither
Living nor dead, and I knew nothing,
Looking into the heart of light, the silence.

(CPP, 62)

Sexual and religious implications are here blended, as they are in
the rose garden of 'Burnt Norton', with its image of the 'lotus'. But
the passionate experience of the *Waste Land* garden is overwhelmed
by that poem's pervasive theme of sexual failure and degradation,
whereas in 'Burnt Norton' the experience becomes the central
theme, as a different voice ponders the meaning of such a glimpse
into the 'heart of light' – the meditative voice that Eliot describes
in his essay 'The Three Voices of Poetry'. It is a voice that springs
from an 'obscure impulse'. The poet 'does not know what he has to
say until he has said it, and in the effort to say it he is not concerned
with making other people understand anything.'

> He is not concerned, at this stage, with other people at all:
> only with finding the right words or, anyhow, the least
> wrong words. He is not concerned whether anybody else
> will ever listen to them or not, or whether anybody else
> will ever understand them if he does. He is oppressed by
> a burden which he must bring to birth in order to obtain
> relief. . . . and when the words are finally arranged in the
> right way – or in what he comes to accept as the best
> arrangement he can find – he may experience a moment
> of exhaustion, of appeasement, of absolution, and of some-
> thing very near annihilation, which is in itself indescrib-
> able.

(OPP, 98)

– indescribable, except in the lyrics that constitute the fourth
movement of each quartet.

The change in voice is signalled in the second line of 'Burnt
Norton' by one word, 'perhaps': 'Time present and time past / Are
both perhaps present in time future, / And time future contained in
time past' (CPP, 171). One remembers how Pound twice queried
Eliot's use of the word 'perhaps' in part III of *The Waste Land*
manuscript, writing 'dam per'apsez' and 'Perhaps be damned' in
the margin (WLF, 31, 45) and then cancelling the word 'may' with

an annotation that Hugh Kenner calls 'almost a free-verse stanza' (Kenner, 32):

> make up
> yr. mind
> you Tiresias
> if you know
> know damn well
> or
> else you
> don't.   (WLF, 47)

Ezekiel would never say perhaps.

In 'Burnt Norton' the note of uncertainty continues: 'But to what purpose / Disturbing the dust on a bowl of rose-leaves / I do not know' (CPP, 171). Here the speaker works within a cloud of unknowing: he gropes toward the meaning of his experience of momentary reconciliation between the worlds of sense and spirit, a reconciliation celebrated in the formal lyric that opens part II (matching the formal verse that opens the second part of *The Waste Land*): 'The trilling wire in the blood / Sings below inveterate scars / And reconciles forgotten wars.' Eliot later changed the last line here to read 'Appeasing long forgotten wars' – apparently to avoid the repetition in the lyric's concluding lines:

> We move above the moving tree
> In light upon the figured leaf
> And hear upon the sodden floor
> Below, the boarhound and the boar
> Pursue their pattern as before
> But reconciled among the stars.   (CPP, 172)

I think the original repetition is better, because the lyric deals with a double reconciliation: one within the human body and the other within the outer universe – to say nothing of the unfortunate implications of 'appeasing' under the wartime circumstances.

Then follows, as in *The Waste Land*, a section of broken utterances, clipped sentences, cut apart by periods or semi-colons, but of course not expressing the hysteria of the frenzied woman in *The Waste Land*:

'My nerves are bad tonight. Yes, bad. Stay with me.
Speak to me. Why do you never speak. Speak.
   What are you thinking of? What thinking? What?
I never know what you are thinking. Think.'

(CPP, 65)

In 'Burnt Norton' these broken words are converted into the thinking, probing voice of the meditative seeker, the sort of philosophic probing that one might feel in the fragments of Heraclitus or the other pre-Socratic searchers after the Logos:

> At the still point of the turning world. Neither flesh nor
>   fleshless;
> Neither from nor towards; at the still point, there the dance is,
> But neither arrest nor movement. And do not call it fix-
>   ity,
> Where past and future are gathered. Neither movement from
>   nor towards,
> Neither ascent nor decline. Except for the point, the still
>   point,
> There would be no dance, and there is only the dance.

(CPP, 173)

Then comes a rounded cogitation, quite unlike the pub scene of *The Waste Land*, but retaining, perhaps, a distant echo of 'HURRY UP PLEASE ITS TIME', in the concluding lines:

>   Time past and time future
> Allow but a little consciousness.
> To be conscious is not to be in time
> But only in time can the moment in the rose-garden,
> The moment in the arbour where the rain beat,
> The moment in the draughty church at smokefall
> Be remembered; involved with past and future.
> Only through time time is conquered.   (CPP, 173)

  But what does that closing aphorism mean? Section III attempts to tell us, in the mode of rational discourse – what was called the working of the intellect in the old meditative procedures. The voice now ponders two ways of using the world of time to conquer time: either through the sort of sunlit transcendence represented by the rose garden –

daylight
Investing form with lucid stillness
Turning shadow into transient beauty
With slow rotation suggesting permanence   (CPP, 173)

– or by 'darkness to purify the soul / Emptying the sensual with deprivation' after the manner of the Spanish mystics
(CPP, 173–4).

All these cogitations are then blended into the short lyric that
is part IV, a lyric that is highly formed within an appearance
of informality suggested by the way the line-lengths vary from
one syllable to fourteen. The words are subtly woven together
by rhyme, assonance, alliteration and repetition, moving towards
the one word 'Chill' that stands by itself in the sixth line; but
this word of fear and death is countered by the hopeful word
'still' ambiguously repeated in the succeeding lines. Thus linkages
of sound reinforce linkages of imagery ('curled', 'world', 'cling',
'king-', 'wing'):

> Time and the bell have buried the day,
> The black cloud carries the sun away.
> Will the sunflower turn to us, will the clematis
> Stray down, bend to us; tendril and spray
> Clutch and cling?
> Chill
> Fingers of yew be curled
> Down on us? After the kingfisher's wing
> Has answered light to light, and is silent, the light is still
> At the still point of the turning world.
>
> > (CPP, 174–5)

The lyric moves around the word 'Chill' by a slow rotation
suggesting permanence within the transient movement of life
from day to darkness, from abundance of natural life to death.
The kingfisher's flashing wing is an image of natural beauty
and vigour in a transient world, but the light that the wing
briefly reflects is an image drawn from the 'heart of light'. So,
through this shaping, 'Burnt Norton' moves to its retrospective
conclusion, summing up in many different ways the effort of the
poem to achieve a goal beyond the reach of the sad time of *The
Waste Land*:

Only by the form, the pattern,
Can words or music reach
The stillness, as a Chinese jar still
Moves perpetually in its stillness. . . .

Sudden in a shaft of sunlight
Even while the dust moves
There rises the hidden laughter
Of children in the foliage
Quick now, here, now, always –
Ridiculous the waste sad time
Stretching before and after.

Thus the prophetic mode of *The Waste Land* has been absorbed and transcended by the probing, inward, meditative voice. The five-part structure, renewed and transformed, now stands ready to serve the poet's need as wartime unexpectedly calls forth the further exploration of that 'burden which he must bring to birth in order to obtain relief.'

In that exploration 'East Coker' also finds its 'moment of exhaustion, of appeasement, of absolution', in the lyric that constitutes its fourth part. This is a lyric deliberately performed in the 'metaphysical' style that Eliot admired in his essays and echoed in his stanzaic poems around the year 1920:

The wounded surgeon plies the steel
That questions the distempered part;
Beneath the bleeding hands we feel
The sharp compassion of the healer's art
Resolving the enigma of the fever chart.

(CPP, 181)

Now, in 1940, the lines that open part V discard that style, adopting a relaxed, conversational, intimate manner of speech:

So here I am, in the middle way, having had twenty years –
Twenty years largely wasted, the years of *l'entre deux guerres* –
Trying to learn to use words, and every attempt
Is a wholly new start, and a different kind of failure . . .

(CPP, 182)

This 'metaphysical' lyric, then, as Eliot has said of the rhetorically inflated lyric that opened part II, is a 'study in a worn-out poetical fashion, / Leaving one still with the intolerable wrestle / With words and meanings' (CPP, 179). It is self-consciously 'witty', 'conceited', paradoxical, while its strict stanza-form of five lines rhyming *ababb* suggests a variation on some of George Herbert's stanzas. At the same time the use of hexameter in the final line evokes a reminiscence of Milton's Nativity Ode, while the stress on 'blood' may carry connotations of eucharistic celebrations by Herbert and Crashaw, along with implications of a world now concentrated upon the prosecution of bloody warfare:

> The dripping blood our only drink,
> The bloody flesh our only food:
> In spite of which we like to think
> That we are sound, substantial flesh and blood —
> Again, in spite of that, we call this Friday good.
>
> (CPP, 182)

The lyric thus brings to a climax the Christian implications that have emerged in part III, with its opening echoes of Milton's *Samson Agonistes*, its central meditation on faith, hope and love, and its closing quotation from St John of the Cross. The traditional significance of Good Friday has, in the past, provided surcease from the flux and turmoil imaged in the first three sections of this quartet. Will its meaning still prevail in this world at war?

The conversational, intimate style that ends 'East Coker' continues at the beginning of 'The Dry Salvages', as Eliot further disclaims the prophetic mode: 'I do not know much about gods; but I think that the river / Is a strong brown god.' Here is the mode of quiet pondering that dominates this quartet and is especially evident in part III ('I sometimes wonder if that is what Krishna meant — ') as Eliot renews his memories of Hindu religion and poetry. 'The Dry Salvages', with its prevalent imagery of the ocean, is broad and deep enough to include 'Many gods and many voices', but all is controlled by the quiet voice that hears the clanging of the bell and knows 'the hardly, barely prayable / Prayer of the one Annunciation' ('Be it unto me according to thy word').

So the lyric of the fourth part binds this quartet together in its quiet prayer to the Virgin, remembering the dangerous voyages of wartime convoys, while the closing allusion to the sea bell and the angelus bring together the bell and Annunciation of the poem's first two parts:

> Lady, whose shrine stands on the promontory,
> Pray for all those who are in ships, those
> Whose business has to do with fish, and
> Those concerned with every lawful traffic
> And those who conduct them.

The flexible, easy, natural movement of these five-line stanzas marks the poet's renunciation of the prophetic mode and the metaphysical style.

Finally, in 'Little Gidding', Eliot is able to create a blending of the formal and the intimate: in the rhymed stanzas of the lyric that opens part II, in the modified *terza rima* of the air-raid warden's communication with the dead, and, climactically, in the Herbertian lyric of part IV which blends the wartime bomber with the tongues of fire at Pentecost:

> The dove descending breaks the air
> With flame of incandescent terror
> Of which the tongues declare
> The one discharge from sin and error.
> The only hope, or else despair
>   Lies in the choice of pyre or pyre –
>   To be redeemed from fire by fire.   (CPP, 196)

The imagery returns to the imagery at the close of the opening part: 'the communication / Of the dead is tongued with fire beyond the language of the living' (CPP, 192). Thus 'The Fire Sermon' of *The Waste Land* has been transformed, while the five-part structure remains, implicit recognition of an older, earlier self:

> And as I fixed upon the down-turned face
> That pointed scrutiny with which we challenge
> The first-met stranger in the waning dusk
> I caught the sudden look of some dead master
> Whom I had known, forgotten, half recalled
>   Both one and many; in the brown baked features
>   The eyes of a familiar compound ghost
> Both intimate and unidentifiable.   (CPP, 193)

That compound ghost includes the many voices of *The Waste*

Land that were drawn together in 'I Tiresias'; but, as the ghost here says, 'last year's words belong to last year's language / And next year's words await another voice.' That voice has been emerging throughout *Four Quartets*, interrupted by moments of high rhetoric or low-keyed didacticism; but in the last two quartets the truly meditative voice, concentrated in its quest, grows more and more confident, until, in the middle of 'Little Gidding', the voice can say: 'See, now they vanish, / The faces and places, with the self which, as it could, loved them, / To become renewed, transfigured, in another pattern' (CPP, 195). This is the 'pattern / Of timeless moments' that the meditative voice has sought to discover, and now discovers in this place of the 'secluded chapel', 'A symbol perfected in death.'

Notes

1 On 2 December,1919, Eliot sent across London to Pound a cryptic message opening with the exclamation 'Ελεναυζ!' adding the comment, 'I am absorbing this matter slowly', and ending with the query 'Who is Tyro?' This, it seems, can only be an allusion to the lines in the middle of Canto VII: 'But *is* she dead as Tyro? In seven years?/ 'Ελεναυζ, ελανδροζ, ελεπτολιζ' [destroyer of ships, destroyer of men, destroyer of cities] – the words of Aeschylus describing Helen of Troy which also occur in what is now Canto II but was originally Canto VIII, written several years later than Canto VII. This correction of the annotation in the *Letters* is important, because later that month Eliot declared in a letter to his mother (18 December 1919) that his New Year's resolution is 'to write a long poem I have had on my mind for a long time.' (L1, 350–1)

2 Eliot, 453, cited in Litz, 19: 'Even *The Golden Bough* can be read in two ways: as a collection of entertaining myths, or as a revelation of that vanished mind of which our mind is a continuation.' This is written with regard to Stravinsky's *Sacre du Printemps*, of which Eliot here remarks (significantly, when one thinks of *The Waste Land* and the *Quartets*): 'It did seem to transform the rhythm of the steppes into the scream of the motor horn, the rattle of machinery, the grind of wheels, the beating of iron and steel, the roar of the underground railway, and the other barbaric cries of modern life; and to transform these despairing noises into music.'

References

Bush, Ronald, *The Genesis of Ezra Pound's Cantos*, Princeton, Princeton
University Press, 1976.
Eliot, T.S., 'London Letter', *Dial* 71.4 (October 1921), [452]–5.
Kenner, Hugh, 'The Urban Apocalypse', in A. Walton Litz, ed., *Eliot in
His Time: Essays on the Occasion of the Fiftieth Anniversary of* 'The Waste
Land', Princeton, Princeton University Press, 1973, 23–49.
Litz, A. Walton, '*The Waste Land* Fifty Years After', in A. Walton Litz,
ed., *Eliot in His Time: Essays on the Occasion of the Fiftieth Anniversary of*
'*The Waste Land*', Princeton, Princeton University Press, 1973, 3–22.

Index

Words in Time